THE RULING TRINITY

To my parents whose sacrifices educated me

The Ruling Trinity

A Community Study of Church, State and Business in Ireland

CHRIS EIPPER
Lecturer in Anthropology and Sociology, Department of Sociology, La Trobe University, Australia

Gower

Published by
Gower Publishing Company Limited,
Gower House, Croft Road, Aldershot, Hants GU11 3HR,
England

Gower Publishing Company
Old Post Road, Brookfield, Vermont 05036,
USA

British Library Cataloguing in Publication Data

Eipper, Chris
   The ruling trinity : a community study
   of church, state and business in Ireland.
   1. Community development——Ireland
   I. Title
   307'.14'09417   HN400.3.Z9C6

ISBN 0-566-05173-7

ISBN 0 566 05173 7

Printed in Great Britain by
Richard Clay (The Chaucer Press) Ltd,
Bungay, Suffolk

Contents

Tables and figure

Acknowledgements

My first debt is to the people of Bantry. They overcame their misgivings about what I would be writing to co-operate and befriend me. Without their help I could not have continued with the research. I will not single out individuals, but those who put themselves out for my sake are particularly fondly remembered.

Also in Ireland, Damien Hannan and Paddy O'Carroll at University College, Cork, assisted me at a critical time. Paddy's advice and comments were invaluable to me while in the field, and he has continued to be of assistance since.

In Sydney, several people read and commented on part or all of earlier drafts of the manuscript: Michael Allen, Jeremy Beckett, Linda Connor, Gill Cowlishaw, Marie de Lepervanche, Andrew Metcalfe, Doug Miles, Lorraine Mortimer, George Munster, Gretchen Poiner, Kathy Robinson, Peter Ross and Ron Wild. Of those mentioned, I must stress the contribution of my former fellow students. Our discussions and seminars, and their advice and encouragement, were extremely important for my work.

Special thanks to Marie de Lepervanche who sympathized with and understood what I was trying to do and counselled perseverence. Having chosen Ron Wild as my Ph.D supervisor, I benefited from his efficiency and effectiveness. He had enough faith in me to give me the independence I needed, he was always available for consultation, reading and commenting on material quickly and thoroughly — rare enough qualities, but his support for my work did not cease then, and for that too I remain grateful to him.

Robyn Wood in Sydney, and Bronwyn Bardsley, Ros Giddings, Jill Gooch, Barbara Matthews and Elaine Young in Melbourne were all involved in the typing of one or another of the various drafts. I am as thankful to them for their patience and diligence as for their typing skills.

Kathy Henenberg helped with miscellaneous tasks. Betty Moore acted as copy-editor and proof-reader. Typesetting was provided by the Arena Printing Group. Again, I must thank them not only for their contribution but also their helpfulness.

Two people have had a profound effect on the thinking behind this study, Michael Matteson and Lorraine Mortimer. Michael educated me in class analysis. Lorraine has been shaping my ideas for over a decade. She accompanied me to the field, debated points of interpretation, and helped with editing and proof-reading.

The research was funded by a Commonwealth Postgraduate Scholarship, funds from the Carlyle Greenwell Bequest, Department of Anthropology, University of Sydney, and a C.T.E.C. Special Research Grant, Department of Sociology, La Trobe University. La Trobe University also generously subsidised publication of the work.

1 Introduction

The relationship of forms of power and consciousness to class is today a central problem of social thought. It is no less of an issue for conservatives and liberals than for socialist theorists and activists. Thus, in attempting to make a modest contribution to the analysis of class, this book addresses issues and raises questions for social thinkers of a variety of persuasions.

Although the concerns of the book are theoretical, the mode of expression is primarily empirical, the argument being presented and illustrated through the extensive use of ethnography. In what follows I do not merely wish to analyse the relationship between the church, state and business in one of Ireland's remoter communities, but to try and reinterpret the conceptual parameters of community studies. Offering what is in effect a critique of community studies on their home ground, I argue that the local 'level' cannot be analysed in isolation from the national or international 'levels', nor treated as a 'micro-system' within a 'macro-system'.

No attempt is made to present a complete account of 'community'; all that is offered is an analysis of important features of class relations in the Bantry area — though they are features common to local communities everywhere in Ireland. Unlike most community studies which take a stratificationist stance (be it Warnerian, Parsonian, or Weberian in orientation), this one is in the tradition of class analysis. Accordingly, it has a more pronounced historical emphasis than is usual for a community study. Again, few community studies have considered the importance of the localized interventions of transnational corporations, which is a feature of this book. However, whilst it emphasizes the impact of Gulf Oil's transhipment terminal on local life, this is only one aspect of the study. A detailed narrative account of Gulf's intervention — certainly the most dramatic influence upon localized social change in the town since independence — is the subject of another book: *Hostage to Fortune: Bantry Bay's Encounter with Gulf Oil — a case study of the multinational corporation, community change and capitalist development*.[1]

Irish society and history evokes images of economic truculence, political turbulence and cultural effusiveness, it seems to demand a vivid depiction of person, place and period. Important as such evocations are, unless they are to remain little more than a sensuous enigma, analysis requires that we go beyond the kaleidoscope of appearances and impressions to see what they express and what they camouflage. Ethical considerations become relevant here. Undertakings given during my fieldwork meant that I could not use names or explore individual personalities. Pseudonyms were not a solution for I was given the distinct impression that they would have been taken as evidence of bad faith. Nor was I prepared to fictionalize. Consequently, I came to the uneasy conclusion that I would refer to people according to the social activities they undertook. A few personalities would be recognizable, but only to the extent that their participation in local affairs was public and well-known. Hence only influential key figures are identifiable from the text and even they appear less as personalities than representatives of specific tendencies and trends. This undoubtedly takes a lot of the colour out of the book. I am not even sure it is a good solution to the problem. But at least it has the virtue of fitting well with my conviction that in many community studies the personalities of key figures loom too large, obscuring the social processes at work. This encourages the reader to see social structures as at root a matter of interpersonal relations and to see the study of 'communities' as essentially different from the study of 'society'. If my approach helps counter those views then the sacrifice of evocative immediacy will have been more than justified.

Overview

The premier theme of the book is the issue of the relationship of macro to micro processes and class dynamics as these influence the reproduction of power and consciousness. This theme is explored by tracing the class character of the relationship between the church, state and business nationally and locally in Eire.[2] Obviously, and this needs to be emphasized, there is no pretence that this study constitutes a comprehensive treatment of all aspects of this relationship; it simply attempts to deal with those features of it directly relevant to the analysis of the situation at Bantry as revealed by my fieldwork. It also needs to be stressed that an analysis of the *links* between the church, state and business from this perspective by no means exhausts the analysis of each of these institutions in their own right. Such analyses should not be *reduced* to that presented here but, hopefully, will be *informed* by it.[3]

The macro/micro distinction as a conceptual problem

In the community studies tradition certain aspects of the issue of class dynamics would be conventionally treated in terms of processes pertaining to the macro level. In this tradition such processes tend to be taken into account only as 'external' factors contextualizing or intruding into the local situation. Yet a central feature of the nexus between church, state and business in Eire is that it has been forged and exerts its influence *simultaneously* locally as well as nationally. In fact, the nexus is itself a product of, and in turn reproduces, the complex but continuous imbrication of nationally-general and locally-specific forces and events. This interleaving creates a symbiotic processual unity, a reciprocal interdependence of macro and micro processes.[4]

From this viewpoint, the familiar disclaimer that specific communities cannot be understood without locating them within a wider context, is usually an excuse for leaving the relation between the macro and micro level untheorized. It does not seem to be generally recognized that the formulation itself implies a prior logical distinction which bifurcates what might otherwise be regarded as a unified social totality. Where some such implication does seem to be acknowledged, it would appear that no serious theoretical consequences are deemed to follow from it. No argument is ever brought forward to explain the grounds for the differentiation between the one set of processes and the other.

But if we cannot analyse specific communities as isolated wholes — especially given the spatially and temporally diffuse character of many social processes — what justification do we have for speaking of them as discrete entities at all? If we do find some such justification, what does it tell us about the processes which constitute the community as a distinct entity and locate it within an enveloping totality?

This book is premised on the assumption that we can no longer unquestioningly assume that different methods of analysis must or can be used to account for macro and micro processes. Rather, we have to regard the micro/macro distinction as purely a question of scale: it does not denote different types of 'system', nor does it separate the study of interactions within institutions from the study of structural dynamics. Micro analyses are only macro analyses on a small scale. If we want to do a different kind of analysis for small scale events then that raises the question of whether that type of analysis can also be applied to large scale events.

Hence to show how class, power and consciousness in the Bantry area were moulded by the evolving relations between the church, state and business, required an examination of the way macro and micro processes were structurally and institutionally interlocked. By identifying the key connections it has been possible to show how class worked in Bantry (and in a number of other places also).

Structural processes get institutionalized and work themselves out in a variety of different ways. Some processes are highly localized in their manifestations, with the result that local idiosyncrasies often mark events with a vivid (and therefore frequently mystifying) character. Other processes are more geographically diffuse and leave a more generalized (if no less pervasive) trace. Sometimes the full import of what has happened is best grasped through national outcomes; sometimes it is local events which are most revealing. That is, although Bantry remains the subject of analysis throughout, in order to understand the changes that were occurring there, it is necessary to shift back and forth between generalized discussion of national developments and a more detailed treatment of local ones. Hence at times I am concerned not only with the way international forces and trends were *dealt with locally* but with the way these forces and trends *shaped the locality itself*.

I must emphasize that no attempt is made to analyse nation-wide processes of social change as such. At most I am concerned to indicate some of the major processes associated with the development of what I have called the ruling bloc of church, state and business. Even then, they are dealt with *only to the extent that it is necessary to do so in order to understand key aspects of the shaping of social action at Bantry*.

Because of the range of issues involved, topics which warrant much more detailed and subtle treatment have had to be dealt with rather schematically whenever the focus shifts from Bantry to the nation as a whole. Unfortunately, such strictures are one of the deficiencies of a study of this type and length — and an indication that it cannot stand alone, but requires other researchers to fill in (and correct) the details of the larger picture which has only been sketched here.

However, by adopting this approach I have tried to counter the tendency in the community studies tradition to proceed as if general macro level structural constraints simply contextualize specific micro level patterns of institutional interaction. Complacency about this procedure is usually coupled with another unexamined assumption: social relations are conceived of in interactional terms. That is, the analysis of social relations is accomplished simply by the observation of interactions between individuals. One problematic implication of this is that the social structure is conceived simply as the product of this network of interactions. Moreover, the interactionist approach commits us to an exclusively subjectivist view of social action and social structure. Social action is seen simply in terms of the strategies and tactics of individuals (including individuals in groups), and social structure as the outcome of these. But it could be argued that interactions between individuals constitutes only one aspect of social relations. And a subjectivist focus, however necessary it may be, cannot by itself provide an adequate understanding of social relations and social structure.

We can make a distinction, for example, between what people do as acting subjects — *institutional configuration* — and what they do as social agents — *structural configuration*.[5] Configuration here denotes the different ways social action is shaped or catalysed, the ways patterned sequences of events are generated and reproduced. The two forms of configuration thus represent different kinds of processes, an interplay of two orders of determination — a societal dynamic embedded in given social forms, these forms thereby giving expression to that dynamic. The aim of the distinction is to stress both the importance of human agency and the social (institutional and structural) limitations upon it. That is, it allows us to distinguish between the reproductive consequences of social agents as incumbents of given social positions carrying out designated functions, and the reproductive consequences of social actors as calculating subjects carrying out various tasks of their own. This entails recognizing that only a delimited range of activities is compatible with functioning in any given social position. But equally importantly, it also entails recognizing that only a delimited range of the activities carried out in any given social position is accountable in terms of the functional requirements of that position.

This latter point perhaps needs frequent reiteration if the argument presented here is not to be badly misinterpreted. For example, in those sections of the study where I discuss nation-wide processes (especially chapters 3, 4 and 5), I am primarily concerned with *outcomes* of the *functioning* of institutions and structures. Because of this some critics may want to claim that the analysis thereby becomes functionalist. Yet such a claim would be quite mistaken. For to argue that a determinate sequence of outcomes demonstrates the interconnected functioning capacities of given institutions and structures is quite a different thing from arguing that such outcomes were teleologically pre-determined, that things turned out this way because it was *functional* for them to do so. At no point does the argument rest upon a purported necessity or inevitability. To emphasize the processual patterning of human agency is not to demean the significance of agency in determining the outcome of events. It is simply to focus on the fact that while other responses to events were possible, we must, in the end, come to terms with history as it happened.

Delineating the society and community

The way the macro/micro issue gets dealt with of course depends very much on what is meant by the terms 'community' and 'society'. Defining these terms entails taking a theoretical position on a number of other important issues as well. Rather than canvassing the various definitions now current, I will here simply state how the terms will be employed in this study and let the theoretical ramifications and empirical applicability of this usage speak for themselves.[6]

By *society* I mean, for the purposes of this study at least, that amalgam of material and ideological conditions which, as an economic, political and cultural totality, is marked off by the existing state. It has been conventional for the term 'social' to be used to refer both to a particular sphere within society as well as to the totality. In this study if I refer to 'the economy and society' it is because I wish to point to influences on the whole society while stressing the economy; the same applies to the phrases 'politics and society' and 'culture and society'.

By *community* I mean a collectivity of people imbued with a particular kind of social solidarity. That is, it denotes the way people see themselves as bonded together, in spite of their differences, by ecological, historical and social circumstances. Usually such things as locality, tradition, custom, vested interests, etc. make powerful bonding agents (as they have in Bantry), but any number of other things may also be important. The key thing is that for self-identified community members (and by implication those thereby identified as non-members), community is flexibly defined, its boundaries are malleable and permeable: people find and make themselves members of several different kinds of community simultaneously. An essential feature of this notion of community is its *ideological* character: community is defined and redefined in relation to specific conflicts as well as perennial antagonisms, i.e. by the way people become conscious of their conflicts and fight them out.

Most readers will have at least a passing awareness of Irish society, its predominantly rural and underdeveloped character, and the fact that this is in part due to it being deprived of industry during the island's long subjugation by British colonial rule. They will be aware too of the nationalist war of independence and the subsequent treaty with the British which made a 'free state' of the southern twenty-six counties where the overwhelming majority of the population were catholics — and in so doing mapped in a slender protestant majority for the remaining six. And thereby manufactured the conditions for a virulent and festering sectarianism which has inhibited the further renovation of the power structures of both the North and the South and the consciousness of the mass of the population either side of the border. It is this artifact of historical struggles delimited by the 'free state' of republican Ireland which I refer to in this study when speaking of 'Irish society'.

The community I am concerned with will be unknown to most readers. It is located in the far south-west of the country, in the region known as West Cork. Bantry Bay is one of the world's spectacular harbours, albeit

6

one of its least developed. Roughly twenty miles long and three to four wide, it once served as a major British port capable of sheltering what was then the largest navy in the world. In 1966 the Gulf Oil Corporation announced plans to build an oil transhipment terminal and tank-farm on Whiddy Island in the Bay. The site was selected because the deep and sheltered waters of Bantry could accommodate on a year-round basis the new generation of supertankers Gulf Oil planned to build to transport crude oil from Kuwait. Many of the changes occurring in the area after 1966— at least until the tragic explosion of a tanker discharging oil in 1979 caused the terminal to cease operations — were directly or indirectly traceable in one form or another to the Gulf Oil intervention. But Bantry had been subject to outside influences dating back to the early years of English colonialism, and at least since then Bantry people have been no strangers to events possessing both drama and historical significance.

Until Gulf Oil came the town itself was a small market centre for a poor agricultural and depleted marine hinterland which bolstered its income in the short and unpredictable tourist season. Tourists were attracted to the beauty of the Bay itself and the sub-tropical gardens of Garnish Island just offshore from the resort village of Glengarriff eleven miles around the Bay on the scenic route to the Killarney Lakes.

Bantry began to experience a new prosperity in the 1960s based upon a combination of tourism, light industry and the Gulf Oil project. This constituted a reversal of several years of decline. To Bantry people these years were symbolized most vividly of all by the Gulf Oil terminal on Whiddy Island.

Although Bantry's new prosperity was largely due to international developments in the oil industry, it fitted into the national trend in those years of growing affluence in both the countryside and the cities. One result was that, like the nation as a whole, the town finally arrested its previously endemic demographic decline, the population actually beginning to rise for the first time since the Famine — passing the 2500 mark sometime after 1966.

The presentation of the argument

The book is organized in the following way. On the basis of the approach to the study of macro and micro processes outlined above, I begin my analysis by arguing for an approach which offers a solution to another problem of crucial significance for community studies: the question of how to analyse class as it is lived in a specific social habitat. This serves to introduce the conception of class which provides the theoretical framework for the analysis of relations between church, state and business in the remainder of the study.

My argument is that the contemporary nexus between church, state and business is, in large measure, an outcome of the reconstruction of power in the post-colonial period. This process, among other things, depended upon and helped foster the interpellation in the consciousness of all classes of ideologies concerned with: a) economic development and the provision of a better standard of living; b) the nationalist heritage and electoral representation through the dispensation of patronage; and c) an integralist catholicism preoccupied with hierocratically safeguarding the spiritual and secular welfare of the nation.

The institutional forms assumed by this structure of power have a corollary in the part played by owners and managers of businesses, politicians and civil servants, and the clergy and lay functionaries, in mediating the hegemonic deployment of power locally as well as nationally. An outcome of this at Bantry was the division of town affairs into distinct spheres of influence — as revealed by the mobilization of influentials, activists and townspeople around development, government and charity projects and controversies.

Examining the way class relations at Bantry were politically expressed through localized mobilization around issues of significance in town affairs, entails an investigation of how power was personally and collectively wielded in the town, and the means by which it was organizationally implemented. This in turn entails relating the major ideological cleavages differentiating the various participants in local projects and controversies to the status cleavages and alignments through which class relations were culturally expressed. The main feature of this discussion is the way it serves to demonstrate the correspondence of the spheres of interest and influence in local affairs with the tripartite structure of national power.

In making this argument I have tried to show how as acting subjects, these people personified the reproduction of a catholic-nationalist capitalism in Eire through the functions they performed as social agents occupying key social positions nationally and locally. Throughout the emphasis is on the contested and contingent nature of class processes, and the tensions and points of friction in the emergence and maintenance of the hegemonic ruling bloc associated with the interlocking of macro and micro processes.

Finally, I examine the impact on Bantry of a related but more imperious version of class power and class consciousness: the impersonally instituted authority of corporate property, of capital accumulated and organized monopolistically on an international scale. The emphasis here is on Gulf's capacity to subordinate all other objectives to its pursuit of profit. Many of the wider effects of the company's intervention in the Bantry area raise issues which go well beyond the scope of this book.

Hence I restrict myself to addressing the conceptual problem of dealing with interventions which, from the local standpoint, seem gargantuan and exceptional. Thus, although this book does not provide a comprehensive narrative account of the Gulf Oil operation, it does offer an analysis of that intervention to illustrate and draw together the study's major theme. It does so by showing how Gulf's presence influenced town affairs and realigned the balance of class forces locally, as well as how its activities in themselves partially reconstructed the relationship between macro and micro processes of social change at Bantry. Gulf's impact locally is then linked to the changing character of the ruling bloc nationally. The point of interest here is Eire's increasing dependence upon investments by transnational corporations, and upon transnational management of the nation's economy through its membership of the European Economic Community.

2 Class in its social habitat

In history as it is lived, class structures exist only as they are embedded in definite social institutions. It is those institutions which give class — and the abstract principles which govern its functioning — social being as empirically manifested in historical events. The processes by which classes are formed and re-formed thus always need to be analysed by locating them within the social habitat in and through which they work themselves out. In the nature of things, new social forms necessarily emerge from within pre-existing social habitats. Shaped by their origins, such new forms eventually come to exert an influence of their own upon these habitats. Understanding such processes requires not a functionalist conception of social reproduction but a dialectical one. We need to grasp processes of continuity and change as a unity — albeit a contradictory one.

One way of doing this is *to regard duplicative and transformative social processes as twin aspects of social reproduction* in that (as, for example, with biological evolution) *the very mechanisms which work to duplicate existing reality in fact transform it.* This conception of an ongoing, systematically patterned, but contingent and ever-changing, reproduction of social forms provides a way of relating processes of class formation to diverse expressions of power and consciousness so as to explore the interplay between them.

Class as relations of power and consciousness

In this study I am concerned not just with how class derives economically from material conditions, but with how it is embedded culturally in a social habitat which provides the forms and the emblems out of which political objectives find ideological expression.

Processes of class formation

Class does not intermittently influence social events, its influence is ever-present and all-pervasive. Class is 'not this or that interest, but the *friction of interests*' which characterizes the structure of society and its institutions. Conceived in this way, class is not a static category. Rather, as a delineation of modes of social relationship, it possesses 'a fluency which evades analysis' if not approached from an historical perspective (see Thompson, 1968: 939, 9).

If we are to account for the way actual, observable social change occurs, we must try and find ways of relating distinct processes of social determination to a logic of historical causality. It is one thing to argue that those processes which generate and transform social classes thereby change society, it is another to demonstrate how this occurs. Using the concept of class to explain social change entails using social change to explain class. That is to say, we cannot understand how society changes without looking at how classes themselves change.

It is not the evolution of classes as such, which explains change, but the evolution of the processes forming classes; it is the processes which create classes more than the classes themselves which are important (see also Connell, 1977b; Connell and Irving, 1980: 19–21). Moreover, the ongoing transformation of the processes themselves means that social change seldom appears to be correlated in any simple or obvious manner with clear-cut class divisions.

By using the term *processes of class formation* I am therefore not necessarily referring to the creation of entirely new classes — since this is a relatively long term phenomenon which in some way coincides with the development of a new mode of production — but to those processes which reconstitute already existing classes. Because of mechanisms and limitations built into well established structures, processes of class formation very often do not result in the formation of actual classes so much as distinct fractions, strata and milieux. This, however, does not in any way affect their character as processes of *class* formation (see also Thompson, 1978a: 146–50). An analogy can be drawn, for example, with biological evolution where processes which have the potential for creating distinct species seldom actually do so.

The commodity form and the status form of class

The notion of class as a lived experience contains the idea that class has to be analytically grasped both as an ideological encounter and as a material condition. The problem is how to conceptualize these two aspects without abstracting one from the other, or reifying the distinction. Although this problem is frequently side-stepped or glossed over in class analysis, it must be confronted if the concept of hegemony is to be made central to the analysis. For the concept of hegemony also unites within itself the idea of class as an *encounter* — the acts entailed in the exercising of hegemony calling forth a response from those hegemonized; and as a *condition* — a pervasive reality principle which occludes resistance to itself by the very way in which it pressures conformity to its dictates.

A major problem which tends to be passed over by theorists of class centres on the difficulties entailed in translating the abstract categories of capital and wage labour into the substantive classes of bourgeoisie and proletariat (see Parkin, 1979; Giddens and Parkin, 1980). The approach outlined here goes some way towards offering one particular solution to this problem.

The difficulty in fact really arises when we try to move beyond treating people merely as representatives — because owners — of commodities, to analysing social events in all their lived complexity. In order to analyse class as lived experience, to understand the complexities of social life in an actual social formation over time, we cannot satisfactorily treat people as merely personifications of economic relations — however necessary that may be for the analysis of the capitalist mode of production in the abstract. We may agree that it is as bearers of these economic relations that people come into contact with one another, but we can also agree that once in contact on this basis, their relations cease to be merely economic. In fact, we may want to argue that people originally come into contact not only as the bearers of economic relations — however decisive these may be — but cultural and political ones too.

For the actual flesh and blood people who empirically relate to one another in real life are not only agents of commodities (owners of capital or labour power). In order that commodities may enter into relation with each other *as commodities* it is of course necessary for people to place themselves in relation to one another *as persons* (cf. Marx, 1974, I: 88–9; 179 in Penguin).[1] In placing themselves in relation to one another as persons, they do not merely relate economically, for the economic relation presupposes, and empirically depends upon, other modalities of relationship being simultaneously socially effective.

The problem, then, is how to relate the analysis of the social actions of people as sentient beings to the fact that these people can at the same time be regarded as the 'bearers' of the social relations which they enter into. In other words, we have to deal with the fact that even though persons have no necessary identity with the relations they are the bearers of, because they come to have a contingent identity with these relations, they can be validly regarded as the personification of them. Or, to put the emphasis the other way around, we can say that they personify these relations only insofar as they are bearers of them. To recognize this is to allow that we can characterize a person by the social relations they enter into while at the same time still distinguishing between the person as a person and the multiplicity of social relations with which they are identified.

It would appear from this that we can — indeed have to — distinguish two forms of class relationship. In the first instance, functioning as their agents or representatives, the capitalist and the wage labourer personify the commodities capital and labour power. This gives us what we might call the commodity form of class relations which specifically typifies the capitalist mode of production.

But in order that this commodity form can come into being and enter into — so as to shape and be shaped by — the real historical process, it must become a part of the reality of people living a distinctive way of life within a given social habitat. That is, the abstract economic logic must acquire a tangible cultural form.

My argument is that when this occurs class in its commodity form (what we might metaphorically call the 'soul' of class) acquires its real materiality (its 'embodiment'), the form which it assumes in the world of appearances where the bourgeois and the proletarian meet. That is to say, the form which makes it available to experience.

Now since a given way of life constitutes the embodiment of determinate principles, codes, meanings, norms, ideas, values, beliefs, rules, etc., any given culture is thereby also the embodiment of a determinate moral rationality. A culture thus constitutes an ethical realm which confers an inherently evaluative character on human experience. Whatever else they may be about, then, social struggles are always moral issues and people habitually experience conflict in ethical terms. An argument can be made, then, for saying that in a quite fundamental way class is experienced evaluatively.

This evaluative character of class experience, I suggest, is habitually expressed through the forms of status.[2] That is, by the ideological way class relations are reproduced through the generation of social positions which are the repositories of privilege (whether in the form of rights or prerogatives, obligations or duties) and to which accrue (either as returns to property or labour) some portion of social wealth. This is not to claim that there is a neat fit between the commodity and status forms of class. On the contrary, it is just such disjunctions which make the distinction necessary in the first place.

The advantage to be gained by analysing class in this way is that it enables us to pay heed to the intricacies resulting from the translation of the polarities of capital and labour into those of the bourgeoisie and proletariat. At the same time it also allows us to heed the complexities and contradictions associated with interstitial positions and the experiences they engender.

Taking a more encompassing view, though this cannot be pursued here, the distinction between the commodity and status forms of class in capitalist society can be seen as a particular version of a more general distinction which seeks to relate the ontological and phenomenological aspects of class — class as a condition to class as an encounter, social being with lived experience.

Power

Because of the translation of the commodity form into the status form, class relations always appear more complicated in empirical reality than in abstract analyses of 'pure' modes of production. There are at least four factors at work here. Firstly, actual societies usually contain nascent or subordinate modes of production; secondly, contradictory class locations develop as a result of disjunctions between control of different aspects of the system of production and the surplus generated by it; thirdly, variable political and cultural conditions stamp their own indelible mark upon the development of the relations and forces of production; and, finally, the intersection of processes shaping interactions within institutions and those shaping these institutions themselves further multiplies the way class relations are lived out. All of these factors profoundly condition people's class consciousness, i.e. the way they comprehend their conflicts and the stance they take towards them. And it is this power struggle *in, for* and *over* consciousness which is the acme of class struggle, of class formation.

Now, if power refers to the capacity of people as social agents to realize objectives which determine the conditions under which they and other people live — either in the face of their resistance or by controlling their capacity to resist — then at root power is a matter of whether people are able to individually and collectively self-manage their affairs or not. To what extent is this a class question?

In dealing with this issue it must be remembered that power may be wielded personally or impersonally, by an individual, a collectivity or a corporate body, and that there is a close connection between personal and impersonally institutionalized means of wielding power (e.g. as in the relation between the market mechanism and propertied power). (See also Connell and Irving, 1980: 17, 18.) It is not just who wields power or how it is wielded that is important, but what it is wielded for; we have to relate how power is deployed to the interests it serves and the objectives of both the powerful and the powerless. This necessarily involves analysing how a particular structure of power both maintains itself and develops, i.e. how it is socially reproduced. Since the maintenance and development of a society's productive capacity is essential for its successful reproduction, it can be argued that at a fundamental level power and class relations are empirically symbiotic. Generally speaking, at the point where the issue of reproduction becomes a question of the perpetuation of a system of exploitation and appropriation and the structure of domination necessary for it, the problem of power becomes a class question.

Although the concept of power is of a different order from that of class — and is logically distinct from it — class analysis thus hypothesizes that there is a universal empirical connection between the two. That is, *class relations are relations of power and in class society power relations empirically assume a form to some degree designated by relations of class.* This does not imply that power follows class lines, only that in actual empirical reality power relations are decisively configured by the conflictual evolution of class antagonisms. It follows that although only certain kinds of power relations are class relations, in class society power relations are always premised upon specific kinds of class relations. It would be fallacious to go on and suggest that, logically, class relations are founded on power relations, just as it would be to suggest that power relations are founded on class relations. The point is not that one concept is more important than the other, but that neither can be satisfactorily *empirically* defined without the other (cf. Poulantzas, 1973: 99, 103; Therborn, 1978a: 131–2).

To say that class cannot be conceptualized without conceptualizing power is to stress that the point of departure for an analysis of class relations cannot be a grid of positions or locations from which we read off certain propensities and dispositions (cf. Poulantzas, Carchedi and Wright). Rather it is to argue that class relations can be characterized as a *societal field of force.* That is, social groups align themselves, as if magnetized, around antagonistic social poles, with some clustered at one pole and some at the other, and those in between aligned more sketchily and vicariously as if dependent upon the vicissitudes in the influence of the opposing poles. That is, those in interstitial or contradictory positions are 'bound down by lines of magnetic dependency' to the rulers, or in a different way, to the ruled (see Thompson, 1978a: 151).[3]

More specifically, we can say this. As a social dynamic constituted by relational antagonisms, class can be regarded as a dialectical process set in motion by the relationships of control (economic, political and cultural) generated by specific divisions of property and labour. The forms of ownership of property and the use, appropriation and disposal of labour and its products, are the key features of this dialectic. If class can be regarded as a structure of material and ideological control, then it is the ramifications of that control function which is its premier attribute. Put this way, the concept of control is not a synonym for ownership but a concept of a different order. It neither supersedes nor refines the concept of ownership. Nor is it ownership generalized to take account of and overcome the discrepancy between legal and real forms (cf. Poulantzas, 1975: 18–19). It denotes the impositions and prerogatives which derive from and react upon a given form of ownership.

If class society is not merely an amalgam of haphazard or coincidental controls, but an ensemble of consciously organized institutional prerogatives which pressure people to behave in certain ways, then to speak of class as a structure of control is to speak of a conscious use of power. The possession and exercise of power calls forth certain forms of consciousness and suppresses others. By the same token, different types of consciousness facilitate and suppress certain kinds of power. For this reason we can speak of *a dialectic between power and consciousness,* and we can say that *class processes are constituted simultaneously and indivisibly as relations of power and consciousness.*

Consciousness

Now since power has multiple sources and people are conscious of this and act accordingly, the crucial issue here concerns the way conscious uses of power connect up with the deployment of classes in struggle. If we regard class consciousness in an empirical sense as denoting the actual understandings people have of the class relations in which they are enmeshed and the stances they adopt towards them (cf. Connell, 1977a: 135), and if we regard class struggles not as intermittent events but as the ongoing friction of interests between antagonistic social groupings, classes do not first exist and only then enter into class struggle, but are formed as they fight, negotiate and collaborate (see also Thompson, 1978a: 149; Wright, 1978: 32; Poulantzas, 1975: 14). Classes do not struggle because they exist, rather they come into existence out of struggle, discovering themselves as classes by becoming conscious of class as a reality. Hence class and class consciousness are not the beginning but an arduous outcome of a diversely constituted historical process (Thompson, 1978a: 149).

People are made aware of, develop, articulate, and fight their battles using an enormous variety of ideas and expressive devices which react upon and condition the actual character of their struggles. It follows from this that the way in which they become conscious of and experience conflict is a crucial, perhaps *the* crucial process determining the direction of social change. For how people understand their situation and explain it to themselves and others determines how they organize, and this establishes the terms on which they are prepared and able to fight or co-exist.

If ideologies are those ideas by means of which people become conscious of their conflicts and fight them out (Marx, 1977: 21), then they are socially active manifestations of consciousness — examples, that is, of consciousness mobilized, voiced and acted upon. It follows that only some forms of consciousness can be said to be specifically 'ideological' (see Williams, 1977: 65). This view of ideologies and ideological domination as emerging out of more general consciousness directly relates ideology to material social processes. It is not the mere existence of people under given social conditions that is important, but their conscious experience of those conditions and the stance they adopt towards them. Consciousness is not something tacked onto the social process, but a central feature of the way in which it is materially manifested (see Williams, 1977: 59–60).

Nor is consciousness just what individuals carry around inside their heads. For the subjective motives of individuals *as* individuals are always conditioned by their subjective motives as members of a collectivity, i.e. people often find their personal lives determined by forces which make them think and act in one way as individuals and in quite another way as members of a collectivity which *as a collectivity* is subject to these very same forces. For example, individuals can behave one way when confronted by their rulers but in solidarity with others, their behaviour can take a more militant form, and when militancy is shown to have strength, both individuals and collectivities may develop a new assertiveness. At the very least, then, consciousness has to be defined in terms of the subjectivity of collectivities, not just individuals (cf. Wright, 1978: 89, fn: 73).

But the term consciousness denotes more than the subjective awareness of either individuals or collectivities. For consciousness is *materially manifested* — on the one hand in actual material culture (e.g., architecture, art, or decorated, adorned or scarred bodies and personalities), and on the other, in material practices which empower people by providing them with knowledge. Of course such a denial of knowledge may mean people come to believe what they are told, but the ideological domination exists regardless of whether it results in such beliefs or not (see also Wright, 1978: 38, fn: 18). For example, those in control of production are in the best position to be 'improvers', the innovators. They command or have access to knowledge, say, of new technology, scientific findings, or bureaucratic procedures, and have the means to put it to use. They also largely dictate the terms on which such knowledge will be used and what it will be used for. In resisting the uses to which such knowledge is put — in resisting the way it is used *against* them — exploited classes have often been forced to oppose the knowledge itself.

In analysing consciousness we must always consider these kinds of connections between objective, material consciousness and subjective phenomenological consciousness; between the ideological forms embedded in the culture itself, and the meanings, ideas and values of individuals and groups living under specific empirical conditions within that culture.

Class consciousness, then, is a measure not just of whether a class has come to 'know itself' and what it can do, but of the success or failure of particular kinds of *ideological domination*. This is why the struggle *in, for* and *over* consciousness is so central to class struggles, why the specific ways people become conscious of and experience class conflict are among the most crucial processes determining the direction of social change.

A central feature of this is the interdependence of the organization of coercion and consent, repressive force vis-a-vis directive, intellectual and moral leadership — might vis-a-vis hegemony. By focusing on the 'spontaneous' consent given by the mass of the population to the general direction imposed on social life by a dominant class and its auxiliaries (cf. Gramsci, 1975: 12, 57–8, 105), we can identify and define the ongoing 'friction of interests' in society under circumstances of apparent quiescence and willing compliance. What this conception of hegemony suggests is not a monolithic imperative, but an occlusive ideological pressure, which in coping with real conflict, prevents the claims of antagonistic social interests from being negotiated on an equal footing (cf. Rowse, 1978: 104–5; Thompson, 1978a: 164).

Class domination and the church, state and business

Using this perspective, it can be argued that the church, state and business came to function as a ruling bloc in Eire in the post-independence period.

The point of departure for the argument is that the nexus between church, state and business can only be understood historically in terms of the reconstruction of the relationship between class, power and consciousness in the post-colonial period. The trajectory of social change in Ireland had been one of repeated advance, ossification and rupture, as the capitalist mode of production implanted itself in ever more developed (albeit 'impure') form in Britain's oldest colony. This long and virulently contested process entailed the formation of a succession of what we might call *ruling blocs* within which new modes of class formation came to maturity. Eventually the result was a revolutionary overthrow of the colonial order itself.

That is to say, with the founding of the Free State in the south of Ireland, the conditions for the emergence of the most recent of these blocs was created. Developments in following decades were symptomatic of a new departure in class relations. There was a transfer of effective economic power locally to catholic entrepreneurs. Protestant wealth remained important, but with the loss of their estates the gentry's power was impoverished and marginalized. This abatement and submersion of protestant influence naturally dovetailed with the expansionary ambitions of enterprising catholics. Their appropriation of economic power was simultaneously an assertion of cultural prerogatives and a quest for final political dominance — not only of the remnants of the ascendancy but also their more humbly placed allies who were in trade, on the land, or working for wages.

Although the War of Independence ended in 1921 and there was an indigenous government by 1922, it took a Civil War and another decade of precarious civil harmony and political manoeuvring for the final form of this new bloc to become apparent. Until that time the coalition of forces which had brought the independence struggle to a head was still engaged in determining the shape of the revolutionary victory itself. The Treaty which ended the War of Independence fractured the popular front which Sinn Fein had become. A schism of some kind was probably inevitable. Neither the bourgeois nor the petty-bourgeois wing of the nationalist movement had managed to achieve hegemony. But once the Treaty split the party and the army, the bourgeoisie quickly reasserted itself. The support of both protestant and catholic business went against the Anti-Treaty Republicans, and this as much as military superiority and British aid to their adversaries, lost them the Civil War. Military defeat, however, does not guarantee political immolation, and the victory of the Pro-Treaty forces only extended and further complicated the already arduous transitional period.

The prolonged failure of the bourgeoisie to establish an effective hegemony over the predominantly petty-bourgeois population — particularly in the poorer western half of the country — meant that de Valera was able to abandon Sinn Fein to the revolutionary rump and lead the newly formed Fianna Fail party to a popular majority within six years. The quick consolidation in 1933 of the party's 1932 electoral victory, together with the emergence of Fine Gael as a successor to the former governing party, Cumman na nGaedheal, effectively brought the revolutionary period to a close. Henceforth, bourgeois supremacy in the Free State would be contradictorily mediated by petty-bourgeois modes of representation.

In practice, the main outcome of this sequence of processes was that the church, state and business became the major supports of a new class field of force in Eire. Because of the interlocking of the nominally autonomous institutions of church, state and business class power in Eire became inextricably tied up with the dominant position of the bloc itself. That is to say, since classes always wield power through key institutions — remaining beholden to these institutions and dependent upon their successful functioning — the reproduction of the bloc itself became central to (though not necessarily essential for) the maintenance of class power.

Contrary to what social scientists sympathetic to theories of power elites might want to argue, the autonomy exhibited by church, state and business in Eire does not necessarily indicate a weak form — let alone an absence — of class domination. Indeed, it may well be a measure of its strength. Given that this domination has been structured institutionally as a trinity, we would not expect relations within the bloc to have been necessarily harmonious. Rather, we might expect them to be tension-ridden and constantly renegotiated as changing circumstances have had differential effects upon the members of the bloc and the society over which it has ruled.

3 Business interests and economic development

Robbed and starved of capital as a colony and then partitioned from its industrial heartland in the North, the new state's economy was still in an underdeveloped condition half a century after its foundation. There had been major changes even so. In this chapter I analyse the way the local community was transformed by the ever more extensive incursions of capitalist economic relations. Section I is a general account of the way capital increasingly took control of agriculture, and the influence this had on rural communities in the west, with particular reference to the Bantry Rural District. Section II focuses more narrowly on Bantry to show how the catholic bourgeoisie took control of local commerce, consolidating its position in spite of stagnation and crisis. Section III looks at how local business people tried to improve their profit base by securing industry for the district, and at the way local prosperity became linked to increasing control of the economy by foreign capital.

The transfer of land to capital

The founding of the Free State realigned and postponed, but did not seriously fetter, capitalist domination of agricultural development. The landlords had been the agents of the supercession of feudal property relations, but tenant pressure prevented them from developing a fully capitalist agriculture, and eventually led to their expropriation. Peasant proprietorship of land parcels presupposed a disproportionately large rural population, and restricted development of the capitalist mode of production (Marx, 1974, III: 805–6, 811–2). But this too would change as the expropriation process was taken a step further.

The reshaping of rural life [1]

In the early years of the century the greater portion of agricultural produce was apparently consumed directly by the producers themselves, only the excess finding its way onto the market. This was soon to be true of only a rapidly disappearing minority on the poorest land in the poorest regions of the country. Dating back even before the founding of the state, Irish agriculture had developed a distinctive regional pattern. Store cattle from the west were fattened in the midlands and finished-off for the market and exported in the east. This was associated with a polarization within the country between the urbanized and industrializing east and the underdeveloped and agriculturally-subservient west. The application of science to agriculture, the increasing differentiation and specialization of farming, the decline in tillage and switch to pastoralism, and the dictates of the export market, helped render mixed farming uncompetitive, and eroded the viability of the small farms of the west.

The distinction between the small farmer and the large grazier or 'rancher' was not just a regional one: although the majority of farmers in the west were of the former type, there were always a number of medium-sized farms and a few large farmers. The big farmer was a 'man of business' who was totally oriented to the market, often combining farming with cattle dealing (i.e. acting as a middleman between the small farmer and the buyers in the east) and/or credit-retailing. Commercial capitalists, the big farmers usually relied on casual, seasonal, and full-time labour to make their profits. By contrast, for the small farmers only the surplus of what they raised entered the market and brought in a money income. It constituted a relatively small percentage of the total income, but because of the small farmers' dependence on the market (for both buying and selling produce as well as key consumer goods), the money share of their income was the key to their survival. On small farms, the direct controls on labour were not those of capital, but kinship mechanisms. Between these two poles stood the medium farmers, consolidating their holdings and increasing their livestock inputs. Thoroughly dependent upon the market they did not themselves farm in a capitalist manner, but continued to rely on family labour.

The prevailing cultural economy meant that inter-personal relations in the rural community were based upon an authority structure of patriarchal familism sanctioned by both the nationalist movement and the church. Women and younger men were subordinated to the husband and father; an individual was first of all a member of a family and carried that identity prior to any specifically personal one. Reciprocated ties of family and neighbourhood generated strong parochial sentiments. These overlapping and multi-stranded ties helped to limit a family's dependence on market forces and aided production for consumption, since production for profit was beyond the means of all but the few. But kinship increasingly lost its capacity to organize economic relations within and between families and more and more land entered the market, either because holdings were no longer viable, or remunerative relative to other pursuits. Inheriting sons, as well as non-inheriting sons and daughters, sought off-farm employment. As well as bringing in additional income to the farm, wage-labour brought independence to farming children, altering their marriage prospects and encouraging new lifestyles in the countryside. Improved transport, the telephone, electrification of the home, electronic mass media, better schooling and the cumulative effects of migration all had an abrasive effect on traditional perspectives. As the ideology of progress, equated with commercial competence and modernization, permeated the consciousness of the young, the authority of age and tradition was forced to adapt itself to the inexorable advance of the authority of the market. Continued mechanization also had an effect. As machines particularly farm implements and cars, replaced traditional means of work and transport, old crafts and trades and the employment they gave were swept away along with the agricultural labourer. Mechanization also wrought major changes in *the way* labour was employed. Mutual aid practices succumbed as did the wage labourer himself, for the use of labour was increasingly dictated by the availability and use of machines. Although the technological accompaniments of economic development were gradually introduced to more and more of the population, these innovations did not alleviate the depressed conditions of the countryside; in fact, in many respects they aggravated them: the introduction of farm machinery undoubtedly made work easier for the operator, but it also made additional labourers superfluous and forced more labourers and farmers' sons to join the emigrant queue.

The cumulative effect of such changes on the communities of the west began to show in the 1950s. These years of depression created a crisis in the countryside from which many people, indeed whole communities, never recovered. Traditional ties and relationships had gradually broken down, either because they were no longer viable or because a threshold had been passed beyond which they ceased to have social efficacy or meaning. The immiserization and demoralization of residual segments of the rural population had entered a new phase. In the late 1950s the Irish economy was put on an entirely new footing with the implementation of a national plan for economic development (see below). In order to survive, in order to receive a share of the advantages and not just the disadvantages of industrially-led growth, local communities, quite literally, had to broaden themselves. As one area amalgamated its local institutions with neighbouring areas (its sporting groups, recreational facilities, schools, even its clergy), townlands and villages which once formed the locus of community life imperceptibly surrendered their focal role to the nearest town. A family's immediate locality, while remaining important to it, was relegated to being little more than a neighbourhood. In this way local groups became even more directly incorporated into the wider society.

Many people were marginalized and isolated by these processes. In fact, the bulk of the poorer areas of the west of Ireland became ghosts of their former selves — socially marooned by many of the changes that had overtaken them. But it would be a mistake to describe the decline of individual townlands, villages and parishes as evidence of rural decline or an eclipse of community — even if the people themselves saw it that way — rather, it constituted a re-alignment of community around larger centres.

It also signified the ever more pervasive erosion of the economic, cultural and political distinctiveness of the peasantry — encompassed, constituted and re-constituted as it had long been by the contradictory emergence and consolidation of capitalism in Ireland. That is to say, contrary to what appearances might seem to suggest, we can simultaneously accord importance to the predominantly peasant character of these communities *and* the formative and transformative influence of capitalism *upon* and *within* them. Their 'traditionalism', in other words, was more the product of the process of modernization than a simple antithesis of it.

The logic of expropriation [2]

Whereas in the past the prosperity of the entire country depended upon agriculture, the percentage of the population engaged in farming fell rapidly after World War II, from just over 50% to just under 30%. Meanwhile the gap widened between the success-oriented entrepreneur for whom farming was a mean to an end and the survival-oriented peasant for whom farming was an end in itself. A growing percentage of small farms were declared to be non-viable, whilst the larger were producing a growing share of output and making a higher return per acre. Increasingly, production was controlled by capital — either through the market, directly by management of farm finance, or by taking possession of the land itself. Farmers depended less and less on credit from shopkeepers and merchants as loans from the Creamery Co-operatives, the banks and the Agricultural Credit Corporation became available. Petty usury though not eradicated, was more and more subordinated to corporate financial practices, and it was the big, enterprising farmers who were in the best position to obtain credit from this source. They similarly benefited from the growing control of the dairy industry by the more and more rationalized, bureaucratic and business-oriented co-operatives. Meanwhile the growth of the national farming organizations, dominated by and representing the larger, capitalistic farmers, further extended the hold of capital on Irish agriculture.

As competition from large-scale agriculture and improvements in technology and production techniques required larger outlays and more extensive material means of producion, small farmers were priced out of farming. They were not in a position to enlarge their holdings nor able to increase their output. They or their heirs left the land, and the proportion of the population engaged in agriculture continued to decrease. Moreover, as farmers sold their holdings and the number of farm labourers contracted, the class character of the rural population changed. Within a few generations, the new nation was transformed into one whose land, though not directly farmed by capital, was nevertheless beholden to it. Integral to this was the fact that so many farms remained in the possession of a financially dependent geriatric remnant of the peasantry.

Small impoverished farmers characteristically clung onto their holdings even under extremely adverse conditions. This was not because of some kind of irrational attachment to the family's land (after all, many more people left the land than ever stayed on it). Rather, small farmers were 'land hungry' because they could not afford to be anything else. Inheriting sons rightly calculated that they had more security (a house, potato garden, a milking cow, and calves for sale) by sticking with the land than entering the workforce without saleable skills when unemployment was endemic. Under-employment presumably was preferable to the risks of no employment. Those who stayed with the land had the security of knowing they could wring out a livelihood under all but the most adverse conditions. The absolute limit to the peasant's exploitation of the land and his family's labour lay only in the wages he paid to himself after deducting actual costs: so long as the price of the product covered these wages, he could cultivate his land, at wages down to a bare minimum. The small farmer often combined some part-time wage-labour with his farming. This was designed to augment the farmer's income and the viability of the farm, i.e. it helped keep the wages he paid himself above that bare minimum. By expanding such opportunities, rural industrialization had the ironic effect of encouraging part-time farming in many cases. The hybrid peasant-proletarian was the product of a hedging of bets.

But a measure of the extent to which the odds were stacked against the small farmer was the fact that marriage was too big a gamble for more and more of them and those who would marry them. Single men tended to be content or able to resign themselves to a lower standard of living; their productive capacity attenuated accordingly, and they more readily came to rely on an increasing range of government subsidies to survive. A corollary of this was that, increasingly, if men stayed farmers they either married late or could or would not marry; small farming became a single man's occupation. As demonstrated by actual behaviour, marriage became increasingly unlikely for a man on less than 50 acres, i.e. one working a farm of doubtful commercial viability. A farm worth marrying into was one which would support a retiring farmer and an inheriting son. About 100 acres was necessary to make marriage a certain proposition. Consequently, between a third and a half of Irish farmers did not have a successor. Since women were not marrying farmers, farms were either worked by bachelors or by couples past child-bearing age. Hence in the most extreme cases productive activity no longer expanded and contracted with the varying phases of the family life-cycle once the farm family was deprived of its reproductive capacity.

This ensemble of forces thus caused a transformation in the relation of the farming family to the land. To the extent that the farmer's retention of his holding was dependent upon state welfare, it could be argued that those responsible for state policies found it more convenient to subsidize his employment on the land than his unemployment off it. That is, by subsidizing unproductive farmers, state policy kept them out of the workforce, which was already swollen with a surplus that could not be employed. Land 'kept out of production' in one generation came on the market in the next, and was bought up in such a way as to enlarge the bigger holdings while keeping down the total number of holdings. Land was also sold for non-agricultural purposes, thus keeping down the total number of holdings but providing investment opportunities elsewhere. The overall result was that although large numbers of farms stayed in the hands of unproductive individuals, the ownership of productive land became more concentrated. By keeping marginal land and large numbers of people unproductive, the competitive position of highly capitalized land was enhanced. Escalating land prices further exacerbated the discrepancy between the opportunities available to the poor and the wealthy farmer as far as reliance on inheritance and use of the market were concerned.

The tenacity of this kin-centred form of production in the face of over-whelming forces intent on destroying it was not primarily due, then, to the idiosyncracies of a peasant mentality, rather it was due to the denial of realistic alternatives to inheriting sons by these very forces: small farmers were simultaneously being squeezed out of production and prevented from entering the workforce too quickly. They were, in effect, caged-in on the land, and forced to scavenge a living from it; they clung to the land because they were unemployable off it.

The Bantry Rural District provides a good example of these processes at work. West Cork could never hope to compete agriculturally with the rich lands to the east. Its farms had low output, low productivity, and yielded low incomes. Because of its barren and mountainous character, the Bantry Rural District had little fertile land. Most farms were measured in 'adjusted acres', with many having more than half their total acreage actually composed of agriculturally useless land; 89.2% of holdings in the Bantry Rural District were valued at £20 or less in the mid 1970s. Between 1901 and 1960 the total number of holdings in West Cork decreased by 15%, the fall being greatest in the most western districts. This trend continued through the 1960s (see Table 3.1). The total number of farms in the Bantry Rural District continued to decrease between 1965 and 1970. Farms of 50 to 100 acres declined slightly in number, whereas those between 5 and 50 acres declined markedly in number. Farms of 100 acres and more increased in number as did holdings of less than 5 acres, indicating that land was simultaneously being converted into viable, entrepreneurial units or, failing that, into non-farmable plots held for leisure, hobby or subsistence-augmenting purposes. In fact, an An Foras Taluntais survey showed that in no instance did holdings of under 15 acres provide the sole or primary source of income for the occupants. In sum, fewer people were engaged in full-time farming on fewer, but larger farms. Just as holdings of less than 15 acres began to be eradicated in the latter part of the nineteenth century, and holdings of 15–30 acres in the first half of the twentieth, farms of less than 100 acres were now subject to similar pressures.[3]

Large areas of countryside were thus allowed to become unproductive. Because it was relatively more profitable to invest in agricultural land with

Table 3:1 The changing stratification of farms

Farm Size Acres	1965 No.	%	1970 No.	%	Change 1965–70 No.	%
1–5	149	10.12	161	11.40	+12	+8.05
5–30	499	33.88	452	32.01	−47	−9.42
30–50	342	23.22	318	22.52	−24	−7.02
50–100	315	21.38	306	21.67	−9	−2.86
100–200	127	8.62	133	9.42	+6	+4.72
200+	41	2.78	42	2.98	+1	+2.44
Total	1473	100	1412	100		
Farms of 5–50 acres	841	57.09	770	54.53	−71	−8.44
Farms of 50–200+ acres	483	32.79	481	34.07	−2	−0.41
Farms of 100–200+ acres	168	11.41	175	12.39	+7	+4.17

Source: Meehan (1974) Appendix from Central Statistics Office, Agricultural Statistics 1965–72

a greater natural fertility and where there was scope for capital-intensive farming. The more marginal land was surrendered to the gorse bushes and let go wild or, in scenic areas, turned over to tourist and leisure settlements. Meanwhile, as more and more of the population left the land, larger holdings owned by wealthier farmers became more common. These developments dove-tailed nicely. Wild, untilled land attracted tourists: land devoted to holiday cottages, second-homes and retirement activities removed land from agricultural production, yet at the same time massively inflated its capital value and the profits to be made from it.

Regional dependency and international finance [4]

After the depressed years of the early 1950s the Irish government embarked upon a New Economic Plan which was based upon capital imports to aid economic development (see below). One of the outcomes of this policy was the drive to join the European Economic Community or Common Market (EEC). The Irish Land Commission had long encouraged the creation of viable land holdings; membership of the EEC hastened the state's drive to get smaller farmers to quit their few acres. In fact, the expropriation of small holders now became explicit government policy and the majority of Irish farmers were threatened.

Ireland joined the EEC, following Britain, on 1 January 1973. Almost immediately the country began to feel the effects of the Common Agricultural Policy. Under the Mansholt Plan, 'nonproductive' European farmers were to be removed from the land and pensioned off to make way for 'development-oriented' farmers, thus reducing employment in agriculture by rationalizing holdings and providing incentives for more capital-intensive methods. The Irish government commenced to implement this plan in 1974 with a modified version known as the 'Farm Modernization Scheme'. Virtually all funding of Irish agriculture was now channelled through this scheme. Farms were divided into three categories, based on acreage and the revenue each was capable of producing. The viability of *commercial* farms was assured. Farms which were thought capable of becoming commercial by means of the development plan were designated *development* farms. Those labelled *transitional* farms were to be eradicated as part of the consolidation program. Although modification of these policies diluted them considerably, it was consistent with their rationale that it was the larger farmer, the big producer, who was the one to benefit most from the higher product prices which came with EEC membership.

The push for modernization equated development with capitalism, i.e. with 'adaptation' to modern commercial agriculture symbolized by the enterprising farmer. Such things as 'efficiency', 'viability', 'productivity' and even 'rationality' were now assessed according to capitalistic criteria whenever state policy was being formulated or assessed. The preoccupation with improving the performance of the agricultural industry as a national priority nevertheless tended to be construed as a concern with rectifying anomolous inequities.[5] State policy was ostensibly aimed at creating a situation where incomes and living standards in the agricultural sector were comparable with those in other sectors. Purporting to rectify inequities, this program in fact also served as an ideological gloss for the expropriation of non-capitalist farmers who were increasingly being rendered unproductive by these very same policies. That is, the agricultural support schemes, whilst perhaps having the intention and certainly the appearance of aiding the small farmers, in fact improved the competiveness of larger farmers. They functioned as a pension-scheme for the unwanted surplus of farmers. In some measure, government agricultural policy was the cause of the crisis among small farmers — including those who got into financial difficulties *because* they attempted to modernize. By its failure to act against the tendency of the market to erode the competitive position of small holders (which included a failure to move against land speculation), the state had helped make it necessary to subsidize small holders. The subsidies were designed to politically buy off those who could not be forcibly removed from the land though they had been rendered economically impotent on it. Of course, every attempt was made to reduce the amount of subsidies that had to be paid. One of the reasons why an emphasis was placed on locating small and medium-sized industries in remote areas was to provide factory jobs for men leaving farming.

The high rate of emigration, the stagnation of agricultural production, and the slow erosion of the ranks of small farmers and shop-keepers at a time when the national economy was expanding rapidly, reflected the growing domination of the post-colonial economy by capital. It was a paralysing predicament to be in. As labour fled the west of Ireland so did the region's capacity to generate productive development. Meanwhile, the highly capital-ized agriculture of Western Europe and Ireland's Golden Vale out-competed the poorer regions in the west of the country.

This argument suggests that the gradual marginalization of the peasantry was consistent with if not necessary for the advance of capitalism in the post-colonial period. Seen in this light, the perpetuation of peasant proprietor-ship represents a distinct phase in the development of capitalist agriculture in Ireland, an interregnum between an entrenched aristocratic commercialism and an incursive corporate agribusiness. In this sense, peasant proprietorship, at least as a relatively autonomous form of farming, was doomed as soon as it came into being. The family farm may not have been disappearing, but the number of farms run on capitalist lines increased both in absolute and relative terms. Meanwhile, to remain viable, family farms became more and more subject to the dictates of bank finance, corporate-control of expertise, inputs (e.g. seeds, pesticides, herbicides and fertilizer), mechanization, processing and outlets, that is to say, wholesale corporate, state and EEC sponsored intervention in and regulation of production, marketing, and 'efficiency-based' financing. That is, though the process was disguised by the continuing numerical and social salience of the family farm, this type of production was gradually succumbing to the incursions of corporate agribusiness in all its diverse forms.

As in the days of the landlords (though without such drastic human consequences) the miserable economic circumstances of the majority of the rural population were due to the inexorable advance of capitalism. The Land War and the War of Independence fundamentally ruptured the expropriation process, but they did not eradicate it because they did not eradicate capitalism in Ireland. Social conditions in the country remained both an affront to, and a product of, the way in which capital was creating the conditions for its reproduction on an extended scale. The continued depopulation of rural areas was a measure of the country's backwardness; it was also a prerequisite of capitalist economic development in Ireland. This was the new version of consolidation. That is, the impoverishment and expropriation of the small farmers was the stepping-stone to prosperity for the few who farmed large holdings in a capitalist manner, particularly those who lived in the towns and cities and owned the land. In view of the significance of the small farmer in the nationalist struggle it is of course ironic, though not altogether surprising, that one of the key agents fostering these processes has been the post independence state. The prediliction for corporatist solutions in the pursuit of state policy, though interfering with market mechanisms, nevertheless most advantaged those in a position to convert their strength in the market into influence within the state apparatus.

On an international level, the belated development of areas peripheral to the capitalist economy follows from the prior removal of their productive capacity, their relative underdevelopment. The export of labour and the import of capital were two phases of the one process: capital accumulated abroad by the exploitation of Irish labour was then used, it could be said, to develop the Irish economy by means of investments controlled from outside the country. By exploiting the labour of marginal areas such as West Cork the industrial centres of metropolitan capitalism exploited the marginal areas themselves.

The business of the towns

The transfer of land to capital not only affected the lives of the rural population, it also influenced the prosperity of the towns. This is not to suggest that developments in the towns waited on those in the countryside. Even in the landlord days urban-based capitalists had commercially dominated the rural mass of the population. With the overthrow of the landlords the catholic 'merchant princes' in the towns had quickly consolidated their position as did the more astute of the shopkeepers based in outlying areas.

The personalistic character of commerce

In the larger villages, as in the towns, shopkeepers competed for custom, but in smaller hamlets and outlying country areas, the position of the storekeeper remained more securely monopolistic. This was particularly true, for example, of the peninsula and poorer areas of the Bantry Rural District. A larger proportion of customers in these areas tended to be old, without transport and in need of many favours. The number of rural shops declined with the population and much erstwhile custom went to the town, but the rural shopkeeper remained a key figure amongst those who remained.

Credit-retailing had long been the main form of debt-bondage.[6] If accumulated debts became large enough they were sometimes worked off. Otherwise an old client without immediate heirs (widows or incapacitated bachelor farmers) paid off their debts in land. In some cases people sold their house and land in payment of past debts and as an advance on future favours some years before they expected to die. Shopkeepers thus often had to wait years for payment, but profited from doing so. They were able to buy a client's property at a deflated price, then years later when the owner died and prices for land and housing had gone up, they sold at the new market price. Because tourism and foreign settlement caused real estate to skyrocket at Bantry in the 1960s, a number of rural shopkeepers made some very handsome returns from this kind of investment.

Rural shopkeepers engaged in an immensely varied range of activities which in addition to the shop or pub, often included a farm, a sub-postmastership, an estate agency, a holiday guesthouse, a taxi service, or a fishing interest (e.g. as a boat-owner or as a marketing agent). In remoter areas, the shopkeeper might also have a grocery run supplying outlying households, mainly pensioners and people on the farmers' dole. The shopkeeper in outlying areas also often served as a communications link, bringing goods from town and passing on telephone messages.

Ties of monopolistic personal dependence of this kind no longer embraced everyone to the same extent. Some people were not implicated at all; others were, but only peripherally. It was simply a case of whether the customer minimized potential endebtedness or not. The same personalistic manner of transacting business was maintained, it was simply a matter of whether there were any larger ramifications to it than that.

Although these rural 'big men' may have derived exorbitant advantages from their social position, they were *of* the people rather than above them. Some were not to be trusted, but others were well regarded and there was

30

some affection and a good deal of mutuality in these relationships. For people in need of credit, or someone to call an ambulance or doctor, or deliver the occasional message, the services provided by the shopkeeper were all important. As a result, the petty patron was imbued with a special, if limited, moral authority and prestige in the consciousness of country people.

The main thing about these relationships was not merely that rural shopkeepers often made extortionate profits, but that they were able to convert quantity into quality, translating numerous, trivial, and flexibly calculated debts into a store of capital and influence which automatically multiplied itself. That is, 'money made money': once established, the rural entrepreneur was able to extend the size, number and type of services offered to a wider variety of clients, and as well, become a contact point for outsiders intervening in the affairs of the rural community.

It is clear from this that the rural entrepreneur acted as both a patron and as a broker. However, the latter role was either subordinated to, or inextricably dependent upon, the shopkeepers' immediate and direct control of petty patronage. Of course, in the long run, or in terms of wider social processes, it was their role as brokers which was the most important thing (see also chapter 4). But the fact remains that these people usually became big brokers because they were already small patrons.

In the town marketing and employment practices formally followed capitalist lines. But up until the coming of industry to Bantry if a business was in a monopolistic position with respect to its customers and employees, informal calculations helped convert a nominally competitive 'free' market into one where workers and consumers were kept 'loyal', prices were inflated and wages deflated. In this situation, workers were often clients twice over: first as customers and second as employees. The monopolistic position of the Biggs group (see below) was such that, as the local wholesaler, it competed in the retail trade with its customers. It was thus in a position to dictate the terms of trade to its competitors as well as its customers and employees.

With industrialization and higher wages, these relationships were broken down, the Gulf Oil intervention freed a large proportion of the population from indirect or direct dependence on the merchants for employment. Indeed, the Managing-Director of the Biggs group was alleged to have once boasted that there was not a working man in Bantry who had not approached him at one time or another for a job. According to one source, this degree of power had earned him the title of 'The King of Bantry'.

As the market intruded further and further upon all areas of economic activity at Bantry, personalistic ties were subordinated to its requirements. This did not necessarily mean that patronage-type relations disappeared, only that there was a gradual shift in priorities; those modes of relating which could not be accommodated by the market mechanism gradually became redundant, obstacles to more profitable forms of trade, and anachronistic as mechanisms of social control. It was another kind of patronage which remained salient in the popular mind and continued to have universal efficacy, to all intents and purposes untouched by the market, the thoroughly politicized patronage dispensed by politicians (see chapter 4).

The commercial dominance of the merchant princes

Most of the catholic families who were to dominate commercial life in Bantry in the twentieth century rose to prominence after the founding of the Free State in 1922. A number of these people came from relatively modest farming or shopkeeping-publican backgrounds, but they had managed to achieve means, influence and status which set them apart from the bulk of the town's traders. The cycle of upward mobility took little more than one generation, and in some cases not even that. This pattern of ascent resembled the rise of the few already-established catholic families who had come to prominence in the latter part of the nineteenth century.

The final transfer of economic power to catholic business families in Bantry entailed the incorporation of individual protestant families into the new order. Just as the downward mobility of individual protestants was a function of the immobilization of the class structure on which they depended, the upward mobility of individual catholics was a function of the mobilization of the class to which they belonged and its position within the revolutionary mass movement.

The ambience of aristocratic pre-eminence which might otherwise have attached to the owners of Bantry House had been squandered by the time the family was most in need of it. This was not the case in other parts of Ireland (or West Cork for that matter) where the wealth, privilege and prestige of the gentry survived the transition, even if in a somewhat ambivalent and diminished form. But the Whites of Bantry lost ground early because of the parlous state of their finances. It was only by opening the House to tourists that the family continued to make any distinctive contribution to the town's economy.

Protestant business people found themselves in a contradictory position; their prominence in the local economy had depended upon the continued hegemony of the landlords; the hegemony of their own class, since it was dominated by catholics, threatened to erode their economic competitiveness and to isolate them politically and culturally. Some amalgamated with or sold out to local catholic entrepreneurs. Others continued to operate their businesses, gradually scaling them down as competition imposed new constraints, or heirs opted for other pursuits. Two protestant businesses remained prominent in the town in the 1970s. One was Vickery's Hotel, which declined from its former grandeur as the garage and coach service was closed down, its shop sold, and the hotel itself became run-down. Warner's, owned by the former butter merchants, continued to operate an agricultural provisions and grocery store, along with a bakery. The latter was eventually closed, and the rest of the business was being scaled down as the owner neared retirement.

In other West Cork towns, notably Bandon and Skibbereen, the disproportionate amount of wealth that remained in protestant hands was more immediately visible than in Bantry, where the town's leading merchant, G. W. Biggs, had amalgamated his business with that of a catholic family. As an assertive entrepreneur, G. W. Biggs had originally come to work for a merchant, miller and landowner named Wolfe, from whose executors he bought the business which became the foundation of his wealth and influence. Biggs had the first telephone line in the town (a private line from his house to the company offices in the square) and, symbolically, was given No. 1 in the directory once a state-run service came into operation.

Biggs amalgamated his firm with Jas. Lyons and Co. in 1926, leaving his share of the business to his daughters when he died three years later. They remained the major shareholders in the new company, G. W. Biggs & Co. Ltd., even though managerial control passed into catholic hands. The man who was to become Managing-Director and part-owner of the Biggs group came to Bantry from Schull in 1919 to help manage his mother's family's business. In some spheres the two firms had been competitors. After G. W. Biggs's death the new Managing-Director integrated the firms' activities and from the late 1930s set about expanding the group and his control of it. He bought shares from Biggs's daughter, founded a new company, Fastnet Fisheries, and bought Murphy & O'Connor's sawmill and timber yard when it was on the verge of bankruptcy. The shareholding relationship between the Managing-Director and Biggs's heirs was reversed in Murphy and O'Connor's; he became the majority shareholder and G. W. Biggs and Co. became a minority shareholder. The Biggs group's activities thus came to embrace agricultural supplies (including the milling of grain), sawmilling, coal supplies, petroleum distribution, carrying, ironmongering, hardware supplies, and a general store and supermarket. They also acted as shipping and forwarding agents, ship chandlers, Lloyd's agents and insurance brokers.

The Biggs group provides a good example of the way protestants deployed their capital in adverse circumstances and also illustrates how an enterprising catholic could use protestant capital to consolidate his own position and became the town's leading businessman — and arguably, the most powerful single individual in the whole Bantry area (see chapters 6 and 7). The opportunity to amalgamate with and eventually take control of a large protestant firm came to very few catholic entrepreneurs, but there were other options open to them.

Sometimes the manner in which they took advantage of opportunities for profit-making brought an astringent tang to the nationalism of enterprising catholics. Entrepreneurs who rose to prominence prior to the final assault

33

on the old order had often entered into contracts with the British government and the landlords as part of their normal business practice. McCarthy's, a family of butchers provisioned the Beare Island garrison as well as leasing the tolls of the town from Bantry House.[7] W. M. Murphy, who was to become a leading national figure as a politician, press baron and industrialist (see, for example, Lyons, 1975: 243, 245, 263, 282, 284) made his money building railways throughout the British Empire. At Bantry he built the extension line and established the firm of Murphy and O'Connor's. His sister married a draper who, in a formerly protestant-owned business, made money out of the cotton trade during the American Civil War. Cullinane's Ltd. became one of the town's most important retail outlets and an outfitter of the military. Cullinane's sister married her cousin, W. H. O'Sullivan, a flour miller and merchant, who inherited his mother's business and built himself up to become a major town-landlord and JP. This man had once been forced to flee to America because he was a member of the militant Phoenix Society. But this did not stop him from subsequently becoming a landlord himself. Like many of the conservative, nationalist bourgeoisie, he showed himself quite willing to court popular opprobrium in his bid to amass wealth and supplant the ascendancy.

In the early years of the twentieth century he owned many buildings in the town and began to buy out the ground-leases on which they stood, with the result that although the Bantry estate retained two-thirds of the ground-rent of the town, a catholic landlord owned approximately one-third. The tenants resented the hypocrisy of the situation and the heirs and executors of the O'Sullivan estate, like their protestant counterparts, were embarrassed by their predicament and reluctant to press their claims too hard. Leases were re-negotiated with or sold to the sitting tenant rather than being let or sold on the open market, otherwise they were not renewed. Once a move was made to put the affairs of the estate in order it aroused a good deal of discontent and comment in the town.

The irony of the situation was apparent to all. Yet it was the logical outcome of the bourgeois nationalists' position. Their political and economic initiatives had been designed to replace landlordism with a capitalism based on indigenous trade and manufacture. That program was compatible with the catholic bourgeoisie themselves becoming rentiers. It was not, however, compatible with the petty bourgeois version of nationalism which saw ground-rent as the acme of exploitation.

A variety of other catholics founded and expanded businesses and became important figures in the commercial life of the town in these years, under-writing the transfer of local economic power. A number of these people also became influential in public affairs; others were content simply to run their businesses and based their sway in the community on their prominence as entrepreneurs.

Prior to World War II the profitability of local business houses was limited, but in spite of the sluggish state of the economy, the more astute merchants still managed to consolidate their position. As smaller businesses went under those that remained afloat benefited from the elimination of competition, and shrewd entrepreneurs were able to buy out failing businesses at less than their value. That is, even as their profitability was eroded, the larger capitalists were able, in classic fashion, to strengthen their firms and create a more solid base for capital accumulation in the future.

But not everything went the big firm's way. Up until the 'economic war' Bantry merchants were still importing cargo by steamer from Liverpool. In addition to the Liverpool trade, wheat was imported from Canada and maize from the River Platte. The grain trade supported the pig population of West Cork. Government policy on grain imports struck at Bantry's trade and contributed to the decline of the West Cork pig industry. The establishment of the Co-operative Creameries before the War changed the character of dairying in equally dramatic fashion. By acting as wholesalers, and distributors, the Creameries met many of the farmers' provisions requirements, with the result that they no longer had to go to town so frequently. Merchants resented this competition, and town publicans and shopkeepers railed against their loss of the farmers' ancillary custom. Yet the co-operatives became well established and developed into one of the key businesses on the rural scene.

Probably the biggest set-back to Bantry in these years, at least to the working class, was the closure of the Woollen Mill. It had employed as many as 50 people, mainly women, making blankets, coarse tweed and flannel. It finally closed its doors in 1938 when the Electricity Supply Board (ESB) took over from the private firm which had powered the Mill. The Bantry Bay Steamship Company also ceased to function around this time. Meanwhile the trade in coral sand gave way to the sale of subsidized crushed limestone as fertilizer. Contracting employment opportunities, along with the exodus from the land, meant that emigration continued unabated after the temporary interruption of the War.

After the War, or 'the Emergency', as it was called in Ireland, the economy of the country expanded, but agricultural output stagnated. The slump tightened into a stranglehold in the west of the country in the 1950s. Many small farms, shops and pubs were reduced to a marginal existence or bankrupted, and the labouring population was impoverished. Labour was cheap but there was not the capacity in the economy to employ it. Nor was there sufficient consumer demand (with a falling population) to support the amount of capital invested in commercial undertakings — there was too much capital competing for too little profit. As one prominent businessman of the time put it: too many people were trying to cater for too few at a time when there was scarcely any need for a town at all (cf. Jackson, 1967: 24–7).

The town and Rural District remained in an economically depressed state for almost the whole decade and, as residents and commentators of the time unanimously report, the people were dispirited and despondent. Hope for the future was continuously compromised by the exodus of 'the best and brightest' on the emigrant ships. When looking back people may have cast an exaggerated pall of misery over these years, but the evidence suggests their memories were fairly accurate. They erred, perhaps, in suggesting that things got worse, when really it was more that they failed to get better. Many also erred when they implied that the burden was equitably shared. Things undoubtedly were bad for everybody, but in reality the wealthier members of the community seem to have had little difficulty in maintaining an affluent lifestyle, however difficult it was to maintain a profitable business.

Amongst the worst off in the town were the small fishermen and their families who depended upon the in-shore fisheries for a living. By the early 1930s US tariffs had finished off the export of fish from Bantry. For some years in the 1940s the Biggs group's Fastnet Fisheries fielded a small fleet of half a dozen ocean-going trawlers, but with the sale of the boats in the 1950s Bantry surrendered any serious chance of remaining a fishing port of any significance.[8] The Bay was fished out, mainly because of the foreign steam trawlers operating around the 3-mile limit and the use of small-mesh nets. The introduction of the 'disastrously successful' ring-seine for mackerel (Hourihane, 1971: 101) seriously depleted the fisheries within less than a decade. The ranks of the small fishermen (the 'cottiers of the sea') were permanently diminished. One time there were over 200 boats fishing out of Bantry, Gerahies and Whiddy; by the late 1960s less than 50 men were engaged in salmon fishing in the summer months. After the close of the commercial salmon season, about half a dozen men engaged in scallop fishing. The herring season occupied the winter months and up until the late 1950s the seine-boat-and-follower was used, a method virtually unchanged in 200 years until it was replaced by one requiring fewer men, and relying on motor-powered boats. But the fishing was now highly unreliable, and did not provide an adequate income even for the reduced number of men, most of whom had some other form of employment, or drew the dole.

By the 1960s the last Bantry trawler had been sold, and in subsequent years Castletownbere was developed as a major fishing port catering to its own fleet and to the Spanish fleet as well. This was a state-aided project and part of the government's plan to develop the fishing industry. Being 20 miles from the open sea Bantry could not have competed even if it had had comparable facilities. The Irish fishing industry expanded considerably during the 1960s mainly because of extensive capital inputs by the state, and the development of Castletownbere as a major fishing port was an example of the results. In 1970 it ranked fifth in value of landings (these totalled £0.22 million). But deprived of fish, the small inshore fleets of self-employed fishermen were gradually eliminated in a similar fashion to the small farmers. In spite of rhetoric designed to placate the small fisherman, the state devoted itself primarily to the task of providing larger fishing interests with capital.

The tourist industry, by contrast, reached its peak in the late 1960s.[9] There had been an increase in tourism after the War; the first wave of foreign settlers had begun to arrive then as well. Foreign Nationals made up the bulk of the immigration in the 1960s, but returned-emigrants, Dubliners and 'refugees' from the North also retired to the area in these years. Meanwhile, industrial development inevitably brought in a quota of skilled tradesmen, technicians, managerial staff, as well as one or two independent business people. This influx had quite a few financial spin-offs and an important influence on the demography of the hinterland; it also had a profound effect on lifestyle patterns (see chapter 6 and Eipper, forthcoming). These two trends fed into one another and helped boost trade. The Bantry climate with its short summer put a limit on the contribution of tourism to the local economy, yet in the absence of alternative sources of income great hopes were held for the industry.

The town's economic predicament was symbolized by the decline of the weekly markets and monthly fairs. From a Square clogged with livestock, men and various types of vehicles in the early years of the century, the fair had become little more than a colourful anachronism by the 1960s. This was largely due to the establishment of cattle marts in Bandon and Skibbereen where sale was by auction. Some moves had been made to have a mart established in Bantry, but they were doomed to failure because there was neither the quality of cattle nor land in the area to make one viable.

Aside from incoming foreign industry (see below) little other development took place at this time. The opening of the County Hospital in Bantry in 1960 was important for the town. It not only brought health care on a much extended scale, it also boosted trade and employment, providing jobs for between 100 and 130 people (75% of them females). It became, in the opinion of many people, Bantry's biggest and most reliable industry. As one businessman put it, there was 'black despair' in West Cork in the 1950s and the hospital was the first major breakthrough, 'the best factory we have'. The building of the Secondary School in 1960 had a similar if less dramatic effect. But if Bantry gained important facilities, it also lost some. In the early 1960s the government transport authority, CIE, closed the West Cork Railway against strong opposition. The line to Cork City was slow and did not follow the shortest possible route, which increased the competitive advantages of road transport. By this time the railway was badly under-utilized. The decision to close the line and pull up the tracks continued to be heavily criticized by local people. Road hauliers, they claimed, were the only ones who benefited from the decision. The Biggs group, for example, was accused of not helping the fight against the closing of the line. Instead of putting their influence behind the campaign they had argued and continued to argue that the railway was superfluous. Yet within five years Gulf's terminal construction project highlighted the role the railway might perhaps have played in Bantry's industrial development, given the state of the country's roads and rising costs of petroleum.

Industrial development: inviting in the multinationals

A policy of protectionism had been pursued following the founding of the Free State, but this was massively expanded in the 1930s when Fianna Fail came to occupy the Treasury benches. Although these policies helped establish a modest industrial base, there was little production for export markets, industrial exports constituting only a small proportion of either total industrial output or total exports.

In the early 1950s commitment to protectionism weakened as it became doubtful that further measures of this sort would promote sustained industrial expansion, especially as they had not been successful in increasing employment and reducing emigration. From this perspective it seemed that accelerated industrial development required rapid growth of industrial exports in the absence of dramatic increases in domestic demand. The economy was riddled with structural deficiencies. Manufacturing industry still only accounted for less than one-fifth of total employment in the post-war period and still owed its viability to protectionism. Because of their low import content and their influence on the overall level of domestic activity, three industries remained central to the health of the economy: agriculture, tourism, and building and construction — though expanding slowly, they were still depressed for most of the 1950s.[10] Manufacturing exports were also expanding in spite of the difficulties of those years, but it was nevertheless the fiscal incentives introduced from 1956 that allowed a more rapid expansion.

The immediate post-war period saw some tentative expansionary measures taken. This was followed by a retreat from such initiatives which exacerbated the mid-decade depression. Recovery led to a major shift of fiscal policy which fed the 1959–68 decade of sustained growth.

The shift to capital imports [11]

The launching of the Public Capital Programme was a key early initiative. At first it was devoted to building and construction, and in spite of the retreat from expansionary public investment in the middle of the decade, capital investment facilitating future development continued to be undertaken.

Subsequently renewed expansion of the Public Capital Programme and the provision of finance for capital formation in tourism and agriculture as well as industry contributed to the recovery from the 1956–58 depression. The foundation of the Industrial Development Authority (IDA) was another major initiative, a decision taken as early as 1949. This body was responsible for promoting industrial development, with the attraction of foreign enterprises an important priority. Related to this was the setting-up of Coras Trachtala to develop exports and Borde Failte to promote tourism. A grants scheme was introduced in 1952 to subsidize the cost of buildings and equipment for new establishments, a scheme tending to favour new projects oriented to export markets. The 1952 legislation was confined to regions designated as underdeveloped areas — which included Bantry — but the scheme was extended in 1956 to all areas and in 1959 was given a more explicit export orientation. This was in accord with the priorities in the 1958 First Programme for Economic Expansion and with 1956 legislation providing tax remissions on profits from increases in manufactured exports — measures which were to be further expanded and linked to other incentives, including tax concessions on depreciation of capital, improved credit facilities, and so on. Important too — and symbolic of the ideological shift these policies represented — was the 1958 amelioration of the Control of Manufactures Acts which had been designed to prevent foreign control of Irish industry, the restrictions being removed completely in 1964.

Following the mid-decade crisis, then, the government assumed full responsibility for directing the growth of the economy. The 5-year plan for economic expansion channelled state investment into areas designed to solicit foreign capital, the premise being that the domestic market remained unable to support either a stable or expanding industrial base. Capital was being imported so commodities could be exported. Although agricultural employment fell along with its contribution to the gross domestic product, expansion of the service sector was largely determined by the level of demand from industry, and domestic activity and consumption generally were stimulated by the growth in investments, exports and employment, enabling the maintenance of an expansionary fiscal policy. As a result, real incomes increased with the rate of investment.

It was the depths of the crisis which precipitated — in part by legitimating the need for a drastic change of direction — the adoption of policies which reshaped the balance of economic and political ideologies. To say this is not to deny that some early expansionary moves had already been made by the early 1950s. But endemic problems had constrained the effectiveness of policies in that conditions were less conducive to growth in the early 1950s. Realization of the results of the policy change took some time, e.g. growth of exports. But it also took time for economic ideologies to change in a Keynesian direction. The use of pump-priming by the state, of foreign capital for domestic development, were notions that had to gain practical credibility, as did more flexible attitudes to balance of payments questions. What is more, conditions were changing and opportunities opening up as the world economy's long boom took hold and fertilized itself, with growth giving fruit to growth. Thus by the end of the decade there was a sounder basis for growth through export oriented industry and for optimistic expectations. The 1950s, and especially the mid-years of the decade, the years of depression and crisis, thus represent a transitional phase out of which emerged a relatively coherent and unified policy programme whereas before there had been experimental sallies conceived as desperate remedies.

The 1960s may have been years of rapid economic growth, but they were also years in which the country's economy became extremely vulnerable to international market fluctuations. Success depended upon the continuation of of the long boom and the growth of export markets it made possible. In this respect continued dependence on the floundering British market remained a problem. Foreign trade was large in relation to output, and heavier borrowing increased the number and influence of the country's foreign creditors. Its position in this respect was in marked contrast to the years of the great Depression when the Free State's strong creditor position had acted as a buffer against the worst effects of the international crisis.

Increasingly, the Irish government, and the business interests it represented, looked to membership of the EEC as a guarantor of continued growth and development.[12] Yet with Ireland's entry into the EEC, the major decisions of financial management were now made in Europe. By a power-sharing arrangement of some piquancy for a nationalist government, Brussels-based bankers and bureaucrats controlled the state's finances, while the Dublin government put the policies into practice and took the political responsibility (see also chapter 4).

By December 1977, overseas-sponsored companies had set up 692 new industrial projects, representing a total investment of £628.8 million, providing employment for 82 000 people at full production. Even as early as 1966 earnings from the overwhelming majority of exports of new grant-aided projects in manufacturing industry could be attributed to projects entering into production from 1960 onwards. New industry (i.e. IDA grant-aided enterprises)[13] grew rapidly after 1966 in terms of gross output, numbers employed and exports — from 11% of output, 9% of employment and 42% of exports in 1966 to 30% of gross output, 28% of employment in industry and 61% of industrial exports in 1974. From July 1977 Irish industrial exports enjoyed duty-free access to the EEC market. Thus, according to the IDA, Ireland provided countries such as the United States and Japan, with 'a ready-made bridgehead into Europe' and EEC companies with a base from which they could export back into the European mainland, duty free and tax free, at the same time taking advantage of Ireland's surplus of labour.

By 1971 new industry already accounted for 44% of total manufacturing investment. Irish firms featured prominently in new industry activity but a substantial majority of the new jobs resulted from the establishment and growth of new overseas enterprises — meanwhile there was a loss of jobs in industries which once benefited from protection. On the question of overseas penetration of manufacturing industry, the evidence suggests that Ireland was fairly highly penetrated relative to other OECD countries in terms of the overseas share of the manufacturing sector.[14]

Ireland was caught in the classic double-bind of a developing country: in order to increase its prosperity, it had to increase its financial dependence. Exacerbated by a lack of raw materials and energy, and the subordination of Irish to British capital, the policy of self-sufficiency behind tariff barriers had led to recurrent balance-of-payments crises. Diminished dependence on Britain, however, was to be replaced by a more diversified but no less intrusive form of dependence. In fact, foreign capital became the ultimate arbiter of economic development with the government in effect allowing the country to be 'taken-over', donating a large shareholding in future growth to international capital. One aspect of this was that repatriation of profits siphoned off potential investment funds. Another was that the type of industrial activity atracted to Ireland tended to be assembly and processing operation. The corresponding low level of investment in research and development within the country not only limited future growth options, but laid the basis for continued foreign control. Other aspects were the dependence of foreign firms on imported raw materials, the low value added content in their products, a lack of links with domestic industries, and a correspondingly modest contribution to employment spin-offs relative to the level of incentives, investments and expectations.

The Irish government got foreign capital interested in Ireland because it could point to a labour force that came cheap and was threatened by high levels of unemployment.[15] It also had a conspicuously conservative budgetary policy and an impressive record of political stability given the continuing troubles in the North. With these conditions fixed, individual companies then tried to negotiate the best deal they could.

The Industrial Development Authority's official plan was to encourage industry to locate in less favoured areas in order to raise income levels and standards of living and eliminate emigration by providing employment, but the policy did not have this result.[16] Virtually all governmental decisions directly affecting an individual company's immediate operations were made by the heads of the IDA and the County Manager. The IDA was responsible for the selection and promotion of industry, it also controlled the allocation of grants, while the County Council provided all on-site facilities. They denied that they had encouraged the concentration of industry in the major urban centres, but it would seem they did little to discourage it. Obviously they could not coerce cautious industrialists into setting up operations in a particular place, but they were in a position to apply considerable pressure if and when they felt it was necessary to do so.

Unlike the politicians, civil servants were not directly constrained by popular pressures and public ideological commitments and could more easily stave off local and popular political leverage so as to fit in with the requirements and demands of foreign industrialists. Bantry, like many other poor areas deficient in resources, could not attract capital without external aid, particularly when local entrepreneurs preferred to guarantee their profits by investing with large financial organizations rather than undertaking or propping up local ventures. The town was compelled to sit and react to the initiatives of the state or, increasingly, those of multinational corporations. Left in a dependent and vulnerable position, much of the political posturing of the community's representatives was symptomatic of the manipulatory manoeuvres of the marginally powerful. State instrumentalities like the IDA knew this, and acted accordingly. They did a little placatory PR work whenever it was necessary, then went back to deciding policy according to their own priorities. The IDA, for instance, was widely criticized locally for not purchasing land for an industrial site in Bantry. The IDA and the County Council had been attempting to buy land in the area for some time. Negotiations almost always seemed to be at a delicate stage, or else the price asked was too high, and Bantry people were told to be patient.

Local business interests and the drive for industry

Bantry does not seem to have been a particularly exciting prospect for most industrialists. Beyond an unsurpassed but undeveloped natural harbour, and the incentives of cheap labour and capital grants, it only had the disadvantages for industry of any other remote area.[17] By the end of the 1950s the district's demographic structure clearly reflected the massive toll inflicted by more than a century and a quarter of emigration: it had a disproportionate number of children and old people, discrepancies in the sex ratios of the town and countryside, together with a low incidence of marriage and a high age at marriage. The continuing high levels of unemployment created a constant demand for the creation of jobs in the area. In 1961, 36.1% of the workforce were in agriculture, by 1971 this had declined to 26.3%; meanwhile the proportion employed in industry increased from 24.4% to 30.6%, with service employment increasing from 39.5% to 43.1% (IDA, 1972: 16). Although the economy was still not able to absorb the numbers moving out of agriculture and emigrating, there were some indications that the outflow of people was lessening. Although there had been a small loss in the preceding years, by the mid 1960s Bantry town had actually increased its population (IDA, 1972: 14; see Appendix).

Local influentials had been organizing town improvement committees, progress and development associations in an effort to improve the amenities of the town and district as far back as the 1920s. But it was not until after the War that they became actively engaged in seeking to secure industry for the area. The biggest stimulus, it seems, was the Underdeveloped Areas Act of 1952, the purpose of which was to give increased concessions to industrialists for establishing factories in 'the scheduled areas' of the country, i.e. the underdeveloped west.

Local business leaders, politicians and the clergy campaigned throughout the 1950s to bring the Bantry district to the attention of prospective industrialists. The underdeveloped state of the rural economy meant that the larger businesses and farms had generated a small prosperous elite of entrepreneurs and professionals based upon limited markets, cheap labour and monopolization of commercial outlets. Within the limits imposed by their available capital, their business practices, and the opportunities open to them for expansion, it seems that it was more feasible and decidedly less risky for local capitalists to protect themselves from competition and bank their profits rather than heavily invest in their own businesses. They exported their capital, both from the region and from the country.

One device for minimizing competition used by merchants who were also landlords, was to insert a clause in their leases preventing a tenant from establishing a rival business on the premises. Another device, supposedly, was for established businesses to try and threaten wholesalers that they would withdraw their custom if the wholesaler supplied a new competitor. Property was also allegedly bought up to prevent it falling into the hands of developers, and attempts were made to prevent chain stores from setting up branches in the town. It is difficult to imagine that local businesses could successfully have resisted a serious attempt by a large firm to move in. The point is they were able to minimize the chance of it happening. The Biggs group coped with the problem and turned it to advantage in the early 1970s when it quickly took over a small grocery shop which had become linked to the national 'VG' supermarket chain, and made it a major establishment. The Biggs group had the grocery trade tied up as wholesalers, though in one case an employee managed to keep his job and start a shop against his employer's wishes. They continued to supply him, but he subsequently left their employment. An example of a different kind was a secret move in 1972 by two shop assistants from Cullinane's to set up a drapery business in competition with their former employer. They had to resort to subterfuge to protect their jobs in the interim, and make sure they had premises and supplies before their intentions became known. Ironically their premises were part of the estate administered by the owner of Cullinane's, but there was no clause in this particular lease against starting a drapery store. Because of their personal popularity the new partners received considerable financial, customer and personal backing in the town.

The parochialism of the business people reflected their attempt to enforce a local monopoly. Bantry's workers similarly tried to restrict the labour market to locals. This practice tended to be tolerated by employers, in part because of popular pressure, but also because it helped them maintain a special kind of relationship to their employees. Local capitalists had secured their profits largely by resisting the incursions of trade unionism. They were able to do so mainly because they relied upon patronage-style methods of recruitment and promotion to paternalistically construe the provision of employment as a charitable act (see also chapter 4). In fact, trade unionists pointed out that the traditional employers had made 'working class tories' out of many of the older men and even some of the younger ones, particularly when sons followed fathers into the firm. Some workers strongly resented the way their fathers had 'worked and died for Biggs's'. In some cases the Biggs group did not sack workers they wanted to get rid of, they were simply forced to leave. The Biggs group was unionized before the founding of the Free State, but it was not until the 1970s with the unionization of incoming industries that the union really consolidated its position in this firm.

The government's industrialization program gave local entrepreneurs an additional option, a new way of furthering their interests without jeopardizing their established position. Industry offered them an expanded market based on service contracts and a well-paid workforce of consumers. In their own words, it would 'bring money to the town'. They added new incentives to those offered to industrialists by the state, stressing the advantages of their particular district. They offered land, a cheap, pliable labour force and community support. However, because they were competing with similar districts all over the country their bargaining position was not strong.

The one fear was that industrialization would increase the price of labour. Employers were consequently keen to contain wage demands. Since much of the push for industrialization had come from a drive to reduce emigration (in effect, unemployment), demands for higher wages had to be offset against the more pressing demand for extra jobs. The push for industry in the popular mind and amongst trade unionists was equated with the provision of employment, and it was commonly accepted that what was good for business was in general good for workers too. Because of the unemployment problem, labour interests were amenable to almost any development that brought jobs.

Working conditions in the town were bad in those days, according to trade unionists, with many people working 50 – 60 hours per week. Some people were intimidated by their bosses and by threats that the business would close if there was labour trouble. Old men were on low wages but kept their mouths shut for fear of being pensioned off. Even in 1975 there were reports of men who had been retained on around £20 per week (more notorious were the wages paid to junior female shop assistants, who earned about £12 per week).

But if it did not improve everybody's lot, the coming of industry did improve things for many workers. They had anticipated this: after years of trying to get people to join, the unions found men were 'clamouring' to sign up once it was known Gulf Oil was coming.

The main figures in the organizations concerned with promoting economic development were virtually all drawn from business. The Biggs group was represented by its Company Secretary and the Manager of one of its stores. The Managing-Director himself liked to stay in the background, but he was the one who called the shots, and much of the organizing and paperwork was done from the Biggs group's offices. The other firm most actively represented was Cullinane's drapery. The clergy was strongly represented, particularly in the 1960s when Muintir na Tire was in its heyday, under the leadership of a very dynamic curate (see below, also chapters 6 and 7). The politicians were always on tap, but tended not to be directly involved in detailed committee work.

Although the clergy, and sometimes the politicians, were prime movers in these organizations, they were essentially business organizations, with the larger firms' interests dominant. In any case, the clergy tended to be drawn from business, professional or farming backgrounds, as were the politicians, and the politicians were usually engaged in some form of business or farming themselves. Both priests and politicians tended to move in the social milieu of the wealthier, privileged and prestigious members of the community. The one or two professionals and local government officials who were active in these years similarly saw their concern with community development as compatible with, in fact dependent upon, the support of business, and found it convenient to accommodate the strictures placed upon development by local business interests (see also chapters 6 and 7).

The business influentials found some difficulty in marshalling popular support for their objectives. They also had some trouble in maintaining harmony among themselves. Only one serious attempt seems to have been made to establish an indigenous industry in the town. This occurred when money was raised and land bought for a bacon factory. The project came to nothing, as did a plan to establish a cattle mart on the same land. These projects left a residue of legal and financial difficulties, and in many people's eyes symbolized the way local initiatives were continually paralysed by divisions within the community.

The failure of local development projects and the fact that they were so seldom attempted was attributed by local people to personality conflicts, individual self-seeking, conflicts of interest, and insufficient local capital and expertise, coupled with a failure to procure investment from outside the area. Moreover, the influentials were regarded by many as a sectional interest more concerned with their own profits than community welfare. Their inability to pool their capital and 'pull together for the good of the town' fuelled the popular suspicion that they were more interested in 'putting their money somewhere safe and earning interest on it' than in 'creating jobs' with it. In their criticisms of 'the general public' the influentials themselves provided evidence of the effect of this attitude. One of those involved at the time lamented 'the national failing' of Irish people. They were, he said, very enthusiastic at the beginning of a project, but they did not have 'staying power'. It was 'a lack of interest that causes all associations to die out unless they can produce something regularly, something concrete'. In Bantry's case 'the public of the time were not prepared to co-operate to the full extent. The work was left to the few'.

Such sentiments were common among self-appointed community leaders. One of their pamphlets produced in the late 1950s emphasized the need for and difficulty in achieving, community co-operation. The pursuit of sectional interests and the 'ever widening gap between rural and urban populations and between employers and employees' were seen as the main problems. 'Leaders must have no personal interests', argued the pamphlet, 'and must command respect of all sections of the community. The only people with these qualifications are the clergy, so they must take the lead'. Also considered was the question of whether it was

> more advisable to make public our desire for an industry, or whether better interests could be achieved by making discreet enquiries before taking the public into our confidence.

The business influentials undoubtedly preferred the latter option, without seeming to realize that by appropriating all significant decision-making functions to themselves, they thereby alienated popular support (see also chapters 6 and 7).

In the late 1950s the Bantry Development Association became part of the West Cork Development Association. At the time it was thought that an organization representing a larger area would have a bigger impact at the national level. The aim was to show industrialists and tourist agents the region as a whole, pointing out the advantages of each specific district so that the promotional activities of different towns could be co-ordinated in a more effective fashion. The region was promoted, the authorities were lobbied, and government neglect of West Cork advertised. For instance, a booklet entitled *The Scandal of West Cork* (by a Skibbereen solicitor and the leading light of the Association) describing the impoverished condition of the region and castigating politicians, parties and bureaucrats for neglecting the region, was widely distributed with accompanying publicity.

Eventually the Bantry Association joined with Muintir na Tire when the national organization established guilds in the towns of West Cork. Once again it was felt that a larger organization would have a bigger impact. A clerically-led movement organized in accordance with catholic social teaching, Muintir na Tire was concerned to involve all sections of the community, irrespective of partisan divisions, in improving social conditions by self-help (see also chapters 5, 6 and 7). Considerable emphasis was placed on cultural matters, but it was economic projects that assumed top priority in places such as Bantry. Because the guild was dominated by the influentials who had led the Development Association, in Bantry that meant the promotion of tourism and industry. Among other things, trips to the Continent were undertaken (e.g. to Holland seeking a brass factory) as well as to England; a tourist-information office was set up (staffed by volunteers); and support was given to a farm-guesthouse holiday scheme.

Because of their activities over the years, as well as their social standing, the business influentials became a reference group for both politicians and state officials, overshadowing the Town Commissioners whose social com-position was more populist but less luminous (see also chapters 6 and 7). Regarded as the source of the town's prosperity, and thus representatives of its basic interests, the business people were treated less as a pressure group from within the town than as spokesmen *for* the town. As a result they were in continuous liaison with politicians and civil servants from Cork and Dublin. For their part, senior state officials balanced local political pressure and policy guidelines against the 'needs' of different areas in making their decisions. In the last resort, of course, the interests of the state were more directed to siting a factory in any reasonable location than in vainly attempting to satisfy the whims of local interests.

The coming of industry

The first foreign company to set up in Bantry was Rowa Ltd, an offshoot of a German pharmaceutical firm. Beginning in a very modest way, it employed only six people and exported to only three countries when it commenced operations in 1959. Within half a dozen years it had expanded to a peak of over 40 employees (approximately half of them women) with exports to 33 countries. The company initially received no IDA grant, because of doubts about the venture and the nature of the product (upon expansion, which included the building of new premises, a new industries grant was forth-coming). The business influentials did all they could to get and keep the factory. As one young woman put it, the owner of Rowa Ltd was 'treated like royalty' when he was first in Bantry. There were parties out at his house and it was 'like a royal invitation if invited out'.

In addition to feting the owner, the influentials sold him land (far more than he needed for his plant) at a give-away price. In the late 1940s the County Council, one of the banks and the Development Association had been involved in purchasing part of a farm at Newtown, the owners of which were in arrears with their rates and in debt. The influentials organized for money to be raised by contribution on the understanding that if and when the land was purchased by an industrialist the contributors would be repaid in full. When the owner of Rowa turned up a decade later 'he was mad to buy everything'. Except for a small portion that was retained and given free to the Flately factory (see below) and an adjacent area that was developed as an oval, the bulk of the land was sold to the German industrialist. The price he paid, plus the interest from the grazing in the interim, made up the original purchase price and the contributors' money was then paid back to them. Those in charge of overseeing Bantry's industrial future thus relinquished themselves of prime land for less than they had paid under favourable conditions a decade previously. They afterwards realized they had conceded too much, particularly as they could have given away what was needed for the factory and kept the rest. Securing land for an industrial estate subsequently proved to be a major problem in Bantry (partly because of the topography and partly because of price inflation following the coming of Gulf Oil) and potential industries were probably lost to the town as a result. Many local people remained critical, both of the way the property was originally acquired (maintaining that 'no good can come of that land') and the manner in which it was 'given away'.

Whereas Rowa created only small expectations because of the size of its beginnings, the second factory to set up operations in Bantry created an enormous amount of hope. For that reason some of the influentials involved in bringing the firm to the town claimed that it was irrelevant that the plant later closed down. The venture resulted from an advertisement placed in the Irish papers by a small English manufacturer interested in producing electrical driers and similar components. A delegation from Bantry went to England to see him in 1962. As a result of this approach he visited Bantry where he and his family were given a holiday in a local cottage. Wooed, wined and dined by the influentials, he was persuaded to establish a small factory in the town, operating under the name of Flately Driers. Pressure was put on the IDA and the government of the day to provide a grant. The IDA finally overcame its doubts and the plant began operations, expanding to a point where it employed around 120 people at its peak. The IDA's doubts were apparently justified: in 1969 the factory closed down because of the financial difficulties of the parent company in England.

'When Flately comes you'll get a fur coat' was a joking remark of the time which reflected both the inflated ideas generated by the proposed development and the ambivalence and cynicism felt about industrialists with grand plans. Many critics felt that the influentials had been duped by the flamboyant owner. The dubious practices that led the company into bankruptcy confirmed their suspicions.

The third factory to set up operations in the town was another German firm, a small footwear manufacturer operating under the name of King's Shoes. As a result of a survey of areas recommended by the IDA, it began training staff for a proposed factory in 1966. Bantry was said to be chosen because of the town's proximity to the supply of raw materials and the port of Cork. The firm used all Irish materials and exported the finished product to Hamburg. Every possible assistance was given to the German company by the Bantry guild of Muintir na Tire, with the business influentials arranging for the County Council to help purchase and convert the abandoned railway station to factory use. Although the plant was originally advertised as likely to employ 60–70 workers, it only provided jobs for 20–30 people, mainly women on low wages. After a few years operation, it also closed in 1969.

The industrial scene in Bantry was tranformed in 1966 by the Gulf Oil intervention. This softened the blow of the closure of these two factories. But the closures *were* a setback, particularly as they came after the boom period of the construction of the Guf Oil terminal, i.e. at a time when the town was readjusting to a lower level of economic activity and fewer employment opportunities. In fact, the closures underlined the dependence of the town for its continued prosperity on Gulf Oil (see chapter 8 and Eipper, forthcoming).

The factory premises vacated by Flately's remained an important asset, which encouraged the IDA to find a new use for it. It was occupied in 1973 by a Canadian firm, Chesterton International, which specialized in the manufacture of industrial seals and packing. This company's decision to locate in Bantry was not only influenced by the presence of a vacated building; plans for an oil refinery in the area were also an important consideration (see chapter 8 and Eipper, forthcoming). This type of development, particularly if it was related to oil finds in the Celtic Sea, would have provided a ready market for the firm's product. In the meantime, 95% of the product was intended for export: one of the main reasons for siting a plant in Ireland had been to gain access to the EEC market. The company employed approximately 20 people in the beginning. Originally it claimed that this figure would be trebled but these estimates were predictably exaggerated. At its peak the plant employed 44 people (all males except for office staff); by 1977 retrenchments had cut this figure back to 33. The company received no IDA grant, the refinery did not materialize and transport costs proved to be high (the factory was importing its raw materials as well as exporting its product). When the firm began to retrench workers in 1976 (at the same time as Gulf Oil) Bantry people began to wonder whether Chesterton's would soon be closing down.

These four plants constituted only a fraction of the total number of firms which expressed some interest in locating in the Bantry area. Most, of course, were probably never more than 'vaguely interested'. However, many Bantry people claimed that there were another half dozen industries seriously interested, which the influentials had frightened off.[18] The business influentials claimed they were 'unlucky' not to have got more factories than they did.

They saw their position at the time as an extremely vulnerable one: the limitations of the area were so great that Bantry could only compete for industry with other areas in Ireland and abroad if it proved more responsive to industry's demands. They felt that 'within reason' they had to go out of their way to meet any requirements deemed necessary by incoming industrialists: 'It was easy for them to move on. They had to be given the impression of being welcome and of getting every facility available'.

The major claim made by the business leaders' critics was that they attempted to make incoming industrialists 'toe the line' and 'play ball' on wages and agree not to poach workers from local firms; those who refused to co-operate were not encouraged to stay. The second major claim was that the influentials discouraged any industry which might have competed with or otherwise threatened established local businesses, and that their action in this regard, coupled with other restrictive practices, effectively discouraged more development in the town. They only wanted certain kinds of industry, ones that 'suited Bantry', which meant in practice ones that suited them. The third major claim was that the influentials gave too much away in their scramble for industry. For some this was a case of naivety, for others a case of 'greasing the fat pig's backside'. These criticisms were usually made by emphasizing the sectional interest of the business influentials, 'the decisions made behind closed doors', and the ability of the business people, prior to the coming of Gulf Oil, to 'keep the working man down'.

The influentials defended themselves against these charges by arguing that they were seeking industries which 'would fit into the town'. They argued that they offered cheap sites because it was far more important to get jobs than worry about the price of land. But they conceded that as a result of developments they could not have been expected to foresee — notably the arrival of Gulf Oil — land prices rose astronomically a few years later. Citing the short-sightedness of government authorities in closing the railway, they pointed out that they were not the only ones who made mistakes. They either denied or evaded the charge of collusion. As for anti-competitive business practices, they justified themselves by pointing to instances where small, inefficient businesses had not been ruthlessly squeezed out. They also argued that it would have been self-defeating to have bankrupted local businesses, and thrown people out of work, for the sake of an incoming one. As far as wages were concerned, they argued that local businesses could not afford to pay higher wages, even if industry could. In order to compete with other countries and other areas in Ireland they had to 'sell the area' to industry in any way they could. It was better, they said, and to the benefit of the whole town, to have low wages than no wages. It would seem that to these people the future could not be compromised, the plight of West Cork justified their turning the whole community into a commodity to be purchased by incoming industrialists at their own price.

It becomes clear that among the business influentials, at least, the ideology of economic development was in practice motivated more by a concern with creating a favourable business climate than in providing local employment as such, with guaranteeing the profits of business more than the income, living standards or welfare of the community as a whole. This is not to imply that their concern for the good of the town, the jobless and the poor, was anything but genuine and deeply felt. In fact they believed that their way was the *only* way the community's welfare could be guaranteed and jobs created. But however they may have construed their actions to themselves, and however much others may have benefited from what they did, Bantry's capitalists badly needed to consolidate and augment the foundations of the local economy and the profit-making potential of their businesses. By successfully marshalling government, religious and popular support for their interests under the banner of development, they were able, in classic fashion, to present their specific interests as general ones.

It is clear that for those industrialists who did set up in the town the inducements offered were a significant factor. They seem to have fitted in particularly well with local business interests as regards labour relations. The only firm to prove amenable from the beginning to its workers joining trade unions was Chesterton, arriving in the new industrial climate created by Gulf Oil. Rowa, the first to arrive, fairly successfully resisted trade unionism well into the 1970s. In general, the incoming employers complemented paternalistic relations with employees with more bureaucratic promotional and bonus incentives, attempting to buy-off compliant workers while using the argument of the dole queue for militant ones.

Rowa was opposed to trade unions. Any concession had to be 'screwed out of them' according to one unionist. In order to keep the union out, the company had paid above minimum rates and gave extra holidays at Christmas. It sacked four employees in 1973 for attempting to organize the workers, but they were reinstated when the company was threatened with a black ban at Cork airport. Thus, after more than 13 years of operations in Bantry, Rowa became unionized. By contrast, Chesterton had 'gone out of their way' to co-operate with the union from the beginning, negotiating an agreement which gave the ITGWU a closed shop but allowed workers to be put off in the first six weeks of employment if they were unsatisfactory. In late 1976 the company dropped a shift and made about a dozen men redundant, a move which the union was unable to prevent. In this plant the cost to workers was their health. The use of asbestos in the production process and the effect it was having worried a number of people, but they felt they needed the work even if it was killing them.

The owners of the first three plants were personally involved with the establishment and operation of their Bantry factories and they seem to have taken readily to the role of playing the big cosmopolitan fish in the small provincial pond. They basked in the attention paid to them and took full advantage of the opportunity offered to obtain the most favourable deal going. But apart from these activities and public relation exercises, none of the owners involved themselves to any great extent in local business or political affairs. Such things were not so important once a factory was established, given that the plants were (apart from labour, of course) independent of the town. Yet, in general the incoming companies did provide sponsorship for local sporting and charitable organizations in an attempt to create an image of generosity and public-spiritedness — an image which was at times rather hard to sustain in the face of the claims made on it.

Perhaps because it was only a small outpost of a larger firm established without the personal engagement of an owner, Chesterton tended to keep the lowest profile. Flately's owner was more active than the man who ran King's Shoes. The former socialized extensively when in town, although he did not otherwise get involved in town affairs. Rowa showed itself most keen to participate. In the early days the owner, during his trips to town, appeared to many to want to fly in and play the benevolent laird to the local peasants. Later, his manager (a local man promoted from the ranks) was active both in the Bantry Chamber of Commerce and the Cork Chamber and maintained close links with Fianna Fail (see chapters 6 and 7). The company in these ways secured business and political connections for itself that it would not otherwise have had and which, because of internal changes, it found increasingly useful.

Only two of the four factories were still in operation by 1975. The first to close was Flately's. There were conflicting accounts about the circumstances surrounding its closure, and thus the whole venture. Whatever the full story, the manner in which the Bantry operation failed suggests that it was perhaps never really a viable proposition: a company with sounder financial management would perhaps not have committed itself to the original decision to invest in Ireland. The closure of King's Shoes suggests that its decision to set up operations in Bantry might have had less to do with production than accounting considerations. The company claimed the decision to close the Bantry plant was due to a lack of female labour. There was no such shortage, but there were problems in the Irish footwear industry. It was also charged that the owner 'only came for the grant'. Whatever the background to the specific decisions made in these cases, their impact on the lives of Bantry people was direct, immediate, and arbitrary. Although these firms provided much needed employment, when they left they took the jobs with them.

Bantry people were grateful to these companies for bringing employment and money to the area, acknowledging to the full, industry's special contribution to the new prosperity. But as a result of the shrewd property deals at a time of depressed land values, the taint of shady business practices, the appearance of sheer opportunism in regard to grants and tax concessions, and an instrumental aloofness from the public life of the town, there developed a consciousness of a different kind, a feeling common among all classes, that industrialists were not to be trusted. They brought invaluable benefits to the area, but they did so merely as a by-product of their chief concern, which was to bend the town, and the government, to their purposes, creating the most favourable conditions for making profits for themselves. Then, when this was no longer possible, they pulled out as fast and as cheaply as they could, leaving the workers jobless, and the local business people (who did not have that kind of mobility) with a depressed local economy on their hands. But however cynical people sometimes became, they seldom went beyond a fetishized view of the relations between capital and labour and, in the main, continued to see jobs as the patronage provided by the wealthy to the otherwise poor. This sense of social and economic dependence was strongly reinforced by the presence and performance of Gulf Oil.

The Gulf Oil intervention

As already indicated, my discussion here of the impact of Gulf Oil on Bantry will be limited to a brief description of the multinational's contribution to the business of the town, focusing on the way Bantry's business people availed themselves of the opportunities the company's presence offered them for making profits of their own.

In order to reduce its transportation problems and costs, Gulf Oil in the mid 1960s decided to use long-haul mammoth carriers to supply its refinery network. To do so it built a massive transhipment and storage installation on Whiddy Island at Bantry. Here crude from Kuwait was transferred to shuttle tankers for delivery to Gulf's mainland refineries, Bantry being the only port in Europe then capable of accommodating the superships. The Whiddy terminal was thus a pioneering venture in the oil industry. By the time it opened at the end of 1968 plans were well advanced to develop the major European refinery-servicing ports — which suggests the Whiddy terminal was an interim measure designed to be superseded. The upheavals of the early 1970s associated with OPEC undoubtedly caused reappraisals, but there can be little doubt that Gulf's initiative was from the outset based on the assumption that there would be major changes in the industry of one kind or another in the years to come. Hence the Whiddy terminal was designed to be 'nothing if not flexible' (see, for example, Binsted, 1968).

Gulf's interest in Bantry Bay became public in early 1966. The company soon lodged a planning permission application with the Cork County Council and construction began later that year. About one-third of Whiddy Island had been bought, at a reported price of £120 000 for the 350 acre site. The company was already having a profound influence on the area, transforming the Whiddy community, farmers selling land and moving off the island to buy elsewhere or to become wage labourers — even employees of Gulf Oil itself. Farmers who had not sold their land also sought work on the construction of the terminal, or with Gulf Oil after its completion. The Gulf Oil intervention accomplished in less than a year what had taken emigration more than a century to achieve.

An astute businessman, the largest farmer on the island not only sold a sizeable amount of land to Gulf Oil, but established himself as a labour and machinery contractor as well as extending his commercial activities to cater to the construction (he already ran the local Post Office and shop). That is, as a local patron in a monopolistic position, he expanded his activities when the opportunity presented itself, becoming a broker in the industrialization process. Like a number of others in a position to do so, he subsequently purchased land on the mainland in anticipation of a refinery being built. Where others became proletarians, albeit ones paid high wages by local standards, this small entrepreneur began to accumulate capital to an unprecedented extent.

The local area as a whole began to feel the effects once the construction started. The Gulf Oil project and the presence of the other factories in the town undoubtedly hastened and consolidated the reversal of the district's chronic population decline. The town's population increased by over 10% between 1966 and 1971, reaching nearly 2600. But because of the poverty of the hinterland and the associated incidence of part-time farming, as well as the tendency of people to build and live outside the town boundaries, the effect on the hinterland was also important. Although 90% of the terminal workforce resided within a 10 mile radius of the town, only 25% lived within the town itself.

The terminal's construction turned Bantry into a 'boom town', inflating land and shop prices, rents and wages, and changing the tempo of social life. To locals it was 'like the Klondyke' because of the influx of foreign workers, the huge machinery, and the prodigal spending. The shopkeepers and merchants obviously benefited, but so did others, mainly by providing accommodation. The quantity and quality of shop stock was improved, business premises — particularly the pubs — were modernized and extended, and so on. Such changes may well have occurred anyway, but without Gulf Oil they would have been less rapid and less extensive.

The industrial chain-reaction which most locals hoped or expected Gulf Oil would set off did not eventuate. Nevertheless, there was some spin-off employment. Income generated during the construction period included a total wages bill calculated at £4 million, with an annual total attributable to the terminal exceeding £575 000. Approximately 1000 men were employed on the construction; with 60 men employed at the terminal itself, 60 on the tugboats, 12 on the service boats, and about a dozen as clerical staff once normal operations commenced. Gulf Oil provided direct employment, then, for roughly 150 people, and indirect employment for possibly that many again. Something like a quarter of the town's workforce thus became dependent upon the multinational for employment. Since many of these people were on wages regarded as high by traditional standards, the town's traders could now count on an inflated level of sales at boosted prices. The regular arrival of the tanker crews taking some leave in the town injected additional money into the local economy, as did any provisioning of the terminal and tankers which came the town's way.

Local merchants secured numerous small contracts during the construction period, though the big jobs went to large national and international firms. Being the biggest firm in town, the Biggs group cornered as much of the market as it could. It increased its timber sales and carrying trade. It also bought out and expanded the first supermarket in the town. It thus protected its monopolistic position as a wholesaler and distributor as well as guaranteeing itself the largest slice of the expanded market in what was the single most important development in retailing arrangements in the town for decades.

The business people also did what they could to protect their traditional sources of profit, particularly by trying to control wages and conditions of employment. As far as labour was concerned, Gulf Oil had become 'the price-fixer' during the construction period, and it was alleged that as the terminal was about to come on-stream, approaches were made to the multinational concerning wage rates and the poaching of employees. These moves were not particularly successful, but as the supply of jobs contracted with the completion of construction, the business people again tried to directly dictate terms and conditions of employment.

Control of most of the new job opportunities was cornered by a few well-placed business men. The Harbour Constable's family became an important employer by obtaining the contract to run Gulf's service boats. The Biggs group's Managing-Director was made a Director of the Bantry Towing Company, and reputedly came to have a major say in getting men jobs on the tugs; the group also became one of the two major shareholders in the Bantry Tanker Agency which serviced the tankers.

Once the terminal was in operation the number of industrial contracts was limited, but maintenance and additional construction jobs continued to provide work for building firms, as did the expanded market for housing. Self-made men ran the two most prominent local building firms. One of these built and ran the West Lodge Hotel, which in 1969 became West Cork's largest hotel as well as the town's entertainment centre, and a venue for national conferences, conventions and functions. It also served for a time as Gulf's mainland headquarters, which is notable if only because the hotel would not have been built if it hadn't been for the terminal. For its part, the other local building firm, Murnane and O'Shea, grew to become the largest in West Cork. Although the partnership started in 1962, its rapid expansion came later as a result of the opportunities created by Gulf Oil. By the mid 1970s it employed roughly 100 men on projects throughout County Cork. The big opportunity came in 1968 when it won the contract from the Bantry Bay Towing Company to build 36 houses for its Tug Masters and Engineers. The firm then built 32 houses of its own on another estate. Then, in 1972, it won the contract to build 96 houses on a new Council Estate. It also worked on the proliferation of privately constructed dwellings built for the immigrants and the newly affluent locals.

The terminal construction was the first large scale industrial project in Bantry's history, which proved crucial for the processes of class formation affecting the area in coming years. Most obvious was the emergence of 'militant' trade unionism. Over a third of the 1000 men employed on the construction were from West Cork, though many had returned from abroad for the construction work and the permanent employment they anticipated would follow it. Together with the foreign workers, they brought a wide experience of trade union action home with them, which they passed on to the men recruited locally. The most notable example of this was the initiative shown by a group of locals near the end of the construction period in leaving jobs worth £50–60 a week to take up permanent work on the tugs starting at £17 per week. They took this massive reduction in pay to get secure jobs and with the aim of forcing their wages up as soon as possible. By 1975 they had succeeded to the extent that they were earning £95 per week with shift allowances and other fringe benefits. These gains earned the tug workers a reputation for being militants. This militancy led them into wider arenas, the economic struggle becoming a political one (see chapters 7 and 8).

Wages during the construction phase had doubled and quadrupled pre-Gulf levels. Strikes, both official and unofficial had been common, and on-site organization effective. In spite of the push for higher wages and better conditions, a moderate tendency of Bantry workers identified their interests with those of the town and Gulf Oil and attemped to limit industrial unrest.

Another important tendency was the push by West Cork men to guarantee priority for locals in the hiring of workers. A parochial consciousness thus influenced the way workers organized themselves. This dovetailed with the outlook of townspeople as a whole. The business people and Gulf Oil were particularly keen to encourage a parochial view. The town was protecting the livelihood of family, friends and neighbours; the business people were making sure money made in the town stayed in the town. They also believed the locals were more compliant and less interested in going on strike than the outsiders.

For its part, the multinational used and encouraged these sentiments to isolate the militant outsiders. It was also commonly alleged that the company blacklisted certain men. Businessmen, politicians and priests not only got men jobs on Whiddy, through Muintir na Tire they allegedly also co-operated with

Gulf Oil to control strikes and marginalize militants (see also chapter 6). There developed, then, a kind of alliance between the local bourgeoisie and the multinational in their efforts to tame the union leadership as well as the rank and file.

To sum up, Gulf Oil created unprecedented opportunities for profit-making. Local capital realized a market value which was non-existent prior to its arrival. But to make these profits local entrepreneurs had to deal with and subordinate themselves to the multinational; to the extent that they linked their prosperity to a venture over which they had no control, they enhanced their profit-making potential, but at the same time found they most effectively pursued their own objectives by tailoring them to Gulf's designs.

Thus, even if they retained their pre-existing form, social relations were often transformed. Although they continued to pursue their own objectives, business brokers also became the agents of foreign capital; their business practices remained the same, but they acquired a new social dimension. Gulf Oil similarly transformed the relationship of numerous small farmers to their land if only because the price paid for their labour now far exceeded that which it could earn from petty commodity production. In some cases wage labour enabled farmers to keep their land, but their farming now supplemented their wages rather than the other way around. No less significantly, the multinational allowed the Biggs group to expand its activities and consolidate its operating base, but in doing so it broke the economic hegemony and monopolistic position of the town's largest firm.

Final remarks

The attitudes of Bantry people to Gulf Oil — as to the other companies which came to their town — were based upon their differential class experience of industrial development of the local economy. Their response to industrialization depended, not only upon their immediate, local class position, but equally as importantly, on their location in an underdeveloped region in a dependent national economy. Whereas national and international economic forces previously tended to have their effects by way of the economic policy of the state or as a result of general market fluctuations, this was no longer the case. Class relations in the area took on a new complexion when they became directly tied to and dependent on international capital, i.e. when they became confronted by a form of class power independent of local or national constraints.

Of course, it would not have required the intervention of a multi-national corporation (however small) to cause some of these changes; they would have occurred even if the development taking place had been instituted by an indigenous enterprise. But precisely because of Ireland's industrial under-development, few indigenous firms were in a position to invest in such an area. Moreover, the weight of state capital funding was increasingly employed not to directly assist indigenous enterprises but to 'bribe' big business organized on a transcontinental basis, to make their profits in areas drained of their own wealth-creating potential.

The processes of class formation and transformation occurring in areas of the world such as this cannot be understood in terms of local property relations or differential changes in the socio-economic position of specific individuals and groups. I have used the Bantry material to describe in detail processes which were having highly specific localized effects all over the west of Ireland. The Bantry experience offers partial and unique instances of more general tendencies. The Gulf Oil intervention was an idiosyncratic form of development, but it illustrates in particularly clear form how with the support of national states transnational capital becomes the motive force of change in underdeveloped regions.

My main concern has been to show how, under the aegis of state policy, foreign-owned industrial capital was invited in by, served the interests of, but also began to dominate locally-based indigenous commercial capital from the 1950s onwards. In order to place this development in perspective I described how the catholic bourgeoisie took economic power from the remnants of the protestant ascendancy and how they consolidated their position in the post-colonial period. I argued that their profit base was threatened by the stagnant nature of the local economy. And this, I previously explained, was inextricably tied up with the expropriation of the small farmer. My argument suggests that it was no coincidence that EEC financial-planning increasingly came to dominate both agricultural and industrial development in the west of Ireland. It becomes clear, I think, that these seemingly autonomous developments need to be understood as part of a unified process of change, a process in which the key variable has been the accumulation and movement of capital monopolized on a global scale.

4 Nationalist politics and patronage

The social metamorphosis brought about by the catholic-nationalist forces fundamentally changed the character of key political institutions and their relationship to capitalist development in Eire. In the previous chapter I argued that the extended reproduction of capital was the motive force of economic change at Bantry as everywhere else in Ireland. The changing nature of political parties and their relation to the state was an important corollary of the growing power of capital. I am here mainly concerned with the part played by patronage and brokerage relations in this process.

Section I looks at the historical antecedents of political patronage in Ireland and the ramifications of this for contemporary forms. It gives an account of the growth of the party machines, and the transformation by Fianna Fail of its class base. These changes are then related to the process of capitalist economic development in Eire and the growing importance of foreign capital. Let me stress that this does not pretend to be a comprehensive account, but rather a sketch of those processes essential for an understanding of localized party-political relations. On the basis of this argument, Section II focuses on the politicians' dispensation of favours locally, and the connection between their electoral rivalry, and the bureaucratization of both the parties and the civil service.

Patronage, the state and capital accumulation

Party politics and the distribution of petty favours locally cannot be fully understood without an analysis of the changing relation between class and state power in the post-colonial era. The party machines were not built on patronage alone, rather they were strengthened by it. By and large the voter's preference was for a party; it was the distribution of preferences which was decided by the vote-pulling capacities of the individual politician. I will argue that the consolidation of the power of the leadership in the party machines was associated with the centralization of power in the top echelons of the state bureaucracy and Fianna Fail's transformation of its class base. These changes were related to the state's role in fostering capitalist economic development, which led to increased control of the economy by foreign capital.

Patronage and the rise of the catholic nationalists [1]

In the days of the ascendancy when parliamentary representation was regarded as a species of property, the landlords augmented their power by judicious use of favours. These included the juggling of tenancies, rent abatement, the provision of jobs, credit and charity. The landlord in these and other ways put the tenant and labourer in his debt and was able to demand some form of loyalty in return.

But with the removal of the government to Westminster in 1800 when the Union was formed, the landlords lost control of much of the patronage they might otherwise have used to bind the peasantry (particularly their larger tenants) to them. The famine undermined the patrimonial basis of the landlord's rule, the extension of the franchise eroded their political leverage, and their moral authority was destroyed by the corrosive antagonisms of agrarian class relations. By this time another kind of patron had arisen.

The most prominent of these were the commercial capitalists, most notably the famous gombeenman. *Gombeen,* a corruption of the Irish word *gaimbin* for interest, was originally coined to describe the activities of rural money-lenders in pre-famine Ireland. Later it was used to refer to shopkeepers practising usury as a sideline, or combining credit-retailing with usurious relations of exploitation. In return for liberal credit and cash loans, the commercial trader charged interest, inflated prices and monopolized the custom of small farmers and labourers. There were both catholic and protestant gombeens, but as more and more catholics rose in the world and as the alienation between the Anglo-Irish and the catholic masses intensified, it was the catholic gombeen who became the important figure.

The vulnerability of the peasantry to economic crises and to seasonal and social demands on accumulated savings was related to its dependence on the capitalist mode of production. Because production was primarily for subsistence, with only the surplus entering the market, the availability of cash at particular times of peak demand became the key to a family's solvency. In other words, the peasant had a cash-flow problem. The smaller the surplus, the greater the difficulties. Extended credit, even at high rates of interest, often mitigated the problem. The subordination of the peasantry to the capitalist market thus helped create the conditions for wholesale petty patronage. Ironically, this inhibited a more thorough encroachment of purely bourgeois commercial relations, and stamped even the rural bourgeoisie with a decidedly petty-bourgeois character. But because business people equated innovation, efficiency and prosperity with capitalist rationality, capitalist ideology flourished even before it was fully institutionalized. Because it was mobilized to augment practices which were not yet nakedly capitalist, it may well have inhibited the emergence of the capitalist mode of production in its purity, yet its reproduction was guaranteed — albeit in a bastardized form.

This in turn influenced the character of nationalist politics. Key members of the emergent bourgeoisie had tied the peasantry to them by entering national politics. The patronage at the disposal of the nationalist politicians was limited by their strident opposition to British policy in Ireland and their permanent exclusion from government. Yet the Irish Parliamentary Party and its functionaries did manage to become important patrons in their own right, mainly by creating tied blocs of political support and using these to further themselves economically.[2]

Working side by side with the entrepreneurial politicians in the Parliamentary Party were a number of political priests. The business people, the politicians and the clergy worked in with one another in other ways too. Although the church drew its income from all members of each parish, it particularly relied upon the support of the wealthier merchants. While the merchant financed his parish priest's and bishop's earthly dominion, they favoured him with God's attention and publicly acclaimed his contribution to God's work. Thus, for example, the church-building program instituted by the bishops in the nineteenth century not only helped remedy the church's deficiency in land by allowing it to accumulate capital, it also provided local merchants with opportunities for investment in large-scale construction projects.

From this perspective, the business people, the politicians and the clergy formed a power bloc tied by patronage to the mass of the population. As a bloc, these three categories of patron exercised an enveloping but fragile hegemony over the rural masses based upon personalistic bonds which linked material dependence to ideological compliance. They functioned as both patrons and brokers, combining the two tasks within one relationship. The parish priest was a patron, but a broker for his bishop; the politician was a patron, but a broker for his party; the business people, though primarily patrons, served as brokers whenever the chance offered itself (e.g. as the local contact of a national political figure).

Once the power of the landlords was broken, this new ruling bloc reigned supreme. As the local representatives of the nationalist leadership, the political priests and the entrepreneurial politicians interpreted nationalism to the local population and converted their economic, cultural and political grievances into the policy of the Parliamentary Party. With the founding of the Free State the clergy began to interpose themselves in new ways as non-partisan community leaders. Likewise, the politicians began to stipulate what the proper role of the state should be and to present the electorate with settled policy for ratification, i.e. to push for a form of government compatible with the continued pre-eminence of the members of the ruling bloc.

The parties and their social bases [3]

Fianna Fail and Fine Gael were both constructed from the top by leaders who won their position during the electoral and military struggles of the revolutionary period. Within the new context of the Free State these leaders found a ready-made mass base for their respective parties in the class and partisan loyalties of the Civil War. To strengthen their position they subsequently insituted several key changes which had far-reaching effects upon the workings of the electoral system. Unable to get the electorate to change the proportional representation system by referendum, Fianna Fail reduced the system's dispersal of the vote as much as possible. The principle of one-vote-one-value was also done away with by the imposition of a gerrymander favouring the rural electorates of the western areas in which Fianna Fail had its strongest support. Many electorates were also reduced in size because this made it easier to dominate the poll in smaller electorates. Finally, multi-member electorates were divided up into the functional equivalent of single-member districts. These moves helped erode the position of minority parties and increased unity in the major parties. That is, the party leaderships were able to minimize internal conflict and maximize their control of the faithful. Moreover, by binding party cadres to the party line the leadership was able to modify what the party stood for and thus the party itself.

In the early years of the Free State Fine Gael was known as the party of the well-off, Fianna Fail being the party of the common people, appealing especially to the young. Both drew support from all classes, but Fine Gael was predominantly supported by the medium and large commercial farmers and business people and the established professionals of the towns and cities. Meanwhile, Fianna Fail depended upon the support of the small farmers and shopkeepers, especially in the west, as well as the agricultural and town-based workers, with an economic policy which advocated reliance upon agricultural exports, protectionism and import substitution to provide an industrial base, and which equated individual with national self-sufficiency. Over the years this picture changed, with Fianna Fail attracting the support of commerce and industry, as well as salaried professionals, particularly state employees. Whereas Fianna Fail's political support increasingly spanned the social spectrum, Fine Gael and Labour continued to depend more upon the support of specific classes. Fine Gael was weakest amongst the working class and appealed most strongly to big business and large farmers as well as the Anglo-Irish. Labour captured the trade union vote and approximately a third of the manual working class vote, but also drew some support from small farmers and shopkeepers, as well as professionals and intellectuals. Fianna Fail poached a large share of the working class vote from Labour, but its support among trade unionists was much less.

But the fact that party allegiances were skewed along class lines is not the test of the class characer of party politics in Eire. Rather, the key lies in the evolution of Fianna Fail. It was to become more and more committed to the bourgeoisie — and to find this commitment reciprocated — yet it remained in a different position to Fine Gael. It continued to rely heavily on nationalist populism — indeed it took this a step further. Portraying itself as more than a political party, it laid claim to being a national movement, the 'natural' government of the country, all the while mingling its symbolism with that of the state itself. The strategy proved remarkably successful. After coming to power in 1932, Fianna Fail was only out of office three times up to 1977 (in 1948–51, 1954–57 and 1969–77). But it did not just dominate the Treasury benches, it came to exercise a specific form of hegemony which stalemated its opponents, dictated the terms of political debate and closed off virtually all the alternative options. The material benefits provided by party patronage became an important ideological justification for contemporary policies and past struggles. By institutionalizing the paternalistic dispensation of state welfare, Fianna Fail demonstrated that there had been substance in its nationalistic-populist rhetoric. Patronage politics and nationalism thus entered into an evolving symbiotic relationship. The key factor in this relationship was the goal of economic development interpreted as, if not upward mobility for all, certainly a rising standard of living. Of course everyone was not upwardly mobile, nor could they be. Upward mobility was restricted to a small fraction of the population. But if few became wealthy, many prospered. Most people improved their standard of living, which meant they could now afford to live at a level that had traditionally been thought of as 'middle class'. For those born poor that was quite an advance. In a memorable phrase, de Valera's successor, Lemass, was to account for the party's transformation by saying that 'a rising tide lifts all boats'. Fianna Fail rose so far, in fact, that its next leader Jack Lynch, could stress on several occasions that Fianna Fail was a party of property. The party which began life as 'the party of the plain people of Ireland' had become a 'party of mohair suits'.

Although trying to develop and commercialize agriculture, Fianna Fail also tried to protect its electoral base. It could not afford to alienate the small farmers of the west. By pursuing policies which subsidized the small farmers on the land but reduced their share of total agricultural output and increased the competitive advantage of the larger farmers (see chapter 3), Fianna Fail shored-up its traditional electoral base — which was in any case in demographic decline — while buying the support of the larger farmers. The party began to jettison its pristine agrarian-populist image within a decade of achieving government, and began losing western rural votes whilst gaining eastern urban ones. In fact, as the relative importance of the west continued to lessen, Fianna Fail was able to accommodate other interests more easily — especially those who moved out of the country and up in the world. It bought the support of the upwardly mobile business and professional interests in the towns and cities, becoming a party of 'the self-made man' (the more established elite tending to retain their old allegiances along with their condescension). By the late 1960s some of the country's most successful businesses were run by men who had built fortunes with the aid of Fianna Fail. The upward mobility of the ambitious entrepreneur was one of the key features of Irish machine politics, both with respect to the patronage the government dispensed and the policies it pursued. Equally important was the fact that Fianna Fail took control of key sections of the state apparatus by inserting its functionaries into whatever positions were amenable to partisan influence. In addition to creating a civil service sympathetic to its policies, the party in this way began to create a constituency for itself among an influential section of the nation's salaried professionals.

Fianna Fail also gained support from those sections of established business which were the beneficiaries of state patronage and government policy. In addition to government contracts, grants, loans and subsidies, the government's protectionism was for a long time welcomed by indigenous industrialists. They later supported the switch to capital imports and the move to join the EEC because of the enormously expanded range of opportunities (capital grants and loans, an expanded market) for capital accumulation that these policies allowed. In the meantime, successive governments had established a network of semi-state companies run on capitalist lines by chief executives appointed from private enterprise. These not only became a powerful arm of government, they were also important power bases for politically connected entrepreneurs.

In these ways, Fianna Fail not only tied more and more owners and auxiliaries of business to the party, it actually helped a fully-fledged indigenous bourgeoisie to emerge in its own right. Thus though it came to power because of the support of the subordinated classes, it was the growing support of the dominant one which helped keep it there.

It did so by mobilizing and institutionalizing a coalition of support which linked the pursuit of modernization to a defence of the traditional. And so the entrepreneurs who took the podium spoke with an elegaic nostalgia for those who had been 'left behind'. That is to say, though its rhetoric invoked the past, Fianna Fail did so in order to make a claim upon the nation's future: its was a modernizing traditionalism — one whose tensions and polarities, inherent ambivalences and evolving ambiguities, called upon and called forth those of Irish society itself.

Government policy and capital accumulation [4]

The progressive centralization and bureaucratization of politics meant that the electorate in addition to being culturally predisposed to look to party politicians for favours, was actually shepherded into doing so. Each generation of politicians shifted the emphasis further and further from appeals to raw nationalism. In doing so they gradually developed new ways to shore up their electoral support and bind voters to them. This was not a decline of ideology as such, but a progressive outmoding of the nationalism of the Civil War by a different kind of ideology. Political pragmatism did not reflect an absence of ideological commitment, it reflected a particular form of commitment: the calculating rationality of the political entrepreneur.[5] Once economic development became an uncontested priority to be accomplished by means of state intervention and subsidization of private enterprise, the impetus behind entrepreneurial politics was effectively consolidated.

If the economy was to develop it was necessary to have institutional structures which maintained, in fact furthered, capital investment. For this to happen, a growing share of the national product had to be appropriated as profits. That is, the economy had to be organized in a manner favourable to capital rather than labour or the petty producer. Given these exigencies, the electoral strength of the predominantly rural petty bourgeoisie created major problems for the exercise of state power by a small indigenous bourgeoisie subordinated to British capital. If the state was to be administered in a manner compatible with the bourgeoisie's control of the economy, some form of reconciliation had to be effected between the political strength of populist social forces and the exigencies of capitalist investment. The importance of political patronage in this context was that it helped mediate divergent class interests.

The selection of political leaders by means of elections made them representatives of the electorate, but for capital accumulation to continue, the policies and objectives of the state had to be compatible with those of business. This meant that other classes had to be ruled at the same time as they were represented. The key to success lay in placating the petty bourgeoisie without jeopardizing the expansion of the indigenous bourgeoisie. By exploiting this area of compatibility, Fianna Fail evolved a program which ensured a politically safe embourgeoisement of the economy and society. An important factor in this program was the embourgeoisement of sections of the petty bourgeoise, a trend which was in the interests of the bourgeoisie since it grew larger and more powerful as the economy expanded.

Thus although successive Free State governments had claimed to be fostering a nation of self-sufficient small-holders and shopkeepers who would be economically independent, politically free, and spiritually guided by the church, when this ideal proved to be incompatible with that of economic development, the latter ideology prevailed. The irony was that industrialization was to be ushered in using the rhetoric of nationalist independence: those most vociferous in their claims to champion 'the small man' who lived the traditional way of life and fought the heroic struggles of the glorious past, were also to become the friends of foreign industry who were going to introduce a modern cosmopolitan lifestyle and a prosperous future.

Once de Valera retired as leader, Fianna Fail moved even further from the elements of petty-bourgeois ideology inherited from Sinn Fein. The party still paid lip-service to the aspirations of the past, but commitment had been replaced by rhetoric. As already indicated, the policy of protectionism and industrial development through import substitution pursued by the Fianna Fail government from the 1930s was abandoned after the economic crisis of the 1950s. Crucial to this was a change of thinking within the Department of Finance, a recognition of the need for economic planning if development was to succeed. Capital imports were designed to stop the export of labour, establish an industrial base within the country and accelerate economic growth. Henceforth national development would depend upon capital investment by foreign corporations.

This move represents the point at which the bourgeoisie finally decisively found certain of its key interests represented by Fianna Fail. If not before, from that date, at least, there was no question about who held state power in Ireland. The state apparatus itself, particularly in its higher echelons and key departments such as Finance, were in any case oriented in this direction, taking for granted the parameters of bourgeois economic management and increasingly interpreting them as necessities.[6]

It is significant that the utopian vision of de Valera did not permanently stand in the way of an attempt to create an indigenous industrial economy along strictly capitalist lines. Indeed, it could be seen as the logical extension of the building of the party machines, the centralization of the bureaucracy, and Fianna Fail's transformation of its class base. This was, of course, a contested and contradictory process whose outcome could scarcely have been foreseen when Fianna Fail first came to power, particularly since it was then neither an ideological nor a pragmatic objective of the party leadership.

This process of transformation meant that the major parties became more and more dependent upon business for successful economic management. Business, in turn, relied upon the parties to harvest the vote in support of policies which favoured its objectives. On the one hand, factories were bestowed on particular areas as a favour, a prize of government, bringing jobs and profits and holding down emigration. On the other hand, industrialists were given state aid. Grants to large industry, particularly foreign industry, were ostensibly assessed in terms of formal criteria. But bureaucratic secrecy at times undoubtedly cloaked and put an impartial gloss upon calculations influenced by patronage consideration. In such cases formal bureaucratic rationality provided an ideological cover for a type of substantive rationality which was purportedly alien to bureaucratic procedure.[7] At the same time welfare policies, grants and subsidies were increasingly designed to ensure the best possible management of manpower planning. More and more attempts were made to regulate the number and type of worker entering the labour market from school and agriculture. AnCo, the industrial training authority, was established in 1967 and National Manpower surveys attempted to map and mould the kind of labour force available to industry. Budgetry policy was designed to create a favourable economic climate for profit making. In addition, particular firms, projects and industries were represented by politicians in a highly personalized way; planning permission, subsidies, loans, grants, etc. were all arranged to facilitate the operations of particular client firms under the auspices of general economic policy (see also chapter 3).

In sum, the pursuit of national development successfully committed all classes to a state-sponsored program of economic expansion geared to the exigencies of privately controlled capital accumulation.

Patronage and the politicians

'Pull is what it's all about. It's not what you know, but who you know.'[8] This axiom dominated the political consciousness of Bantry people. Some version of it was repeated virtually every time the issue of pull became a topic of conversation. Pull of course usually meant 'the pulling of strings', at least this was the core meaning of the term. But it was also commonly used wherever influential individuals manipulated their inside knowledge, contacts or position to create a reputation for dispensing favours. Although many people doubted, and some denied that pull was effective as the politicians liked to pretend, most admitted that they would use it if they thought it would do them any good.

Personal favours and political support [9]

The most common form of pull consisted of politicians exchanging personal favours for votes through the transfer of preferences. Of course they could not be sure the favours would be repaid with a vote, but they enhanced the likelihood that some form of support would be forthcoming. All politicians — whether members of the national parliament, the Dail (popularly known as TDs (from Teachtai Dala)), or members of the County Council (MCCs), the body in charge of regional and local government — relied upon their reputation for pull to make a name for themselves.[10] Most Bantry people were convinced that patronage was inevitable in politics: 'That is politics the world over'. Whenever they were convinced that a little extra persuasion might be needed to get what they wanted from the government, people went to their politician; sometimes they made absolutely sure by going to more than one politician. At times this entailed a violation of proper procedures, more often it simply meant a bending of the rules, a speeding up, or a scrutinizing, of the bureaucratic process. For the cost of a promise of a vote, pull gave people personalized, preferential access to key decision-makers. As one man expressed it: 'it puts the lowest person in touch with those with power and influence'.

For a growing percentage of the population the government had become a direct or indirect source of income as the state sector grew and the provision of social services was expanded. Together with the centralization of decision-making (see below), this created the conditions for the parties to permanently entrench themselves as intermediaries between the individual citizen and the state. The politicians adopted the style of anti-bureaucratic populist leaders while the bureaucrats, at least officially, cast themselves as paragons of impartiality attempting to combat the favouritism of the politicians.

The number of jobs, grants, subsidies, pensions and loans increased enormously after Fianna Fail came to power in the early 1930s. As public employment and expenditure (particularly on social services) rose, individuals and whole communities became dependent on the state to maintain their standard of living. It was not the size of these benefits that was so important, but the number and variety of them, and the fact that they were so often obtained through the politicians.

Jobbery was frequently denied by the authorities, but the ordinary person viewed these denials with scepticism. Predictably, the politicians had most influence in getting their clients state-paid jobs. These positions were not necessarily well paid, but they were secure. In the past the main ones were: rate collector, sub-postmaster, postman (permanent or temporary), County Council foreman, charge-hand, ganger or labourer. Politicians had a hand in getting jobs for professionals and semi-professionals as well, e.g. teaching appointments, nursing positions, clerical positions in the civil service, the County Council and the semi-state bodies, and even jobs in the banks. They often did little more than write a reference; sometimes they went much further and canvassed on behalf of their client (or clients). Wherever competition was fierce, pull became important. In some cases, the politicians served their client as much by giving them preferential access to key people over a number of years as by actively canvassing for them for a particular position.[11]

For the less well-off the securing of social services was almost as important as the pulling of jobs. Here people were after such things as Council housing, pension-benefits, or other forms of special housing, unemployment benefits (including the farmers' dole), disability payments, widows' pensions, old age pensions (contributory and non-contributory, state and IRA), free electricity and subsidized heating fuel, housing grants, or other forms of special assistance. Even where people knew they were eligible for these services according to the standard criteria, they often made doubly sure by trying a little pull.

At the other end of the scale the availability of government contracts, grants and planning permission were the main things which people tried to pull. Again it was often a case of bending the rules. There was a wide range of grants available to the commercial farmer and a growing number offered to the entrepreneur interested in starting a small industry in the west. Small farmers who were eligible for low interest loans and grants under one or other of the farm improvement schemes worked through their local agricultural adviser, but they used their politician as well. Larger farmers in this way secured grants which were originally not intended for them at all. The use of pull to get planning permission was just as common, with many applications initially rejected being subsequently granted on appeal. In such cases it often happened that more than one politician rallied to the cause in an attempt to support a 'reasonable' application or a 'special case'.[12]

The politicians typically had their political contacts feed them information not freely available, and they strategically released information to an individual or the public so as to make it look like they were the ones responsible for getting something for them, e.g. by being the first to congratulate them.

An example of this sort of thing occurred in 1976 when the labour TD for West Cork 'jumped-the-gun' with an announcement for a fisheries project for Castletownbere. At the time he was a junior member of Cabinet, being Secretary to the Minister for Agriculture and Fisheries. Because of his ministerial position he was able to create the impression that he had done some pulling as a personal favour to the local fishermen. Bord Iascaigh Mhara (BIM), the Irish Fishery Board, had scheduled a reception in Cork City to announce the new project. The TD, well aware that the people from Castletownbere were not going to travel 100 miles to Cork City for a Monday lunchtime reception, announced the full details the previous Friday night to a party gathered in Castletownbere, having first made sure plenty of fishermen were invited. He also saw to it that the Government Information Service released his script to the media. On Monday the BIM Chairman and staff attended the scheduled reception, having plenty to eat but nothing to announce. They were not exactly pleased, especially since the TD did not turn up to the reception but informed BIM he had another engagement. The fishermen were given the impression that the TD had 'pulled' the plant for them, and there was little that the bureaucrats could do about it. Some time later when the fishermen became worried that the plant's Spanish promoter intended using its own trawlers, the TD tipped off BIM that its Chairman might do well to take a trip to Castletownbere to meet the fishermen, which he did. The fishermen might well have got the impression that the Chairman of BIM came to see them at the TD's request.[13]

This is a classic example of what has been called 'pulling a stroke'. To acquire and then use publicity in advance of official communications or before competing politicians know about it helps create the illusion of 'real pull'. Skilled use of these methods engenders not only envy but also admiration amongst rivals as well as the press.

The politicians also used their pull to keep clients in line and to get rid of political nuisances. Many politicians ran public houses, and like most publicans they valued their after hours custom. The trade in drink and the trade in favours was good for both votes and profits. In some places the publicans and the police had come to an agreement. In Glengarriff on the north side of Bantry Bay the gardai were supposedly 'understanding' in the tourist season because there was 'only a few months of the year to make the money'. But in Bantry an 'over-conscientious' young garda was (for a combination of personal and political reasons) purportedly harassing one of the proprietors, the local politician. One alleged attempt to get him transferred failed because his father had political connections in a rival party. The politician approached the garda's superior, a close acquaintance. Still, the young turk persisted. It was reported that another attempt to move him was going to be made, and this time he would know because he would be told about it. Whether this was the reason or not, he was transferred soon after.

The politicians also took advantage of their position to get whatever was going in the form of grants, loans, planning permission, etc. Most were business people, with business interests that brought them into frequent contact with the public, and allowed them to manipulate their commercial and their political clientele.[14] This was particularly important for County Councillors who were not paid a salary but received a generous and flexibly calculated mileage allowance. The West Cork politicians who represented the Bantry district were all businessmen, making profits as farmers, merchants, hoteliers, publicans, real estate agents and auctioneers. These men [15] were typical political entrepreneurs building a career and a personal fortune on the symbiosis of commercial and electoral brokerage activities. The coming of industry to the west of Ireland greatly expanded the potential for this kind of entrepreneurship. All the politicians attempted to insert themselves as brokers between individual industrial firms and their local area. Some stood to earn a considerable amount of money in consultancy fees or from the sale of industrial land. They also had a say in who got the jobs. The politicians thus inserted themselves into a quasi-managerial role, in some cases virtually as labour contractors for employers. This was one of the ways, for example, that people obtained jobs with Gulf Oil (see chapters 3, 6 and 7). This kind of activity was only an extension of the politicians' cultivation of local employers. As I have already indicated, endemic high unemployment had put employers in a powerful position as patrons in their own right, forcing employees to curry favour with them or anyone else who could get them work.

These uses of pull were essentially an outgrowth of, and ancillary to, the politicians' dealings with the state apparatus. Most of the things voters sought through their elected representatives lay within the local government sphere.[16] Politicians assiduously cultivated contacts and friendships and made good use of kinship and marriage connections with state officials. Moreover, as they rose to prominence they made a point of establishing direct links with senior officials in central government departments as well as with the County Manager. For their part, even Ministers were obliged to engage in extensive constituency work.

As couriers between the individual voter and the various departments and offices of government, the politicians were, in effect, mediating between the electorate and the state. This function shaped the various tasks the politicians undertook and gave them personal command of a limited, but very important source of power. The particularistic, personal relationships the politicians had with their clients were mirrored in their bureaucratic contacts. The politicians did not deal with the bureaucracy as such, but with specific individuals within it. This was the case both at the County and the local level. County Councillors and TDs often took county officials aside for a confidential chat or to arrange to see them about some matter at another time. In one case a Bantry politician lamented the loss of a good contact in one of the Welfare Offices in his area; whereas he had 'an arrangement' with the previous official, the new one 'did things by the book'.

Politicians could help with appointments and promotions, particularly where a civil servant was a good party member. They paid off their debts to influentials within the state bureaucracy, the professions and in business, by proposing their names for key positions when they became vacant. They also did favours for their bureaucratic contacts in the same way as they did for everyone else. On important issues the party rather than just the individual politician could bring pressure to bear, e.g. by making things difficult for the County Manager. Because of its long years in government, Fianna Fail was in the best position to do this sort of thing, since the civil service was full of people it had appointed over a long number of years.

At the same time, the growing bureaucratization of all levels of government eroded the power of the ordinary politician as compared with that of senior officials. The majority of politicians (the opposition, the government back-bench and virtually all the local representatives) played little more than a supervisory role in government. The major government departments, while nominally under ministerial control, increasingly had a major role in deciding government policy options, and exercised effective control over the activities of the local authorities. Perhaps an even more important development here was the introduction of the Managerial system of County Council administration in the late 1940s.

With the introduction of the Managerial system there was a separation of policy-making and administration which rested on a notion of 'reserved powers' such that administration of state decisions became the sole prerogative of the county officials and policy-making functions were reserved for the elected representatives. The result was that power normally appropriated in the course of administrative tenure was handed over by legislative fiat. Many matters previously subject to political influence were now dealt with bureaucratically, and the ground was prepared for further encroachments by the bureaucracy on the domain of policy-making. Whereas previously the County Councillors made wide-ranging decisions about how public money would be divided between different services and different areas of the County, and influenced the appointment of local government officials, the County Manager now became the axis around which local and County government turned. This appropriation of power by the bureaucracy created tensions and was resisted. Nevertheless, an amendment to the earlier act designed to reinstate a measure of power to the County Councillors actually did no more than clarify the limits beyond which the bureaucracy could not encroach.

The County Manager and his staff were soon initiating and deciding policy for the politicians to ratify. The County Council had the final voting authority on the Manager's proposals, and he prepared his brief with reference to the policy guidelines of the party in power, but in practice he and his staff were the ones responsible for instigating, planning and executing most workable schemes carried out by the County Council. By playing the parties off against one another, by accumulating credit judiciously, and by lobbying and horsetrading, the County Manager soon became more powerful than most politicians. In fact, few County Councillors were prepared to fall out of favour with him; continued friendly access could be far more valuable electorally than a point of principle or even party policy.

County Managers could perhaps have subverted the use of pull, e.g. by instituting mechanisms for more effectively informing people of their entitlements and the procedures for obtaining them. One reason they did not do so is that their co-operation was necessary for the dispensation of electoral patronage, which encouraged the politicians not to hold their administration to account except in a formal way.[17] As the man in charge of the largest County in Eire, the Manager of Cork County Council was personally as powerful as the top figures in the major departments of the national government and was responsible for a much more diversified portfolio than most of them. Consequently, the party in power in the County Council was beholden to him for the success of its policies. Thus, for example, he rather than the Chairman of the County Council, was the key figure in negotiations with the national government and with foreign corporations concerning investment in County Cork.

The bureaucratic apparatus was the source from which state patronage emanated, but it was the politicians rather than the bureaucrats who were popularly regarded as responsible for the system of pull. The civil service officially encouraged this view; indeed, it was in the institutionalized interest of senior civil servants to do so. It was to their advantage to publicly promote bureaucratic procedures and rationality, and to erode the power of the politicians, and in doing so to equate this with the national interest. They, for instance, liked to emphasize that jobs and promotions were distributed according to merit; to do otherwise would have been to reflect on their integrity and their independence. However, their subordinates who were the victims of actual practice, and politicians and party functionaries who were its beneficiaries, tended to stress that pull *was* important in getting jobs.

This was not the only way in which the bureaucratic underpinnings of this form of patronage politics were manifested. Most instances of pull were little more than personalized forms of obtaining legal entitlements. Of course, some people did not know they were automatically entitled to a given benefit, and very often the politicians did nothing to let them know the truth. This was one of the main reasons the Information Centre opened in Bantry — to bypass the politicians and let people know their rights (see chapters 6 and 7). But sometimes there were advantages to be gained by getting a favour through the politicians that could have been obtained through official channels. A little pull could speed things up and cut through a lot of bureaucratic rigmarole. Each TD, for example, allegedly had a couple of beds 'allocated' to him in the local hospitals which he could fill with clients. A politician could also be helpful when it was necessary to go over the head of an over-officious local official. People also used their politicians to guard against obstructions by the bureaucracy, to uncover and correct needless mistakes. In other words, the politicians 'looked after' their constituents by scrutinizing the bureaucracy: not once things had gone wrong, but right from the beginning. A man of influence would be heeded, whereas an ordinary person might be 'put on the long finger'.

Although politicians were used to get things voters thought they might miss out on, including legitimate entitlements about which they were ignorant, they also used them when they knew that canvassing was unlikely to have any influence at all on the result, e.g. when they knew they were eligible for a medical card or pension. There was quite a sound reason for using a politician in such cases. It was given voice in such expressions as: 'Sure, isn't that what the fellow's there for?' and in behaviour which suggested a similar attitude. Many people came to see the Bantry County Councillor to get him to fill in a form for them when they might just as easily have gone to the Information Centre. These people may have continued to use their politician out of loyalty, habit, privacy, but in effect what they were doing was tying the politician to them. They were creating or maintaining a link, establishing an enduring relationship and investing in the future. That is, they were establishing 'a call upon' their representative. By bringing themselves to the attention of 'the man with pull', the voters sensitized him to their existence as potential clients; by asking for inconsequential favours, voters laid claim to the politician's attentions when something more important was on offer.

Bantry people expressed a great deal of scepticism about the effectiveness of pull, but when they thought it might help, most tried it, they 'chanced it away'. In general they got politicians to intercede on their behalf whenever they believed and had been encouraged to believe that the discretionary powers of the relevant decision-makers were subject to influence. They had to use the system even when they doubted its usefulness. The following example, which many people were fond of, suggests one reason why they felt so constrained. A job was advertised and competition for it was fierce. Several of the applicants approached their TD to make representations on their behalf. When one of them was successful the TD contacted the candidate to say in effect, 'I got you the job'. Meanwhile he contacted his other clients to say 'I did my best for you'. In defence of his credibility the TD could claim that the chances of inferior candidates were considerably enhanced by his intervention. Few would have been convinced by this argument, but the cynicism of the successful candidate would certainly have been tempered by the thought that the TD might actually have kept his promise.

These sorts of carryings-on by the politicians led some people, in a somewhat superior fashion, to express amusement at the belief most people had in the efficacy of pull. But in a sense the cynics missed the point. It was the demand for, and expansion of, state welfare associated with the vulnerability, insecurity and dependence of people, particularly the poor, that gave pull so much of its efficacy: those worst off were, for that reason, the ones most in need of advantageous personal contacts. Although the mass of people found it necessary to resort to pull, they had no commitment to it. It was the logic of the system not the morality of it that they found persuasive. No one defended it, they were amused by it and cynical about it, and they defended their own use of it in a practical, utilitarian manner; it was criticized, but the lack of an appealing alternative muted the criticism. Few people were impressed by bureaucratic administration, and most people were cynical about bureaucratic impartiality. In their eyes bureaucracies also preserved an unequal distribution of privilege, and they valued their existing personal contacts, however small and fragile were the advantages they gave — especially if they found dealing with civil servants intimidating. Moreover, civil servants and politicians consistently gave the impression, by their style of operating, that bureaucratization was a perennial problem affecting every level of decision-making, consequently when the politicians claimed that their intercessions 'cleared the way', or 'cut through the red-tape', the electorate was more than amenable to the suggestion that they might be right. In any case, they could put their faith in the politician because by looking after their interests he looked after his own.

Sometimes the politicians did not get away with trying to pull a job. Most advertisements for government jobs carried a banner saying 'No Canvassing' or 'Canvassing Will Disqualify'. The ban was seldom effective. In general it neither stopped the practice nor led to disqualification, but as the following example shows, state officials did sometimes try to enforce it in a limited way. In this case it was a teaching position that was at stake. One of the West Cork TDs canvassed the selection committee on behalf of his favoured applicant. His client's qualifications were on a par with a number of other applicants, but when the TD left the room this application was put aside. There was no suggestion that the TD's intervention by itself rendered the application ineligible; all it did was provide a way of deciding between otherwise equal applicants. It was an ironical inversion of assumptions. In the educational field there was a strong body of opinion that jobs should be decided entirely on merit. Yet in this case the action taken was contrary to the expectations of all involved: the applicant, the TD *and* the selection committee.

Politicians could resort to more covert means of persuasion when the use of pull was definitely frowned upon. They did not have to make a public plea for their client; if an applicant was genuinely competitive, the politician could help tip the balance by arguing on the merits of the case. Covert canvassing of this kind publicly avowed the importance of impartiality yet privately determined how it would be interpreted. Very often the politicians preferred it this way; they could publicly avoid criticism for rigging the result, yet at the same time confidentially let their client know the 'inside story'.

This tactic was particularly useful if something went wrong, for it was then fairly easy for the politician to deny that he had any say in the matter at all. Applications for local authority housing were assessed on a needs basis under the Housing Act of 1966, the Act being administered by the County Manager who was responsible for allocations. It was nevertheless generally believed that politicians can 'pull' their supporters a house. Bantry's County Councillor was reputed to have been influential in getting his clients houses in the new Council Estate. According to one estimate he was responsible for about one third, i.e. roughly a dozen, of the allocations made. When there were recriminations about this, he denied that people had got houses through pull, claiming that they had gone to the people most in need. He was particularly criticized because not all of the houses had been allocated to local people. Since the

County officials also claimed that the decisions had been made on a needs basis, the County Councillor was able to insist that although there were people everywhere in need, priority should have been given to locals when deciding between applicants. Double-shuffles of this kind were not uncommon, and like most performances of sleight-of-hand the audience was never quite sure at which point it had been duped.

The fact that denials of pull were, if anything, harder to disprove than claims of success is indicative of the importance of the manipulation of secrecy and uncertainty to the whole process. It was why politicians could get away with providing so many illusory favours. The prevalence of 'imaginary patronage was perhaps indicative of limitations upon the power of the politicians, but it was also evidence of their effectiveness within those limitations. Their power in fact consisted of the ability to privatize and divert the distribution of state services from bureaucratic channels and to mystify and conceal how decisions were actually made and thereby subvert accountability.[18] Once we go beyond the terms set by the patronage process itself, the question of whether the politician's pull was real or imaginary becomes less relevant, for the system was a loaded die. The favours were a product of the political structure itself, of individuated needs and wants generated and made necessary by a prior appropriation of power. Pull resulted from a monopolization of bureaucratic access, from the politicization of the bureaucracy, and from the secrecy and calculated mystification of the decision-making process. In this context, imaginary patronage helped reproduce the consciousness the system required that there was 'no harm in trying'.

Although they still used all the old tricks and techniques to trade favours for votes on a personal basis, the politicians had begun to place a greater emphasis on their links with local interest groups. On the lookout for new ways to bind the electorate to them and mediate between popular grievances and state policies, instead of simply doing personal favours for individuals, politicians had begun to place more emphasis on servicing a clientele of interest groups *as* interest groups. This was done in the name of helping 'the community'. Given that interest groups concerned with economic development themselves operated in the name of the community, it was easy to make this sort of identification (see chapters 3, 6 and 7).

Ironically, it seems that in the past the provision of favours in an individualistic, particularized fashion inhibited the emergence of specialized interest groups, except those coming under the umbrella of the church (see also chapter 5). The major parties, particularly Fianna Fail, had tried to encourage the view that party membership was sufficient to ensure a favourable response to sectional demands. But from the 1950s specialized interest groups which were not beholden to either the church or any political party began to assume a greater importance. The most prominent of these in Bantry were concerned with economic development. The relationship of the local politician to these bodies was to become an increasingly important aspect of the distribution of political patronage during the 1960s and 1970s, adding weight to the emphasis the electorate placed on having a good 'local man'. Other politicians might pull for the area, but their first loyalty was to their own district. The 'local man' had a vested interest in developing his own area: as it grew so would he. By lobbying in the county and national arena and by inserting local concerns into wider issues, a successful politician could get his district favoured with benefits and, as well as increasing his chances of enhancing his local vote, he could make himself a lynch-pin in all future struggles for progress and development.

Bantry's Fianna Fail County Councillor, for example, was extremely active in a wide variety of committees and organizations in his home town, but not elsewhere. Significantly, he did not seek election to the Town Commissioners as his predecessor the Fianna Fail TD had done. Whereas in the past, national and county politicians sought a seat on the Commissioners even though they were unable to attend many meetings, these positions now went to local party activists who were unlikely to go further in politics.

The other West Cork politicians also tended to be active in organizations near their home-place (see Table 4:1). When they ventured further afield, they mainly relied upon the pull they commanded through the County Council or the Dail. The Fianna Fail TD from Bandon had little personal influence in the Bantry district; the Fine Gael TD from Clonakilty had somewhat more, but he was also a figure external to the town. The Labour TD from Schull had a much larger personal following in and around Bantry, but this was almost entirely based upon the dispensation of personal and collective favours; outside the Labour party and the trade unions, he had little sway in local organizations and town affairs. Nor did his County Councillor brother, in spite of the fact that he was stationed at Aghaville only half a dozen miles away. Like him, the Fine Gael County Councillor from Goleen spent a great deal of time in Bantry, but his influence did not extend into the major organizations concerned with civic affairs.[19]

The value of participating in organizations independent of the party encouraged the emergence of a new syle of rural politician, the educated, urbane, 'executive-material' type. Within Fianna Fail, these men were referred to as 'the mohair suit brigade'. Although he was critical of their influence within his party, Bantry's County Councillor could easily have been mistaken for one of them. He posed himself as an alternative to the zealous publicity-mongering, tub-thumping backwoods campaigner, the stereotypical parish-pump politician. He looked after his clients as assiduously as his Fine Gael and Labour Party rivals in the County Council (who fitted the stereotype), but he was also keen to project the image of professionalism required by the changing character of government.

Brokerage and electoral rivalry [20]

TDs and County Councillors were selected on the basis of universal adult suffrage by means of a system of proportional representation (single transferable vote) from multi-member electorates. Each Dail (parliamentary) Constituency contained a number of County Council Electoral Areas (see Table 4:1). Most TDs first entered politics through the County Council, and held onto their seat in the County Council after winning a seat in the Dail.[21]

Because of the system of multi-member electorates, on polling day each party faced the voters united across electorates but divided within them. Politicians of the same party competed not just for pre-selection but for the available seats once pre-selection was obtained. Running mates from the same Constituency were pitted against one another in Dail elections; if they also happened to be from the same County Electoral Area then they were pitted against one another in County Council elections as well. This situation made for a certain amount of ambivalence between running mates, particularly between the sitting TD and his colleagues in the County Council. Although electoral success depended upon running mates co-operating (both formally and informally) to augment their pull and improve their standing with the electorate, they also tried to turn these arrangements to personal advantage

Table 4:1 Constituency: Cork South-West

comprising the County Electoral Areas (CEA) of —
  Bandon (part)
  Skibbereen (part)
  Schull (part)

The elected representatives from Cork South-West active in the Bantry Area*

Party	Office	Home Base	CEA
Fianna Fail	TD	Bandon	Bandon
Fine Gael	TD	Clonakilty	Skibbereen
Labour	TD	Schull	Skibbereen
Fianna Fail	MCC	Bantry	Schull
Fine Gael	MCC	Goleen	Schull
Labour	MCC	Aghaville	Schull
(Labour	Ex-MCC	Bantry	Schull)

* NB This list does not include elected representatives from Cork South-West who only intermittently involved themselves in political affairs in the Bantry Area.

by outflanking one another — even to the detriment of their party. The would-be County Councillor or TD often as not had to steal a seat from a member of his or her own party in order to get elected. The competition within each party was finally decided, not in the party room, but by the electorate. On polling day the voters had both a choice between parties and a choice within each party. Given the relative durability of party allegiances, the use of pull tended to influence the latter choice more than the former. Nevertheless inter- and intra-party electoral contests were symbiotically related.

In marginal electorates, and electorates where boundary changes had been common, a fluid situation prevailed, which offered many opportunities to aspirants to political office. In safe seats the aspiring politician was more often forced to wait for the incumbent to retire or die. In the meantime, all that could be done was prepare for that day by building a local power base and isolating potential rivals. Up until 1948 West Cork was a 5-seat Constituency covering an enormous scope of country. It was then reduced in size and turned into a 3-seat Constituency, South-West Cork. The new arrangement created a safe seat for the three major parties. A further redistribution of electorates in 1959 preserved the 1948 arrangement. The situation was little different in the County Council. Fianna Fail and Fine Gael both held two seats in the Schull Electoral Area (which encompassed Bantry), while Labour held one. Since two of the County Councillors confined their activities to the Beare peninsula, Bantry was effectively represented in the County Council, as in the Dail, by one man from each party (see Table 4:1).

From the electorate's point of view there was little to be gained from this set-up. Right through the dark days of the 1950s West Cork people had claimed that the region had been neglected because it had no marginal seats and returned no prominent Ministers. Although things had improved considerably by the 1970s, it was still felt that areas with a marginal seat were getting all the benefits, factories especially. In the mid-1970s the politicians liked to point out that West Cork as a whole had done reasonably well in the industrialization stakes. Nevertheless, individual localities such as Bantry would certainly have gained from a more volatile situation.

By redrawing the electoral boundaries and dividing up the electorates between their candidates, the party leaderships had, in effect, entered into a power-sharing arrangement in West Cork which shifted the locus of inter-party competition to other parts of the country. The result of this was that the number of candidates campaigning in any one electorate was reduced, the party vote was solidified, and the party leaderships were given greater control of their candidates.

Although safe, the electorates of West Cork were well and truly locked into the patronage system: because they were safe they could be neglected; because they were in danger of being neglected they had to struggle harder for patronage.

This was not the only way the electoral system had both helped shape, and in turn been shaped by, the patronage politics of the major parties. TDs were generally more powerful figures than County Councillors, but each politician had a strong pocket of influence centred on his home place. Within this pocket most County Councillors were stronger than all but the most powerful TD. Nevertheless, ambitious County Councillors had to be careful and patient, for the TD was best positioned to manipulate the system to advantage if an ambitious rival threatened to cause him or his allies any trouble.

To minimize friction between running mates and enhance the party vote, electorates were carved up by each party into the functional equivalent of single-member seats. In this way, each candidate's parochial pocket of influence was formalized by the parties into a bailiwick system. The boundaries of bailiwicks were porous and frequent poaching occurred, but officially at least they were respected.

The co-operation between running mates mainly consisted of County Councillors acting as brokers for TDs. This in effect made the County Councillors brokers' brokers. Because County Councillors were centrally placed within their pockets of influence and had continuous personal contact with voters, they did not have the same need for leg-men as the TDs. It was as County Councillor himself that a TD did most of his Constituency work and it was in his home pocket that he dispensed most of his favours. Throughout the rest of his Dail constituency he relied on friendly County Councillors and local brokers to relay clients' grievances to him.

County Councillors were not the only people the TDs used in this way, but they were the key ones. This arrangement increased the County Councillor's reputation for pull and expanded the TD's clientele. If the request was a local government matter it was dealt with directly by the County Councillor, if it was not, the Councillor passed it on to the party's nearest TD. The TD subsequently was supposed to pass the answer back to the client through the County Councillor.

This system created a division of labour and credit between the TD and the County Councillor. But it also enhanced the potential for friction between them. As an aspirant to higher office, a County Councillor with pull was potentially more of a threat than an ally to the sitting member. As a result the TDs developed a circle of local brokers independent of the County Councillors. Bantry's Fianna Fail County Councillor, for example, was frequently sparring behind-the-scenes with the TD from Bandon and his leg-man for control of cumainn (clubs or branches) in and around Bantry. To strengthen their home base, the County Councillors tried to dominate all the party cumainn in their Electoral Area, and to expand the total number of cumainn under their control (thus increasing the support at the party conventions). The Fine Gael County Councillor, for example, owed his electoral success to the number of cumainn he had created throughout the Schull Electoral Area while criss-crossing the countryside dispensing favours and cultivating the vote.

One of the devices the TDs used to strengthen their personal machines and protect themselves against potential rivals was to short-circuit the brokerage process. That is, when a County Councillor channelled a client's grievances to him, the TD could pass the information back to the client directly or, alternatively, he could use a local broker to by-pass the County Councillor.

A local broker who was not a County Councillor could thus be used by a TD as a counter-weight to a threatening rival. To achieve elected office the local broker had to build a clientele of his own and short-circuit the County Councillor's lines of communication. With the help of the TD, a local broker could thus construct a personal power base to rival a vulnerable County Councillor. In the Schull Electoral Area both the Fine Gael and the Labour County Councillors came to power by vigorously out-manoeuvring women who did not have the contacts, or ruthless dedication to a political career, possessed by these men. The opportunities for a local broker to become powerful enough to dislodge a County Councillor were relatively rare in West Cork, where the electorates had relatively stable boundaries and seats were safe. But with enough pull a lot of things became possible.

The man with the most pull in the Bantry area was arguably the **Labour TD**. His personal machine was probably the most effective in West Cork in the 1970s because he was the longest sitting politician in the region and the most firmly entrenched. His career provides the most striking example of machine politics in West Cork, specifically of a politician seeking to make the party's interests coincide with his, rather than his with that of the party.[22]

Although Bantry came within the TD's Dail Constituency, it was not included in his County Electoral Area (see Table 4:1). He was originally elected to the County council from the Skibbereen CEA in 1941 at the age of 22. In 1949 the sitting Labour TD died. Although they were not related, both men had the same surname; this was to be of major importance in the events to come. The deceased TD's hand-picked successor was a Labour County Councillor from Bantry. However, he withdrew his nomination when his ambitious rival threatened to run on an independent Labour ticket if deprived of the party nomination. Such a spoiling operation would have given the seat (perhaps permanently) to Fianna Fail or Fine Gael. It was not all that uncommon for someone to threaten to run as an Independent as a spoiling operation in a situation such as this. The fact that the future TD came from the same part of the Constituency as the deceased TD and had the same surname gave added weight to the gambit. Following the Bantry candidate's withdrawal, the usurper went on to win the seat for the party in the next (1951) election.

Twenty years later he repeated his coup by engineering the defeat of his old rival's widow, installing his brother in her County Council seat. The TD's father-in-law had been a County Councillor for the minority Farmers' party until 1966 when he conveniently retired. The TD put his brother forward as a candidate over the objections of the Bantry widow who claimed there was not room in the Schull Elecoral Area for two Labour County Councillors, particularly ones living only six miles apart. Pointing to the Gulf Oil project and emphasizing that additional development was expected to flow from it, the TD argued that Bantry was on the verge of becoming a Labour strong-hold, and now was the time to move. At the 1967 elections both Labour Candidates were returned, the widow ahead of the brother. The next election in 1973 produced a different result. With his brother ensconced as a legitimate candidate, the TD left nothing to chance. The brothers indicated by their actions that they no longer believed the electorate could elect two Labour County Councillors and set about trying to reverse the proportion of votes going to each of the candidates. It was widely alleged that, although the TD 'officially' endorsed the widow, in 'personal letters' to voters he asked for support for his brother. Actually, most of the groundwork had been done long before the campaign started. The widow had been increasingly by-passed in the flow of favours. When she passed requests on to the TD the reply frequently came back to the voter through the brother. The woman was isolated and rendered ineffective and her pull evaporated. Although she could still count on a 'sympathy' vote and a loyal following dating back to her husband's day, her local vote was eroded by the proximity of her rival, and by her failure to play the political game hard enough, canvassing support, electioneering, and building a machine of her own.

The bad feeling generated by these events persisted. On public occasions the protagonists usually maintained a surface cordiality, but sometimes, per-sonal feelings came through. At the first meeting of the newly established Harbour Authority in 1976 (see chapter 8), the widow took advantage of a unique situation to vote against the brother who had taken her seat from her. The move took him completely by surprise and foiled his attempt to become Deputy Chairman of the new body.

The Labour TD took the manipulation of kinship ties somewhat further than most politicians. Although his father-in-law had belonged to another political party the TD was able to convert his seat into a safe seat for his brother. But then he had always seen the value of kinship connections, even spurious ones: after all, he was only a TD himself because he used a coinci-dence of surnames to secure his predecessor's seat. By installing his brother in a safe seat in the adjacent County Electoral Area, he had the best of all brokers working for him: a loyal bulwark against potential rivals, and a dependable vote catcher — in fact a mini-version of himself.

Final remarks

The kind of brokerage politics favoured by the electoral system in Eire is only a special case of the more general problem of political representation in democratic capitalist states. In a general sense all politicians are brokers mediating between the electorate and the state. But the mechanics of this mediation process take on a special significance when shaped by the dispensing of patronage by party machines. For the purposes of this study I have concentrated on one aspect, relating the pervasive influence of patronage-style party politics in the Bantry area to the quest for development (without denying the importance of other factors common to patronage politics the world over).[23]

I have particularly emphasized the importance of the consolidation of the indigenous bourgeoisie as the dominant class in the face of a politically assertive petty-bourgeoisie, and suggested that in these circumstances patronage politics was associated with a particular form of underdevelopment and state functioning. The state apparatus could not be administered and state power exercised according to universalistic procedures of a strictly bureaucratic kind because of the partisan and popular demands made upon it. Nor was the bourgeoisie in a position to directly control the lives of the mass of the people; consequently it had to rely upon paternalistic dispensations and populist modes of representation and mediation. From the late 1950s onwards the balance of forces began to shift yet again as the state entered into a new type of relationship to foreign capital. The interlocking of populism and patronage was thus taken a step further.

Fianna Fail came to power with the support of the subordinate classes but — not without opposition — increasingly administered the state primarily in the interests of the dominant class. In making this switch, the party increasingly separated the demands of the mass of its supporters from its general policy-making functions. The patronage system helped make it easy to do this, in part because it allowed the state to be depicted in a way which did not bear upon, and actually distorted, its major functions. The politicians were more than just 'messenger boys' between the electorate and government. This is certainly how they appeared to the voter, but they were doing more than just running errands. They were actually representing the interests of the electorate — albeit in a personalized and particularistic way which turned common political grievances into individual personal wants to be placated by the dispensation of state welfare. The use of patronage committed the electorate to a political system wherein the individual voter pursued his or her personal interests in a manner which did not seriously impinge upon the formulation of state policy. In other words, it reduced political citizenship to the equivalent of a fee-for-service relationship in which the client bought a right, not to say in government, but to a quotient of the state's redistribution of resources. In reality of course, the voter was getting the equivalent of something like a tax rebate. Meanwhile, ostensibly bureaucratic procedures glossed the privatization of state activities and impeded the aggregation of political demands, resulting in a nexus of collusion which put the state's impartiality, though not its legitimacy, into question.

As a result of these processes, the state appeared as a paternalistic bene-factor, and the political broker as an ally rather than a gombeen-like figure. The institutionalization of the politician as a channel for complaint-satisfaction helped convert grievances against the system into grievances against the individual politician, the party, or the civil service. What is more, the system of multi-member electorates multiplied the number of intra-systemic alterna-tives available to the electorate. Voters could choose not only between parties but between individuals within parties. Popular discontent was in these ways displaced; instead of challenging the system, dissatisfaction came to serve as fertilizer which helped the system flourish. Political demands became a nuisance rather than a force in politics. Policy making was left in the hands of the Cabinet and the top echelons of the civil service and the County Councils. Of course, the demands of the electorate could not be neutralized, but they could be contained, and the politicians were always there to orches-trate their expression. So long as the state maintained a level of welfare, services and employment sufficient to appease the electorate and allowed the brokerage system to distribute favours, and so long as the politicians remained influential figures having a decisive say in local affairs, broad policy guidelines could be fixed and implemented without any effective control from below.[24]

The institutions of parliamentary democracy welded to a system of state patronage co-opted the subordinate classes. Lacking a viable alternative, their compliance rested on two things: their participation in the system to the minimal extent of voting and demanding petty favours, and the universal quest for prosperity. Patronage politics was one of the means by which control of the state was separated from the constraints of electoral representation, a device which prevented popular demands from compromising the program of economic development. In other words, the brokerage system enabled the political parties to actively mobilize the electorate in support of policies favourable to the extended reproduction of capital. Populist demands were thus successfully prevented from disrupting the public servicing of capital accumulation.[25]

In this context it is worth emphasizing that there was no rupture between illegal or unethical practices, the distribution of petty favours, and the normal means used by business interests to persuade governments to favour them. Each depended upon personalized exchanges of material aid in return for political support of one kind or another. Yet only some of these dealings were of the type conventionally described by social scientists as patronage relationships: those sweetheart arrangements which exuded the whiff of a 'bought' vote, or else personal profiteering or 'corruption'. Yet the doling out of favours to both local and foreign capitalists took the same general form as any other example of patronage politics.[26] There was only one difference. After the 1950s key sections of the indigenous bourgeoisie came close to resembling a *comprador* class beholden to EEC and US finance capital. The Irish State now mimicked its politicians. It had itself become a broker: currying favour and ferrying the patronage distributed by international financiers who depicted themselves as global patrons, creating employment, prosperity and social development wherever they chose to invest.[27] Conflicts within and between classes, parties and the state were increasingly mediated by this growing dependence upon foreign capital, and in their different ways they were all to became ambivalent advocates of its dispensation of development.[28]

5 Catholic culture and civic affairs

The success of the catholic-nationalist forces in the War of Independence ushered in a new era in church-state relations in Eire. In the previous chapter I argued that patronage-style politics came to help guarantee political support for capitalist economic development. Here I am concerned with religion as a mechanism of cultural control, i.e. with the church's ideological domination of key areas of social thought. I will argue that whereas politicians and civil servants used their control of patronage to mediate between the individual voter and the state, the clergy mediated between their parishioners and the state by using their sway over the faithful to establish themselves as civic leaders representative of the community as a whole. Section I briefly discusses the accommodations reached between the major parties and the church in the development of the post-colonial state. The focus here is on how these ties provided the institutional underpinnings for the parish clergy's influence. This does not pretend to be a comprehensive account, but rather a sketch of processes essential for an understanding of localized clerical interventions in civic life. Section II looks at the changing place of religion in everyday life and the clergy as intellectuals, particularly their leadership of a diverse range of local committees and organizations.

Church and state

The influence of the parish clergy locally cannot be fully understood without an analysis of the changing relation between church and state in the middle years of the century.[1] The administration of parish affairs was ultimately the responsibility, not of the parish priest, but the bishop and his diocesan advisers. It was this wider organization, comprising the hierarchy (council of bishops) and its supporting bureaucracy which defined what constituted the 'needs' of each parish and what the appropriate responses to them were. The hierarchy owed its position and influence to, not only the allegiance of the faithful, but also its relationship to the state.

The consolidation of the Free State [2]

In the colonial period the church formed part of the nationalist bloc which confronted the British rulers. With the founding of the Free State, the bishops had to renegotiate their relationship to the nationalist political forces.

From the Easter Rising to the outbreak of the Civil War the limits to the church's power were demonstrated more clearly than at any time before or after. While the revolution mustered its strength, the hierarchy — like everyone committed to constitutionalist politics — could only bide its time. Yet as soon as a government that it could safely support and declare legitimate existed, it invoked the full authority of divine law in its favour.

The influence of the church was always weakest on matters where nationalist political ideology was most powerful. Its influence was traditionally strongest where issues of faith, morals and ethics had no independent political import. Whenever the aspirations and loyalties of the population found a moral expression in political action, the clergy were either forced to fall into line or manoeuvre until they could reassert their authority. Rather than dictate the terms of the struggle, the church was forced to bow to its logic.

In colonial times the church maintained its autonomy from the British state in order to retain its influence with the people. After the triumph of the nationalist forces the hierarchy preferred to preserve its autonomy rather than enter into a formal concordat with the new state. That is, it opted for a *de facto* catholic state rather than a *de jure* one. Whereas a formal concordat would have yoked the church and the governing party together and created a potential for institutionalized conflict and constant friction, conflict became a contextual danger rather than the inevitable consequence of joint decision-making; the threat of schism was replaced by the need for accommodation. This arrangement secured the church substantive privileges while denying it formal ones. It remained free of state control in areas where it had traditionally been independent. The state exerted no influence in the ecclesiastical realm: it had no say in clerical appointments and it did not endow the church. The bishops were thus not under any political obligation to the government, but they could command its attention when they demanded it. For the clergy to remain powerful they had to preserve this power of 'veto': they had to forestall developments which would enable the secular authorities to emancipate themselves from ecclesiastical influence. The aim was to ensure that all major social forces were simultaneously pledged to the will of the church. From the clergy's perspective, by supporting the church, the state protected itself.[3]

The church had remained tied to the Free State government after the Civil War because there was no viable constitutional alternative, but once Fianna Fail was formed and began to participate in the electoral process, the hierarchy moved toward a more truly neutral stance. By convincing the bishops that previous opposition to the church on political questions had not impeded his or his followers' loyalty on religious ones, de Valera secured clerical legitimacy for his party at the very time Cumman na nGaedheal was most in need of its unequivocal support: as the appeal of Fianna Fail grew, Cumman na nGaedheal's hopes of capturing an absolute majority of the vote disappeared; it needed the hierarchy more than hierarchy needed it. Fianna Fail went out of its way to suggest that it was the more truly catholic party of the two. It even went so far as to equate catholicism with Irishness — a common enough view in the countryside but one which, coming from the government, gave the bishops special licence to stipulate what was not appropriate for a catholic state.

In fact, the major parties continued to show they were prepared to uphold the church's position, accepting the authority of the priests whenever it was deemed they had a traditional right to speak. When in government, the parties seldom — and then only very cautiously — attempted to encroach upon ecclesiastical authority. More commonly, they deferred to the moral pre-eminence of the priests and appointed them to influential positions both nationally and locally. Most politicians were committed catholics, and accepted the clergy's right to speak on matters of faith and morals. They also knew that the vast majority of the electorate accepted the church's authority on matters of conscience. But perhaps even more importantly, like the vast majority of the populace, they saw themselves as belonging to a 'catholic nation.'

To the major parties, the church was the guarantor of the existing cultural order and the standards which both priests and politicians held dear. This commitment to the maintenance of catholic values ensured that a whole range of social issues came to be treated exclusively as moral issues. The clergy's views on such matters were usually well known, heeded and abided by — even to the point of taking special account of the particular views of individual clergymen. The church did not establish its own party organization because it did not have to: it had, in effect, its own party in all of the parties. From this perspective, the former Taoiseach, Lemass, was right to say that there were only two parties in Ireland — the catholic and the protestant. The parties' use of state power to protect catholic moral values was done, of course, in the name of the catholic majority, the 'catholic nation'. But the fact that it was felt necessary to protect these values suggests that the populace was less strenuous about holding to them than their rulers felt necessary.

By remaining neutral in the sphere of constitutional party politics, the church was in a better position to deny legitimacy to extra-parliamentary alternatives, the major parties thus allowed the church to become, in effect, the defender of constitutional government. The whole weight of its authority could be brought to bear as an independent voice supportive of legislative and repressive measures, and also to counter opposition to 'the legitimate authorities', e.g. by the IRA. The alternative option of a catholic party would undoubtedly have meant the church would have remained a force in political life both within and without the party, but its power then and its relation to the state would have been quite different — and less distinctive.

The church thus managed to place itself 'above' party politics. All governments were beholden to it, but it remained untainted by unpopular policies and was free to comment on them. It was not predjudiced by partisan loyalties but could speak in the name of the people. It thus remained at all times free to negotiate with the government whenever it was deemed appropriate. The priests were society's guardians not just because they were the spiritual leaders of the overwhelming majority of the population but because they were guarantors of, on the one hand, constitutional government and, on the other, the catholicity of the nation.

The Integralist offensive [4]

From the early 1930s to the mid-1950s various groups began working to make Ireland more totally catholic. Under the influence of the papal encyclicals *Rerum Novarum* and *Quadragesimo Anno,* which stressed class harmony as the christian response to class war, the social movement in Ireland began to advocate the organization of 'vocational groups' or 'corporations' in which employers and workers would collaborate to further their common interests It was to be incumbent upon the state to consult with these vocational bodies, indeed one of the outcomes of the corporate order was supposed to be the reconstruction of the state itself.

The propagation of these ideas coincided with Fianna Fail's rise to power in the early 1930s and the spectre of resurgent socialism which grew out of the Depression. Prior to this there had been no tradition of catholic thought on social questions in Ireland outside the pronouncements of the hierarchy.

However, once they found their voice, the secular ideologues of catholicism made a profound impression. Led by General O'Duffy, the Blueshirts went so far as to advocate the formation of a corporatist state along fascist lines. This program was still-born. The social movement's advocacy of corporatism was designed more to reform the state apparatus than revolutionize it: it was not itself fascist, although a number of its leading ideologues were sympathetic to the Blueshirts.

Although the ideologies of the social movement were concerned about the growing power of the state, it was not the capitalist state as such which they feared, but a supposed insurgent bureaucratic socialism. The aim was not really to do away with the state control so much as replace one kind of state control with another. The proposed method of achieving this was to get the government to act as much as possible through vocational bodies instead of bureaucratic departments. If pursued without resistance this policy would have brought virtually all voluntary organizations under the umbrella of the church. The anti-state rhetoric of the advocates of integralism thus masked an hierocratic impulse which, if successful, would not have weakened the power of the state so much as created a theocratic edifice within it.

The clergy saw in these ideas a way of reasserting their authority in the face of the increasing secularization of social life and the erosion of beliefs and values which were compatible with catholic social teaching. From their point of view, everybody was subject to the church's discipline, even those who denied its sovereignty. The faithful were to compulsorily comply from the moment they were born; protestants were expected to accommodate themselves to the dictates of the hierarchy. In attempting to enforce a comprehensive ethical discipline on the population, the church recognized no substantive limitations on its moral authority (cf. Weber, 1968: 1164–5). This view was taken furthest by Dr Lucey, the Bishop of Cork and Ross and a former parish priest in Bantry. In a speech to the Christus Rex Congress in 1955 he was reported as arguing that 'the church is the divinely appointed guardian and interpreter of the moral law', the bishops being 'the final arbiters of right and wrong even in political matters'. That this did not mean the church should actually be able to veto state policy was only made clear in his 1957 lenten pastoral: the bishops' power, he conceded, 'extends only to the religious and moral implications of what goes on — the Church has no competence to control public affairs itself . . . ' (quoted by Whyte, 1971: 312–3).[5]

The initiatives of the hierarchy and its allies during the integralist period were designed to preserve and increase the power of the church in all areas of social life, with the bishops seeking to extend their influence into arenas in which they had not traditionally had a say, e.g. they spoke out against communist infiltration of the IRA, the trade unions and the Labour Party and even persuaded the latter to remove the phrase 'Workers' Republic' from its constitutional aims; they, among other legislation, attacked changes to the alcoholic licensing laws, and firmly laid down their position on sexuality, marriage and divorce, adoption, contraception and abortion. The preservation of 'traditional moral standards' remained their most obvious preoccupation. But episcopal influence on state policy was unobstrusive because state policy tended to be in line with church thinking.

At their most insistent the advocates of integralism construed the rejection of vocationalist ideas as rejection of catholic social teaching. Yet the vocationalist attempt to combat the secularization of social life was essentially defensive: if the threat could not be prevented, it could be contained. It was more a utopian impulse than the formulation of a viable program for change: the idea that decision-making responsibility should be diffused among functionally inter-related vocational groups ran directly counter to the growing power of the party machines and centralized government departments, neither of which were about to allow vocationalist rhetoric to have an effect on how decisions were actually made and acted upon.

Once Fianna Fail became entrenched in power, the relationship of the church to the state was in key respects a matter of the relationship of the church to Fianna Fail. Neither Fianna Fail, nor the other parties when they took over government, ever seriously showed any intention of remodelling the state apparatus on vocational lines. The party did not even appear conciliatory in the face of such proposals. Even so, the Constitution of 1937 had all the marks of Irish catholic social teaching of the time. Its articles on the primacy of the family in social life, marriage, education and private property, through to the provisions on 'the special position' of the catholic church, clearly illustrate how strong this influence was. Yet these provisions did nothing to alter the actual position of the church, they were merely public acknowledgement of it. If anything (and admittedly this did not seem to be his intention), de Valera's Constitution was important mainly because it set definite limits on the church's claims upon the state. It effectively pre-empted any subsequent moves to enlarge the bishops' jurisdiction. The church was 'special' because virtually the whole population was catholic: Eire was a catholic country run by a secular state — beyond that, closer relations were dependent upon the discretion of the government.

The parties did not defer to the bishops simply because they chose to speak, yet government leaders did show a marked reluctance to involve the clergy in public controversy. When the bishops were prepared to take a stand governments still compromised or consulted with them. The politicians assiduously sought to harmonize state policy with catholic social teaching and the party leaders avoided adopting policies which were likely to meet with disapproval from the bishops. This created the appearance of a theocratic state in which governments were manipulated by the church behind the scenes. Contact between the clergy and government departments was, in fact, a regular and taken for granted aspect of administrative procedures. But unless a clear question of catholic doctrine was involved, the bishops were not automatically informed about government policy proposals. When controversy arose it was usually because there were objections to policy that had already been formulated. In fact, even when their views were taken into account or they were deliberately consulted, the bishops were not party to the policy-making process.

As the advocates of integralism became more insistent, they provoked more resistance and eventually the counter pressures prevailed.[6] This happened to coincide with the switch in state economic policy of the late 1950s. State planning for development was demonstrably effective in remedying the problems which had beset the economy.[7] Instead of the wholesale denunciations of the past, the view developed that in key areas the state did too little rather than too much. Welfare, education, job training and man-power planning, for instance, were seen as more closely related than before and their co-ordination a key state responsibility. Attempts were made to harmonize the defence of the family unit, private charity and self-help with the provision of more and more social services. Indeed, the state was now called to account if it neglected its responsibilities in these areas, and the clergy became mediators and lobbyists on behalf of the needy and the neglected.

Even when relations were most tense, church and state never actually challenged the prerogatives of the other, rather they accommodated them, merely taking one another to task on specific issues. The state always had the power to take exclusive control of health, education, welfare and marriage-related provisions (divorce, contraception, abortion, etc.) if it proved necessary to do so, although it is doubtful whether any individual government could have made such a move without the support of all the parties. This continued to be the case, but by the early 1970s the political leaders had shown an ability or willingness to tackle questions and institute reforms affecting the church's position which in previous years they would not even have considered. The reforms caused some controversy, but the hierarchy did not always oppose the initiatives taken, e.g. changes were made regarding censorship, and the running of the schools, and the Constitution was amended by referendum to delete the clause which accorded the faith of catholics a 'special position'.

The church's acceptance of these renovations of social policy reflected its accommodation not only to the state but the changing nature of society itself. This was partly due to its judiciously pragmatic conservatism with regard to matters over which it had no control and which were capable of making it seem redundant. So long as its own survival was not threatened, if toleration could be reconciled with religious doctrine, and if it might help the flock keep their faith, the church could adapt — however reluctantly. In this respect its stance was defensive, its public campaigns so often rearguard actions from an entrenched position which allowed it to win the battles which staved off the eventual corrosive effects of secularisation and pluralism.

Religious observance and clerical authority

At Bantry, as everywhere else, the symbols of catholic piety adorned the countryside. Religious iconography decorated mountain passes, public buildings and private homes. Children, aeroplanes, ships, trains, cars, suburbs and streets were commonly named after a saint, a martyr, or a bishop. Mass goers filled the streets on the Sabbath; the Corpus Christi procession was the most impressive public ritual of the year; church-affiliated collectors for sundry charities and missions abroad regularly canvassed the city streets. In advertisements for pilgrimages to Holy Places, in the sentiments expressed in the media, literature and song, in the very idioms of the language, a catholic imagery prevailed. Less than 5% of the population were protestants. Indelibly marked by catholic Ireland, they were shadow players who bore witness to the influence of catholicism by mimicking its preoccupations in inverted form. It was this pervasive catholicity — rather than the divide between catholics and protestants — that was the key feature of the relationship between religion and other aspects of social life at Bantry (see Table 5:1, also chapter 6).

The changing place of religion in everyday life

Bantry was abustle with people and traffic every Sunday. The noon mass was the most popular. The 'Chapel' was invariably overflowing, the doorways crammed with the male youth and latecomers. Meanwhile at the Church of Ireland, a small group of worshippers equally assiduously fulfilled the felt obligations of their faith. The rituals of baptism, confirmation, marriage and death figured prominently in people's conversation and were the occasion for much organizing and socializing. Funerals were especially noteworthy events

Table 5:1 Religious affiliation: Bantry Town

Denomination	Males		Females		Total	
	No.	%	No.	%	No.	%
Catholic	1,107	94.78	1,357	96.17	2,464	95.54
Other (including No Religion and No information)	61	5.22	54	3.83	115	4.46

Source: Census of Ireland, 1971

93

which brought large numbers of people into town every week. For the Corpus Christi procession, buildings were spruced up or freshly painted in bright colours, and decorated with flags and bunting. The parish priest and his curates led the procession under a canopy carried by members of the St. Vincent de Paul, followed by the Legion and Children of Mary, with the people of the town in train. Men and women marched separately, the men bringing up the rear. As the procession wound through the town, people joined from the sidelines until both members of the procession and spectators assembled in the Square for mass.

There were also economic and political reasons why religion was important. The business people appreciated the commercial as well as the spiritual value of keeping up the faith: they estimated that a funeral was 'better for business than a wedding'. A death certainly did more to fill the pubs and shops than a marriage. At meetings of the Town Commissioners and the County Council it was the practice to pass votes of sympathy to the relatives of the recently deceased; politicians were also conscientious in their attendance at funerals: the dead could not vote but their relatives did. Since it was the only guaranteed way of getting the whole town to contribute, church gate collections were regularly carried out by local organizations on specified Sundays. At election times the political parties canvassed support by placing their candidates outside the church gates (as a result, they were even known to receive a donation from their rivals). People brought into town for religious reasons often used these visits for other purposes: the Bantry Bay Hotel, operated by the Fianna Fail County Councillor, was a very busy place on Sundays.

Virtually all daily social discourse was expressed in a religious idiom, partly because the English spoken by West Cork people was heavily inflected with Gaelic pieties. Bantry people keenly appreciated the fact that, compared with the English, and catholics from other countries, religion occupied a distinctive place in their life. Discussions of the subject were frequently prefaced with the remark, 'Now you'll think us funny . . . ' or a similar self-deprecatory comment. This attitude was tied up with defensiveness about other kinds of 'backwardness', exacerbated by returned emigrants, tourists and the media. Yet in other ways, Bantry people asserted their beliefs with conviction. It was not their earnestness that was most striking, but the fact that their faith had such deep roots in custom and internalized habit. Many gave credence to notions which they knew foreigners were sceptical about. Although few willingly testified to a belief in fairies, more were prepared to accept claims that houses were haunted. Older people, in particular, clung to their so-called 'superstitions'. For example, they maintained that 'Danish [i.e. ring] forts' should not be visited; that the fish had vanished from the Bay because the fishermen had fought over them; that families and land suffered from having a 'curse' put on them, and that numerous small avoidances and obligations had to be given their due. Women were most punctilious in their observances. They were popularly regarded by both priests and laity as 'the backbone' of the church, and were usually responsible for getting their husbands and families to mass. Older women, spinsters and widows were especially punctilious. Those who attended mass daily, especially the early morning mass, were known as 'craw thumpers' and were the object of mild ridicule.

In spite of the fact that the vast majority of catholics attended mass one or more times per week, many people detected a decline in mass going. This was universally attributed to the new prosperity brought by Gulf Oil: 'affluence makes you less dependent on God'. Social pressure was nevertheless still quite formidable. According to one of the Bantry priests, 'One person not going to mass would cause talk in a family'. The only people who did not attend mass regularly were a few men who seemed to think they should have. even though they did not (one man refused to go for political reasons), and young people temporarily resident in the town whose families could not police them.

Concern was often voiced about young people 'losing their faith' when they moved away from home: 'they're used to having people watching them'. Religious indoctrination from an early age was thought to be the best guarantee of a young person remaining 'a good catholic'.

> If you grow up in a small town and go [to mass] from when you're a child it's just like going to sleep of a night . . . The English thought us all mad the way we'd get up and go to mass — a waste of a day — but we all did it and if you didn't you'd probably feel guilty.

The church attached particular importance to the socialization of children because it saw the sublimation of emotional and intellectual energies as necessary for both social cohesion and spiritual salvation. The family was described as 'the fundamental unit of society' and denominational schooling was seen as buttressing the training the child received at home. It would seem the intention was not so much to inculcate particular secular ideologies, as mould character structures and create ideological predispositions which were susceptible to clerical influence.

Fear of losing the hearts and minds of the youth led the church to make numerous attempts to demonstrate to young people that it was not an authoritarian body, that open questioning and independent thought were not anathema to the clergy, and that the faithful were the spiritually free not the religiously fettered. 'Progressive priests' attempted to embrace and use 'the positive aspects' of the international youth culture for 'a Christian purpose'. In Bantry the folk masses of the Shalom Singers were an outgrowth of these trends. Their performances had been particularly successful; they were often invited to perform at venues in West Cork, had appeared on national television and even travelled to Holland.

Teenage sexual morality was a particular cause of concern. Some people were critical of the church's puritanical attitudes, even going so far as to comment on the psychological effect of celibacy on young priests, and questioning whether they were really fit to speak on sexual matters. Discussion of these topics was viewed apprehensively by the bishops. Wherever they discerned social trends they did not like, they launched a pre-emptive strike against 'permissiveness'. Confirmation ceremonies held in the towns and villages of each diocese every spring were often used by the bishops to voice their opinions on these issues. Such pronouncements were given prominent coverage in the media.

Dr Lucey related the growth of permissiveness to the emergence of a 'pluralist society'. The term 'pluralism' was popularly used to refer to the diversity of social thinking which now characterized Irish society. This diversity posed particular problems for the church; according to the bishops it also posed problems for the laity. The church found it difficult to endorse too much diversity of thought. It could have insidious, spiritually deleterious, effects. It also weakened the clergy's authority to speak on secular issues. In effect, the church could tolerate a pluralism of opinion only if this was not translated into a pluralism of policy.

Whereas many of the elderly lamented the passing of the old latin mass, a new wave of catholic renewal (known as the Charismatic Movement), emphasizing a non-authoritarian, personal experience of Christ, was seen by many young people (including young priests) as an expression of creative growth within the church. For example, a young curate near Bantry who found himself opposed to his parish priest on a number of grounds saw his participation in the Charismatic Movement as a way of establishing a closer, more communal relationship with both his God and his parishioners.

The traditional character of Irish catholicism was also being eroded by non-religious forces, particularly economic ones. The wake was fast disappearing because of expense and inconvenience, 'problems' associated with the declining importance of wide kinship networks, the privatization of family life, and the commercialization of funerals. Funeral parlours were fast taking over. The body was now 'removed' from there to the church rather than from the home. People still felt obliged to attend, and to be seen to attend the funerals of kin, neighbours and friends, but the sense of obligation had been weakened. The eclipse of the wake vividly symbolized the changing place of religion in community life: as religious practices were subtly prised apart from their roots in popular culture, unquestioning obedience to the church declined.

The clergy as intellectuals

As the place of religion in everyday life changed it was the character, not only the extent, of the clergy's influence which was modified. In the colonial period the clergy became the people's advocates, protectors and advisers. Priests mediated in relations between landlords and tenants, state officials and catholic citizenry, employers and employees, creditors and debtors, between neighbours and between kin — adjudicating both inter- and intra-class relations. Priests were recruited from the rising strata of catholic society and in turn helped to socialize the subsequent generation, fostering the emerging counter-structure to the protestant ascendancy. In class terms, the clergy constituted a special category of intellectuals whose relationship to the rest of society was determined by their educative, directive and organizational work. As professional functionaries following a sacred vocation, their distinctive way of life invested the priesthood with a special mystique which could be used to hegemonize the lay population.

I have already indicated that patronage-type relations were a feature of enterprise and government; this was also true of religion itself — for as the term 'Father' suggests, the priest was in many respects the epitome of the patron. He was the spiritual protector of each and every parishioner, indeed, of the parish itself. His influential support created both a spiritual and a monetary debt. Priests received no salary apart from what they collected from the parish, either at mass or in other ways. Outside the towns ceremonies called 'Stations' were held twice a year in the homes of parishioners on a rotating basis. On these occasions the priest read out the names of each household after the mass and they brought forward their contribution. In the towns the priests personally called on parishioners in their home to have a cup of tea and collect their contribution. Each priest depended for his personal income on the amount he collected from the parishioners allocated to him. In addition, people paid to have masses and prayers said for the dead, as well as for baptisms, weddings and funerals, etc. These payments were also made on a personal basis, and were seen by the parishioners as payments to the individual priest rather than the church. The ideological personal dependence of the parishioner on the priest was thus underscored by the direct material dependence of the priest on his parish. Although priests clearly lived well in largish, comfortable houses, they derived only a modest personal income from their vocation. It was the church itself, not the popular priest, who benefited from the spiritual dependence of the population.

Priests were not the only professionals to function as intellectuals locally in the colonial period. Teachers, solicitors and doctors were also key figures. Like the politicians and the business people, these professionals frequently adopted a patronage-type mode of operating. The teacher was the only major counter-weight to the parish priest in daily contact with the peasantry. Assaying propaganda and news, interpreting events, reading and writing letters, translating documents, and negotiating with officialdom, were all tasks that fell to the teacher as 'an educated man'. Far more was at stake when the solicitor was required. The negotiating of trading arrangements, indenture contracts, leases, conacre, dowries, inheritances and land sales were central to rural property relations. Although solicitors ostensibly acted as go-betweens in these arrangements, their intimate knowledge of the finances and affairs of so many families, and their unique ability to act upon this knowledge and convert other people's resources into their own, meant that they were able to influence the passage of wealth not formally in their possession.

Doctors were intellectuals of a different sort. In the syncretic cosmology of folklore and folk catholicism, a link was made between the healers of the body and the healers of the spirit. When someone was mortally ill the priest and the doctor would both be summoned; the priest first, however, because he could still save the soul when no doctor could save the body. This link was once given a public, ceremonial expression:

> The doctors had a higher standing than any other profession. I can remember when the doctors used to walk with the priest in the funeral procession wearing sashes. There's still a legacy [of that] today.

Curing has long been associated with charity.[8] Medical help was overlaid with the stigma of poverty, with a fear of death, and of death incarcerated in a pauper's institution. The historical tie-up between the famine, the workhouse and the dispensary hospital made the doctor an awesome figure to many of the poor: his intervention, however necessary, was still to be feared.

The priests' influence was popularly equated with patronage-type activities of the politicians and business people only where they interceded in the secular sphere. Priests were commonly called upon to write references, approach employers, creditors, government officials and other people of influence. These representations were made on the assumption that those controlling the desired favours would be especially amenable to the authority of a priest's persuasions. For interceding in this way the priest usually received something in appreciation for the church. A priest could develop a considerable reputation for pull because of the say he had in the distribution of secular forms of patronage. Such a reputation augmented his power in other areas.

The parish priest's control over the provision of charity, a particularly humiliating and hegemonic form of patronage, was a powerful ideological weapon which gave him considerable sway over the catholic poor. This form of influence had been eroded by the 1970s, but around the turn of the century the members of the St. Vincent de Paul Society claimed to be 'much edified by the patience and resignation of many of their poor under stress', drawing 'lessons of humility' from 'their patient and resigned endurance of suffering' (O'Keeffe papers).

Dispensing charity was not the only way the priests mingled private and public aspects of their power. Using the pulpit and the confessional, the public meeting and the private conversation, they stipulated codes of conduct and interpreted social events in terms of their sinful dangers, saving graces and exemplary features. Because they held themselves responsible for the spiritual and moral welfare of their parishioners they felt free to intrude into the private lives of their flock — for example, to counsel against a teenage marriage or to pressure a reluctant father-to-be into marriage. What gave certain of the priest's actions a coercive character was that they could respond to private opposition with public retribution, and vice versa. That is, a priest could treat as a public matter (or threaten to do so) something which was the private concern of an individual or family, or take up privately something which was really a matter of public concern. Priests in Bantry had been known to use the pulpit to obliquely criticize particular individuals who had not bowed to their wishes. Sometimes they took stronger action. In one case, the parish priest refused to confirm a child after its parents had taken it away from the National school and put it in the Protestant School.

The interventions of the clergy were often not only unsolicited but also unwelcome. Bishop Lucey was notorious for the conservatism of his pronouncements. He, for example, tried to insist upon children being given Saints' names, and thought the clergy should have a greater role in determining the fitness of young couples for marriage. Both catholics and protestants charged him with impeding ecumenicism in County Cork.

The clergy was also accused of meddling in things which were not religious issues and so not its concern. The Gerahies fishermen near Bantry allegedly refused to ask a young curate to bless their boats after he criticized them for dishonestly exaggerating their losses from oil spillages. Similarly, some workers resented the clergy's anti-labour activities during construction of the Gulf Oil terminal. With the support of the protestant clergy, the catholic priests once called a public meeting to break a prolonged strike. Under the umbrella of Muintir na Tire, they joined forces with the politicians and business people to allegedly co-operate with Gulf Oil in dealing with strikes, 'troublemakers' and 'reds', even going so far as having a list of 'known communists' compiled.[9]

The scope of clerical leadership

The active participation of the clergy in civic affairs was premised upon the church's control of key ideological institutions both nationally and locally and upon the support it received from the state for its secular activities. Religious orders ran most of the major hospitals, orphanages, reformatories and other welfare and charitable institutions supported by state aid. The church also ran, or influenced the running of, most of the nation's educational institutions. In fact it saw denominational education as central to the socialization of the population both as regards their faith and the clergy's authority. From colonial times the church's control over education had underwritten its influence in other areas, as well as being a major source of revenue. National (primary) schools were locally run by a manager, who was usually the parish priest. Most secondary schools were owned by religious orders or the Diocese. The parish priest controlled school finances and hired and fired teachers: he 'held the purse and held the reins'. Only the Vocational Schools (called Technical Schools by most people) were under the direct control of state-run Vocational Education Committees. These committees were made up of County Council appointees. Even so, there was always a large number of clergymen (catholic and protestant) among the nominees. In addition, each Vocational School usually had a priest on its board.

Successive governments had shown themselves extremely reluctant to do anything that might cause church-state conflict over education; indeed, they had helped buttress the church's control of it. In the late 1960s and 1970s, some important reforms were introduced. The main innovation was the introduction of Boards of Management to which the school manager (usually the parish priest) was accountable. These boards were made up of nominees of the school's patron (usually the bishop), representatives elected by the parishes, and, if the school was large enough, by the school staff. These reforms were accepted and even approved of by the clergy. This is not altogether surprising since the changes did not so much erode the power of the church in educational matters as give it a gloss of democratic accountability.

The clergy had some say in most voluntary organizations and a major say in the running of a number of the key ones (see Table 6.5). Most voluntary organizations in Bantry were single-issue associations with an informal club structure and membership, formed and kept going on an *ad hoc* basis. Some had been in existence for many years, but several which had taken a key role in town affairs had not been particularly durable. More traditional modes of organization, such as neighbourhood ties, kinship and friendship networks, had not yet been effectively superseded by the development of formal associative linkages. In fact, it was the newcomers, the 'blow-ins', to the town who were most active in clubs and associations. This enabled them to establish and maintain connections, friendships and influence which would not otherwise be open to them.

Many locals suggested that 'the pubs are the clubs here'. They certainly provided an important base for a diffuse range of casual activities and a meeting place for more formally organized groups. Quiz competitions between club, pub and other teams was a popular form of fund-raising entertainment. Some clubs were associated with a particular pub. This was the case, for example, with the Bantry Bay Hotel, owned and operated by the town's County Councillor. As well as being the Fianna Fail stronghold, it was also the GAA's main drinking spot. The clergy had little influence within the pubs and had consistently attempted to weaken the links between alcoholic consumption and other leisure activities. Consequently they tried to promote the formation of clubs which were independent of the pubs. These efforts had had only limited success, and then more with women than men, for the pubs were almost exclusively male clubs. Young women were acutely aware of this. In the 1970s they had begun to infiltrate 'respectable' bars. Husbands more and more took their wives out for a drink together. These trends were changing the character of many of the pubs, but not weakening their links to other aspects of comunity life.

All the major charitable organizations were church-led. In fact, the church tried to channel state funding of charitable and social service projects through its own organs, emphasizing that this saved government money, and encouraged private initiative and voluntary effort. The St. Vincent de Paul, the Care for the Aged (which ran Meals-on-Wheels, ran entertainment evenings and provided housing), the Homes for the Aged (an alliance of the St. Vincent de Paul and Care for the Aged), and the Children and Legion of Mary, were the major dispensers of charity in Bantry. Charity work was closely linked to community welfare organizations such as the Credit Union, the Information Centre, the Youth Centre, the Community Centre and the Boys Club. The priests usually worked through an executive which had a group of business people at its core, but they also tried to get a number of 'the ordinary people of the town' on church-organized committees. Each priest tried to build a group of trustworthy supporters and helpmates who were able and conscientious organizers. This enabled them to pursue their objectives even without the support of those influentials upon whom the success of local projects normally depended (see also chapters 6 and 7).

The establishment of the Credit Union in Bantry was a typical 'community self-help' project of this type. The priest-principal of the Secondary School started a study group on the aims and operation of credit unions which ran for nine months. The participants then decided they were well enough prepared to start a credit union. Unknown to anyone, the priest had kept a record of attendance. When the time came to elect officers for the organization, he put up the attendance record for all to see. 'Who was going to be on the committee?' he asked. The answer was never in doubt.

The Credit Union proved to be extremely successful, with 700 members and sizeable assets and loans. Those involved in it were strongly motivated by the principles of mutual aid. They saw what they were doing as just a different form of the traditional co-operation between farmers, arguing that it was not physical help that was needed now but money. As might be expected from these collectivist sentiments, the Credit Union had a strong working class flavour. A trade unionist (who was later co-opted as a Town Commissioner) employed by the Biggs group was active in it. Its Secretary was a female employee of the Biggs group and its Treasurer was the Biggs group's supermarket manager (a supervisory position). The priest-principal remained as Chairman. In his opinion, these 'were good, ordinary people who were known to mind their own business'. All work was voluntary and a new committee was elected annually. None of the town's charity influentials (see chapters 6 and 7) was actively involved in this particular project. If they had been it would probably not have been so successful. According to the project's organizers, the people most in need of a Credit Union would not have been likely to support an organization run by such people, preferring to have their finances scrutinized by their own kind.

The parish priest was his bishop's representative, while each curate functioned as a 'community organizer' for the parish priest. Bishop Lucey liked to have grass-roots contact with his parishioners. Since he had formerly been a Bantry parish priest it was popularly thought that he had a special affection for the town and took a keen interest in its affairs and development. In return, he had 'great influence and support and loyalty — especially in the older stock'.

In general, each curate was given responsibility for specific projects which then came to be seen as 'his' venture. In this way the parish priest could co-ordinate separate projects while allowing them be organized independently. It might have seemed that each priest was dealing with things in a piecemeal fashion, but each project was part of an amorphous, yet more or less concerted approach, to the perceived 'needs of the community' instigated on a broad front. At the same time, if one priest became embroiled in a dispute, it was easier for the others to remain aloof from the controversy. By delegating responsibility to his curates, the parish priest was thus able to distance himself and the church from unpopular actions. He also put himself in a position where he could over-rule his curate or try and conciliate.

This type of co-ordination of diocesan and parish initiatives was apparent in the Homes for the Aged project. This was the most imporant venture undertaken by the parish clergy for many years (see chapter 7). Bantry's parish priest consulted closely with the bishop and received diocesan funds and public support from him. The running of the Boys' Club exemplified another aspect of the bishop's influence. It was led by a committee personally known to him from his time in Bantry. He did not interfere in its running, but knowing the men on the committe helped ensure that the uses to which the facilities were put remained compatible with diocesan control (see chapter 7). The bishop similarly knew influential figures in the Care of the Aged and St. Vincent de Paul. These contacts put him in direct touch with key individuals. They could also prove important if the local clergy fell out of favour with their parishioners or when new priests were appointed to the parish to carry out projects initiated by the bishop.

This was an important consideration, for the clergy (like many others) were troubled by what they saw as inherent divisiveness in local organizations.

Some organizations in local terms, had fairly long histories; they may have had their internal conflicts, but these had not destroyed the organizations themselves. The really brittle bodies had been those concerned with that elusive objective, 'community development'. These were special interest groups which devoted a lot of their energies to lobbying, negotiating with, and bringing pressure to bear on government departments, the County Council and the political parties. Politicians were used as spokesmen and intermediaries (see chapter 4), but so were the clergy. There was a variety of reasons why these organizations had proven so fragile (see also chapters 3, 4, 6 and 7), not the least of which was that they were trying to effect major changes from a low resource base. Most of them were, in effect, single-issue associations: formed for a specific purpose, they had no alternative basis for cohesion when that purpose was achieved or lost. The priests were important figures for they could rally support quickly for a new project or even lean on people to involve themselves in a project for which support was lacking. Even so, given the west of Ireland's economic predicament, major changes could not be brought about by local organizations on their own, but only by large infusions of capital. Even when local people did organize to get something done, the effectiveness of their actions was severely circumscribed by the contingencies of county and national-level policy-making.

In fact, it seems that the clergy wielded the greatest influence in smaller, poorer parishes where morale was low, resources limited, where the business people were small in number and size and were disinterested or politically impotent, and where votes were few or partisanship and factionalism mitigated the influence of the politicians. In such a situation the clergy was the only group of influentials in a position to mobilize a broad coalition of popular support for ambitious projects whose chances of success were doubtful. It would appear, then, that the long years of rural poverty helped keep the clergy influential. Whereas the business people geared their public activities to the pursuit of profit, and the politicians attempted to tie voters to them on a partisan and particularistic basis, the clergy attempted a grand consensus. It tried to unite a materially divided society by emphasizing the need for spiritual solidarity and the importance of the common good over the profits and pull of the few, and to this end brought together a broad coalition of interests in the name of a strongly felt 'community-wide' sense of concern.

Once the drive for state-aided industrial development got going in the 1950s new opportunities opened up for pressure groups, including church-led ones, to do something effective to improve things for themselves and the areas they represented. The organization which probably made the biggest impact in rural areas was Muintir na Tire (the name meant 'People of the Land'). Formed in 1931 by a Tipperary priest, it started as an economically oriented body, but grew into a nationwide, vocationally-organized movement which was concerned with the total social uplift of the countryside. The

Bantry guild did not really come into its own until the mid-1960s when a curate with a record as an activist organizer was sent to the town to aid the push for industrial development (see also chapters 3, 6 and 7). He helped make Muintir become one of the most important organizations in the town's history. Its significance can be gauged from the fact that it gave rise to most of the major organizations in the 1970s: the Chamber of Commerce, the Community Centre, the Development Association, the Golf Club, the Care for the Aged and Homes for the Aged. Although the Bantry guild of Muintir did not itself survive, and in spite of the fact that the fortunes of its numerous offspring waxed and waned, it had a lasting impact on the town. As its example shows, a conscientious, enthusiastic and able priest could forge a united front of community activists using the combined weight of his office and personality. The Bantry guild of Muintir was successful because it had the active support of the town's business influentials and because it made good use of the politicians — but it was a priest who gave the organization its unity, drive and focus (see also chapter 7).

Coming in as an outsider, usually without kinship or other local connections, an activist priest had considerable room for manoeuvre. As a professional 'doer' without prior allegiances to local factions, the new priest (particularly if he brought a reputation with him) was looked upon as a man who could 'get things done'. Purportedly untainted by the vested interests of the secularly powerful, the priest was seen as 'filling a gap' which could not be bridged by secular influentials. A popular priest could mobilize the bulk of the community; the secular influentials needed to be able to tap this support and use it for their own purposes. If the clergy could not always overcome the cynicism, apathy and suspicion of the mass of the population, it could nevertheless often neutralize it.

Unlike government bodies, the organizations run by local influentials were not answerable to anyone but themselves. Although the activities of the business people and the politicians were fairly closely scrutinized by their critics, church-led bodies were in certain respects allowed to be an authority unto themselves. Priests were not immune to criticism but opposition had to be legitimate in terms of standards laid down by the clergy itself. Because the church purportedly represented 'the community interest', it became necessary for opponents of the clergy to demonstrate that they too had 'the community's' interests at heart. They had to prove they were not just a sectional group or motivated by private gain. An outright attack on the clergy was both difficult and dangerous: such an attack could easily become a matters of controversy itself.

Even where the priests did not have working authority, they often held positions in clubs which gave them formal or honorary authority. They were frequently guests of honour at public functions and dinner dances. The parish priest or one of his curates was traditionally always invited to chair or participate in meetings and functions of community-wide significance. Many people, particularly older individuals and a lot of women, were willing to endorse the clergy's every move. It could thus always draw upon a large body of people to provide voluntary labour and, less often, expertise and finance for church projects. Each priest had a following of friends and supporters on whom he could draw to do administrative work, engage in fund-raising or help out in an emergency. Sometimes these people were also available to take over and run projects instigated by the clergy. In fact the curates spent a lot of their time organizing things so that they could delegate responsibility to people who had 'proved' themselves. They could then keep an eye on things but they did not have to be concerned with every detail.

Many projects did not require a priest, but there were other occasions when, as one of the curates put it: 'the people expect the clergy to be in it. If the clergy are not in it there is no enthusiasm'. Things were changing, however, 'Some people' he added, 'do not like the clergy. I have no veto power as in the old days'.

Curates were purportedly now trained to instigate projects and then hand over control of them. A few progressives were willing to further demystify their position and authority. The laity were also keen to dispense with the clergy more than in the past. People had once 'stood in awe of the clergy'. 'Some old people would never contradict a priest at a meeting whereas younger people would, without any disrespect'. These changes appealed more to the junior than the senior ranks, more to the 'progressives' than 'the conservatives'. The bishops, for instance, had shown no desire to divest themselves of their power, and if the parish clergy lost its sway, the influence of the bishops at the grass-roots would wither too.

Even when trying to lead the population to reject their leadership, members of the clergy were still acting as leaders. Moreover, when they felt they must intervene decisively on some issue or other, they were still inclined to marshall all their resources and traditional sanctions to get their way. When a definite commitment to substantive objectives came into contradiction with a formal commitment to democratization, it was the latter which suffered. The clergy tended to see democracy as desirable in principle, but inefficient, ineffective, and even utopian in practice, hence its tendency to delegate responsibility for church-led projects only to hand-picked committees over which it retained a supervisory (if not always controlling) influence.

Even catholics who harboured no anti-clerical sentiments recognized the essentially undemocratic nature of this kind of decision-making. They attempted to justify it by pointing to the ineffectiveness of many democratic organizations and the efficiency of those entrusted to clerical control. They also argued that church-led organizations were usually internally democratic anyway, that the priests were only the first among equals. Of course, this was not how the clergy's critics saw things. They usually felt the need to defer to a priest's opinions in public. This meant that people were more likely to withdraw from an organization rather than openly oppose a priest and his policies.

The priests had to wield their power publicly to be effective. They had to advertise their usefulness and indispensability to the community. In this they were rather like the politicians (except that the politicians often privately promised much but publicly disclaimed responsibility when it suited them), but very different to the business people (who primarily used their public power to aid and abet privately organized initiatives). As 'consensus-makers', the priests continually had to wrestle with the twin problems of mobilizing popular support for projects instigated by other influentials, and of getting projects going which did not have the support of other influentials (see also chapters 3, 4, 6 and 7). They were thus acutely aware both of how important it was to get the business people and politicians on side, and how much it mattered to have church backing for a project. One of the Bantry curates, for instance, emphasized that the secular influentials could 'do a lot of harm if they're against you'. There were two aspects to this. One was the power the influentials wielded in the eyes of the townspeople:

> You won't get so-and-so speaking out against Biggs's because he knows what they stand for, because they are large employers in the town. Like the landlords of the past it may be resented but it takes a brave man to oppose them. They are a kind of local aristocracy.

The other aspect concerned the manner in which the business influentials wielded their power. 'By and large', they didn't 'get involved in public meetings'. They believed that 'democracy is all right in theory, but [that] a few people know what should be done and what is needed'. This priest readily admitted that the church was not always enamoured of democratic procedures either. Similarly, he saw the party machines as more interested in winning votes than in democracy as such. Summing up, he described the situation this way:

> Here still, it is the establishment. Religious, commerical, political too. And if you wanted something accepted you'd need the support of the religious [bodies], commercial [interests] and the major political parties. And it is the people who represent these rather than the personalities that is important.

Final remarks

Other people at other places have been strong in their catholicism without the church's position resembling the Irish situation. In fact, it could be said that in Eire religious belief was becoming less reflexive, less enveloping, less authoritative even, but for a time the church as an institution grew stronger. This is because the significance of the church in Eire had as much to do with the prevailing pattern of social domination as it did with the personal beliefs and customary practices of everyday life. There was clearly a dialectic at work here: ideological compliance was both a condition for, and a creation of, institutionalized domination.

I have argued that capitalist development in the post-colonial period in Eire took place within a petty-bourgeois integument. The church's relationship to the state reflected this. Its stance towards capitalism — both before and after the founding of the Free State — was decidedly ambivalent, even contradictory. Suspicious of all power independent of it, and claiming to speak in the name of all catholics, the church attempted to impede the arbitrary, indifferent and haughty use of power by any or all secular institutions. The state may have been its prime target, but it was not the only one. In the church's eyes unregulated capitalism could be harsh in its effects. Its excesses had to be moderated, and the clergy fulminated against poverty and denounced profligacy. But the church did not advocate the redistribution of wealth; rather, it saw the sanctity of private property as an important guarantee of freedom. It condemned 'unnecessary' exploitation and 'excessive' profits, but championed the spirit of enterprise. It lamented the decline in 'traditional values' but urged industrial development. It also attempted to arbitrate between capital and labour. The tasks of both employer and the worker were inscribed with moral worth and reciprocal obligations: a 'fair day's work' called for a 'fair day's pay'.

Capitalism claimed the support of the church before any alternative economic and social system primarily because any force capable of threatening the capitalist system — e.g. socialism — also potentially threatened the church. It supported capitalist social relations more as a practical reality than an ideal in itself. A corollary of this was that although it often championed petty-bourgeois ideals, it did not advocate the establishment of a petty-bourgeois economy. Therefore, like the major political parties, it praised the virtues of a society organized around self-sufficient families of farmers and shopkeepers, but simultaneously advocated industrial development to rescue the small and poor communities of the west.

This ambivalence expressed itself in the advocacy of certain forms of development in preference to others, for example projects of rural reconstruction. But though modernization, urbanization and industrialization had their dangers — including materialism, pluralism and permissiveness — and though the traditional rural community might have virtues best suited to catholic values, the championing of development initiatives was seen less as an option than as a necessity.

Bishop Lucey, for instance, in the 1960s and 1970s vigorously attacked opposition to industrial projects. In the 1950s he had accused the politicians and the parties of abandoning their ideals and neglecting the small farmers of West Cork who had done so much to throw off the British yoke. On this, as on other occasions, the church was able to use the rhetoric of nationalism against the political parties and claim that their commitment to the people who had brought them to power was based on expediency. The holders of secular power were condemned, but in language which confirmed the foundations on which their power was based.

But even if they did not always approve of what one another were doing, the politicians and the priests clearly respected the institutionalized prerogatives of the other. Conflict between them was premised on a prior structural relation. By supporting one another (whether tacitly or actively), they buttressed their respective influence.

I have already argued that the evolving class character of the major parties, particularly Fianna Fail, was central to the development of the state in the post-colonial period. Taking this further, I have now proposed that the class character of the church's position in Irish society lay in the fact that (whatever its other activities) it functioned as an ambivalent ideological auxiliary of the state. The church provided the state with independent legitimation, and cast itself as the guardian of the common interests and values of both rulers and ruled. The state in turn protected the church's position and pursued policies compatible with its social teaching. This was not a static, functionalist relationship, but an evolving one: church-state relations in the mid-1970s had changed considerably from what they had been at the height of the integralist period a quarter of a century before.

For this reason it is important to recognize that the influence of the parish clergy locally cannot be understood unless it is recognized that the integralist period helped to underwrite and extend the parish priest's traditional authority at a crucial time, i.e. during the post-colonial reconstruction. This authority began to be whittled away in the 1960s and 1970s, but it had by no means disappeared. Along with the business people and the politicians, the priests remained key influentials locally as well as nationally.

6 Town influentials and the basis of their influence

Class characterizes social institutions by the way it becomes embedded in them and so comes to function through them. It is in this sense that we can speak not only of business enterprises as class institutions but the state and the church also. A constitutive feature of this institutional form of class power in Ireland, I have suggested, has been the delineation of distinct but overlapping spheres of influence in social life both nationally and locally. I will now examine how this manifested itself in the running of town affairs in Bantry. The analysis will centre on power as it was individually and collectively wielded locally and the means by which it was organizationally implemented. The aim is to establish not only who wielded power within the town, but how they wielded it, and what for, so as to delineate the character and limits of different forms of locally significant personal power.[1]

In this chapter I present the findings of a survey used to identify and characterize local influentials, and to distinguish them from activists and other townspeople. On this basis I discuss the class nature of the influentials' power insofar as this is revealed by the status characteristics of their social position. I thus relate the changing political form to the changing cultural form of class relations at Bantry.

In the next chapter I elaborate on these findings by discussing the various organizations active in Bantry and the projects and controversies with which they were concerned. On this basis I discuss the class nature of the influentials' power as revealed by their attempts to organizationally mobilize one another and the town around key issues of local significance.

Identifying the influentials

In order to examine how different types of organizations operated within distinct spheres of influence it is first necessary to establish who the powerful were. We can then look at what they did with their power, and what they used it to achieve. This requires an analysis of the major issues preoccupying the town during the period under review. Those issues in which Gulf Oil became the central actor have not been included in this review. The reason for this is that it is questions of *individual* and *collective* power that are being considered here. The limited nature of these kinds of *personal* power when compared to the *impersonal, corporate* power of a multinational company, the state or the church raises different questions which require separate treatment (see chapter 8).

The survey: its uses and limitations

Many people were active in town affairs in Bantry but few were influential. There was a marked clustering and overlap of a small number of people in a few key areas, i.e. in areas where decisions were made of potential consequence for the whole town. This much was obvious to Bantry people themselves. A young worker summed up the prevailing opinion when he said, 'We in Bantry believe there are a certain few always in all organizations, any committee set up'. From the outside, it was not always easy to distinguish activism from influence; nor was it easy to tell if reputed influence was based on real power, status symbols, or some less visible factor. Because of the peculiarities of a particular issue, it could also happen that an individual who might have been expected to have a say in a decision did not participate at all, and so on. To clarify the picture I undertook a formal survey to buttress more informal participant-observation methods, and related the results to the distinctions already made between the church, state and business as discrete spheres of influence in social life (see Tables 6:1, 2, 3, 4, 5, and 6).

The survey distinguished people active in public life according to their reputation for influence. These findings were then compared with those indicating which people occupied authoritative positions in locally important organizations. Comparisons were then made between both sets of results and the survey findings relating to those people who participated actively and decisively in issues of local significance. A wide range of townspeople, activists and influentials (present and past) were informally and formally interviewed as part of this survey. Meanwhile, the actual involvement of influentials, activists, and townspeople generally, during the fieldwork period was recorded and checked against the survey information.

The survey used three methods of determining who *possessed* and who *exercised* power. These have come to be known as the reputational-snowball, the positional and the issue methods (see Wild, 1974: 147–55). Used in isolation, each method has its limitations. The reputational-snowball is an artificial device in that it relies upon a forced-choice system of ranking. It thus gives a certain hierarchical skew to the distribution of power which distorts the real picture. It tends to emphasize power possessed (potential power) regardless of whether or not it is exercised. The positional method involves identifying the office holders and officials of the major local organizations, councils and committees which make decisions of potential consequence for the community as a whole. It tends to emphasize authoritative office as an accoutrement of power (formal power) without regard to the substantive relation between the two in the possession and exercise of power. As used here positions of authority in the church, state and business enterprises have been taken into consideration since to exclude them would be arbitrary and inadequate, and would give unwarranted prominence to the holding of authoritative positions in voluntary organizations. The issue method entails a detailed analysis of local projects and controversies. It tends to emphasize the exercise of power (actual power) regardless of whether or not this is an adequate measure of power possessed. This method enables us to chart how conflicts develop and are dealt with, to see the characteristic stances people adopt to different kinds of issues. It also enables us to focus on what the powerful actually *do* with their power. Used in conjunction with one another, the three methods allow us to relate public postures to the covert activities of the powerful.

For the reputational survey 36 local knowledgeables were approached and asked the following question during the last six months of fieldwork: 'Please nominate, in order of importance, those people whom you consider to be the most influential in making community decisions with wide consequences for the community as a whole'. The responses to this question were used to obtain a list of influentials, to rank these and discriminate between them. The longest list of reputed influentials obtained from the survey contained 20 names. When ranked, this gave a total possible score of 720 (36 × 20). A division was made where people received 15% or more of the total possible score. This was an arbitrary division, but one which, given the formal survey's inadequacies, proved much more realistic for handling the data than divisions at 10% or 20%. A division at this point meant it was feasible to distinguish between visible, concealed and assumed influence as outlined below, though a division at 25% would perhaps have been more realistic in terms of total and percentage scores and number of first mentions (see Table 6:1).

The problem with this sort of methodological device, of course, is that it converts tendencies into rigid distinctions. It also takes no account of the personal vagaries which influence the promotion or suppression of certain names by some respondents. The value of the device is that it allows comparisons to be made between the rankings of the top influentials and the remainder. Anyone featuring on the original master list will therefore be described as a local activist. Anyone obtaining more than 10% on any one list will be referred to as an ordinary influential, unless they received more than 15% on the original master list, in which case they will be called a top influential.

By comparing the names mentioned by the top influentials with those mentioned by the ordinary influentials and activists, it theoretically becomes possible to formally distinguish three types of influentials as follows: (a) *visible* influentials: people who were presumed to have similar influence by both the

Table 6:1 Master list solicited replies

	Individual	Score (Total: 720)	No. of Mentions	%
1	County Councillor (MCC)	439	25	60.97
2	Dentist	389	21	54.03
3	Company Secretary, Biggs'	263	16	36.53
4	Motor Dealer	216	14	30.00
5	Canon	212	12	29.44
6	Solicitor	204	13	28.33
7	Manager, Biggs'	133	9	18.47
8	Engineer	132	9	18.33
9	School Principal	119	9	16.53
10	Retired Draper	97	7	13.47
11	Chemist	94	6	13.06
12	Draper	92	6	12.50
13	Manager, Rowa	81	5	11.25
14	Restaurateur–Publican	76	5	10.56
15	Business Woman	76	5	10.56
16	County Surgeon	56	4	7.78

NB The ordinary influentials and one of the 'Extras' nominated by the top influentials filled the first 16 places on the Master list. This 'Extra', the County Surgeon, received four nominations from top influentials. The other two 'Extras', the ex-MCC/Trade Union Official and the Chairman of the Town Commissioners, were ranked 32nd and 33rd on the Master list. They were both only nominated once — by a top influential who gave them a high ranking. The two Catholic curates were ranked 18th and 21st on the Master list, each receiving four mentions from top influentials.

top influentials and others; (b) *concealed* influentials: people who were pre-sumed to have more influence by the top influentials than by others; and (c) *assumed* influentials: people who were presumed to have less influence by the top influentials than by others. According to this scheme, the visible influentials (who may, like the other groups, have been composed of both top and ordinary influentials) would tend to play a recognized part in public affairs; the concealed influentials would be likely to have more say among the top influentials, and therefore in public affairs, than was generally realized; the assumed influentials would be likely to have less of a say than was generally thought, but be of high status or otherwise conspicuous (see Wild, 1974: 145–55). The formal distinction between these three types of influentials can then be refined by relating their influence as revealed by the reputational-snowball to whether they held formal positions of authority in key organiza-tions and the nature of their involvement in major issues.

Of the 36 local knowledgeables I approached for the formal survey two would not participate. Several others felt that trying to list local influentials in a rank order was difficult. A characteristic reluctance to name names was a factor in this. Although the majority of these people were on friendly terms with me and were very co-operative, some were still extremely cagey about ranking their fellows and, of course, some were also blatantly partisan. More significantly, most respondents found the task a meaningless one. Many left out names which they definitely wanted to include when these were mentioned to them or when they came up later in the course of the interview. I noted these variations and processed the data three times. I first ranked the names in the order that they were first mentioned; I then ranked those names which were entirely unsolicited according to the priority of the respondent; finally, I ranked the full number of (solicited and unsolicited) names according to the priority of the respondent (see Table 6:2). In this way I hoped to cancel out some of the inconsistencies and inadequacies of the formal survey data. For reasons of economy I have only given the figures for the solicited replies (see Table 6:1). But as can be seen from the rank order tallies the differences between the three sets of results is only minor, and in my estimation the solicited replies were the result of more considered opinions. Note that all lists have been shortened to include only those people obtaining 10% or more of the total possible score.

Although I constructed the usual diagrams illustrating the patterns of interaction between the different influentials, they were not particularly revealing. There are two reasons for this. Firstly, I was not able to complete this part of the survey with five of the influentials. Secondly, respondents betrayed a remarkable flexibility in describing friends. Although most distin-guished between 'close and intimate personal friends' and 'personal friends', they did so according to varying criteria. Some reserved the first category for confidants. Others did not distinguish between those with whom they socialized as status equals and those they liked and mixed with in situations where status differences were minimized. These responses may tell us a lot about the politics of naming friends, and the diverse meanings attached to notions of friendship, but they were totally unreliable as far as actual patterns of interaction were concerned. Interpretation of the significance of friendship networks was therefore based on an interpretation of the survey material in the light of other evidence.

Table 6:2 Master list rank order

Solicited replies	Unsolicited replies	First mentioned
Top influentials		
County Councillor	Dentist	County Councillor
Dentist	County Councillor	Dentist
Company Secretary	Company Secretary	Company Secretary
Motor Dealer	Motor Dealer	Motor Dealer
Canon	Canon	Canon
Solicitor	Engineer	School Principal
Manager, Biggs Group	Solicitor	Engineer
Engineer	School Principal	Solicitor
School Principal	Manager, Biggs Group	Manager, Biggs Group
Ordinary influentials		
Retired Draper	Retired Draper	Retired Draper
Chemist	Chemist	Manager, Rowa
Draper	Draper	Draper
Manager, Rowa	Manager, Rowa	Business Woman
Restaurateur–Publican	Business Woman	Chemist
Business Woman	Restaurateur–Publican	

Influentials as ranked by the top influentials

Top influentials		
County Councillor	County Councillor	County Councillor
Canon	Canon	Canon
Dentist	Dentist	Dentist
Solicitor	Solicitor	Solicitor
Company Secretary ⎱	Company Secretary ⎱	Manager, Biggs Group ⎱
Manager, Biggs Group ⎰	Manager, Biggs Group ⎰	Company Secretary ⎰
Motor Dealer	Motor Dealer	Motor Dealer
Engineer	Engineer	School Principal
School Principal	School Principal	Engineer

Ordinary influentials and extras nominated by the top influentials

Manager, Rowa	Manager, Rowa	Manager, Rowa
County Surgeon	County Surgeon	Restaurateur–Publican
Chairman TCs ⎱	Chairman TCs ⎱	Chairman TCs
Ex-MCC/Trade Union ⎰ Official	Ex-MCC/Trade Union ⎰ Official	County Surgeon
Restaurateur–Publican	Restaurateur–Publican	

Solicited replies	Unsolicited replies	First mentioned
Influentials as ranked by the ordinary influentials (and extras)		
County Councillor	Dentist	County Councillor
Dentist	County Councillor	Dentist
Company Secretary	Company Secretary	Company Secretary
Motor Dealer	Motor Dealer	Motor Dealer
Solicitor	Canon	School Principal
Canon	Engineer	Retired Draper
Manager, Biggs Group	School Principal	Engineer
Engineer	Solicitor	Canon
School Principal	Manager, Biggs Group	Draper
Chemist	Retired Draper	Chemist
Retired Draper	Chemist	Business Woman
Draper	Draper	Solicitor
Manager, Rowa	Business Woman	Manager, Biggs Group
Restaurateur–Publican	Restaurateur–Publican	
Business Woman	Manager, Rowa	

Some of the formal survey's deficiencies are apparent from the problems associated with distinguishing between visible, concealed and assumed influentials (see Table 6:3). The clarity of these distinctions was perhaps lessened by the fact that the two men who did not participate in the survey were top influentials; and by the fact that of the other top influentials, one bracketed five names together and did not include himself, while another listed Gulf Oil and Rowa and the County Manager but no locals, and another was among those who could list no names at all. A further three of the ordinary influentials were also unable to provide me with a rank order of names. They were not being unco-operative; to them the task was either meaningless or impossible. In their view no local person had power to compare with the TDs, the County Manager and Gulf Oil.

For these reasons, the formal typology of visible, concealed and assumed influentials turned out to be only of limited usefulness for the analysis of the Bantry data. It helped to schematize the presentation of tendencies but it also reified, and to this extent, distorted them. Nevertheless, it still has some value. Even where the distinction between visible, concealed and assumed *influentials* has only limited validity and could even be misleading, it can still be useful to distinguish between *influence* which is visible, concealed or assumed. That is, specific individuals may prefer to exert their sway in one way rather than another, without exclusively specializing in the use of any given *type* of influence. This suggests that in analysing personal and collective power, it

Table 6:3 Types of influence

	Concealed influence	Visible influence	Assumed influence		
1		Fianna Fail MCC [G & D] (1)		(5)	Top Influentials
2			Company Secretary Biggs Group [D]	(7)	
3		Dentist [D] (3)	Motor Dealer [D]		
4	Canon [C] (2)				
5	Solicitor [D] (4)				
6					
7	Manager, Biggs Group [C & D] (5)				
8		Engineer [G & D] (8)			
9		Principal, Vocational School [G & D] (9)			
10			Retired Draper [C, D & G]	(17)	Ordinary Influentials
11			Chemist [C]	(16)	
12			Draper [D]	(15)	
13	Manager, Rowa [D] (10)				
14		Restaurateur–Publican [D] (14)			
15			Business Woman [C & D]	(18)	Extra influentials nominated by the top influentials
16	County Surgeon [G] (11)				
17	Chairman TCs [G & D] (12)				
18	Ex-MCC/Trade Union Official (woman) [G & D] (12)				

NOTE: Rank order as presented is from the Master list of solicited replies. Rank order as designated by top influentials is given in round brackets. Sphere of influence is given in square brackets — [D]evelopment, [G]overnmental and [C]harity.

would be wrong to uncritically subsume the analysis of *types of power* under the categories appropriate to *types of power holders*: they will certainly be related, but they are not necessarily the same thing.

There is, for example, only a very restricted sense in which any of the Bantry influentials could be said to be 'concealed'. This is especially true of the top two influentials characterized as wielding 'concealed' influence, the Canon and the Solicitor. Both men may have exerted influence behind the scenes but they were also highly visible figures. Indeed, the success of their concealed influence was often premised upon the maintenance of a high public profile. In the Canon's case, this was essential to the authority of the clergy. In the Solicitor's case, it reflected a penchant for flamboyant displays of his wealth and the power of wealth. It also reflected his desire to wield power as an individual, such that if he could not control an organization, he preferred to work outside it and bend it to his will. By contrast, the other top influential wielding concealed influence, the manager of the Biggs group, kept an extremely low public profile and was even quite reticent behind the scenes, but that was where he made his presence felt. Of course it may well be the case that if Bantry was a larger town where business influentials were more remote and their doings less well known, certain activities which remained accessible to the public gaze would have been more camouflaged, and worn the cloak of behind-the-scenes manipulation. While it is true, then, that those wielding concealed influence were presumed to have somewhat more influence by the top influentials than by others, this cannot be taken as meaning that the rest of the town failed to recognize their importance. Rather, it means that the top influentials had inside knowledge or direct experience which reinforced the presumptions they shared with others about the influence of these men.

At the other extreme, there is less difficulty in characterizing the Biggs group's Company Secretary and the Motor Dealer as men assumed to have influence. Both carried past reputations with them. They had been key figures — the Company Secretary for many years past, the Motor Dealer in more recent times — but they no longer held centre stage, even if it was not inconceivable that they could do so again.

As far as visible influence is concerned, this 'visibility' has quite a different character depending on who we are talking about. As reasonably popular figures active in the public arena who were universally recognized as top influentials, the County Councillor's and the Dentist's influence was starkly visible. Yet in the case of the Engineer and the Vocational School Principal, the visibility of their influence was due to the fact that, despite them having different jurisdictions, judgements about the influence they wielded, for one reason or another, happened to be quite informed. This perhaps reflects the fact that they were middle ranking figures and it is this that was universally acknowledged. Significantly, their influence was estimated less highly by the very top influentials than by more middling figures such as themselves.

Under certain circumstances the survey approach can produce quite elegant results (e.g. Wild, 1974). What, then, are we to make of the problems encountered here? In one sense they are simply the result of methodological hazards. These centre, firstly, on whether key figures consent to participating in the survey, and if they do, whether they answer questions truthfully. Secondly, they centre on whether survey participants can in good faith fit their view of social reality into the framework of the survey, particularly as regards the forced-choice ranking procedure. (Of course the abilities and personality of the fieldworker are as important as any other factor in the equation.)

Important conceptual issues are implicit in these methodological problems. For example, the problem of how to theoretically and practically cope with evasion, dissimulation and outright lying. And, even more seriously, the problem of the distortions introduced by the methodology itself, the artificiality it introduces, particularly the temptation it offers the researcher to try and squeeze square answers until they fit round questions.

This is particularly likely to happen in that the approach encourages the delineation of distinct issues and organizations and thus lures the researcher into perhaps arbitrarily seeking out criteria which allow a melange of issues and a jumble of organizational forms to be given a coherence compatible with systematic tabulation. The use of such a survey also encourages a tendentious distinction between 'the community' and 'the wider society', in its search for 'local' or 'community' influentials. As such it has built into it the unexamined assumption that local figures can and do make decisions of local consequence when compared to those made outside the locality or community by individuals, collectivities and corporate bodies. It thereby also presupposes a highly individualistic conception of power which, though it allows the identification of collective power, tends to direct attention towards key personalities *as individuals.*

These problems are not ones easily eradicated. But, if taken into proper account, nor are they insurmountable. In fact, the tensions they create in the analysis can highlight the need, and facilitate the search for, further *theoretical* and not just methodological refinements. This was the case, for example, with two of the key concerns of this study: the relation of the local to the national 'level', and the relation between personalized individual and collective power and impersonal corporate power.

The difficulties entailed in carrying out and tabulating the results of the formal survey also underscores the point that the use of a formal survey by itself would not only be inadequate but culpably misleading. The results of the survey can only be made sense of by bringing information produced by other participant-observation techniques to bear upon them. That is to say, as a tool of field research the survey did not serve as an alternative to participant-observation techniques, but was used *as* a technique of participant-observation. It obviously allowed more systematic investigation through standardization of results for comparative purposes. Beyond that, it also proved a valuable device for making and deepening contact with otherwise inaccessible respondents, and for expanding interviews beyond the survey itself into more informal open-ended discussions of matters relevant to the fieldwork, and in this and other ways, generally extending the boundaries of participant-observation into new areas.

The organization of influence

I have already argued that as part of the institutionalization of enterprise, government and religion in Eire, distinct spheres of influence were created within which different categories of influentials wielded their power. The business people did not merely act as economic influentials, the politicians as political influentials, or the clergy as cultural influentials. Rather, it was *as* business influentials that the first group wielded political and cultural power; *as* governmental influentials that the second group wielded economic and cultural power; and *as* religious influentials that the third group wielded economic and political power. In other words, their spheres of influence were functionally distinct, but overlapped. If, as I have indicated, this demarcation of power was reproduced locally, then the influentials controlling town affairs could be expected to operate from a number of interrelated but independent organizational bases.

The division of influence

In fact, three main types of organization crucial to the power wielded by the influentials could be identified: *charity* committees, *governmental* bodies, and *development* organizations. The clergy and their lay associates dominated the first, politicians and civil servants the second, and owners and managers of business firms the third (see Tables 6:4, 6:5 and 6:6). However, on closer examination it becomes apparent that the key governmental influentials were either business people themselves, or closely connected to them, and that the key charity influentials were predominantly business people also.

The development influentials dominated decision-making in the town, and visibly did so. Among the top influentials, all but the Canon was in some way associated with this sphere. The Biggs group's Manager, the only other top influential who was not a development influential, nevertheless belonged to the Chamber of Commerce. What is more, his interests in this sphere were looked after by this firm's Company Secretary. The Company Secretary, unlike the rest of the development influentials, had a long history of involvement with development bodies in Bantry. He was Secretary of the West Cork

Table 6:4 Areas of influence

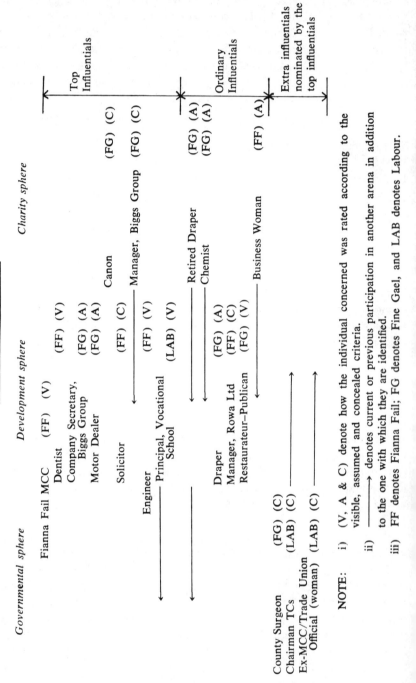

Governmental sphere	Development sphere	Charity sphere	
	Fianna Fail MCC (FF) (V)		⎫
	Dentist (FF) (V)		
	Company Secretary, Biggs Group (FG) (A)		Top Influentials
	Motor Dealer (FG) (A)		
		Canon (FG) (C)	
		Manager, Biggs Group (FG) (C)	⎭
	Solicitor (FF) (C)		
	Engineer (FF) (V)		
	Principal, Vocational School (LAB) (V)		
		Retired Draper (FG) (A)	Ordinary Influentials
		Chemist (FG) (A)	
	Draper (FG) (A)		
	Manager, Rowa Ltd (FF) (C)		
	Restaurateur–Publican (FG) (V)		
		Business Woman (FF) (A)	Extra influentials nominated by the top influentials

County Surgeon (FG) (C)
Chairman TCs (LAB) (C)
Ex-MCC/Trade Union Official (woman) (LAB) (C)

NOTE:

i) (V, A & C) denote how the individual concerned was rated according to the visible, assumed and concealed criteria.

ii) → denotes current or previous participation in another arena in addition to the one with which they are identified.

iii) FF denotes Fianna Fail; FG denotes Fine Gael, and LAB denotes Labour.

Table 6:5 Leadership of local organizations

Organization	Type	Leadership
‑wn Commissioners		P
‑rbour Authority		P
‑cational School Mgment Cte		P, C
‑tional (Boys) School Mgment Cte	Local Government	C
‑nvent (Girls) ‑chool Mgment Cte		C
‑otestant School Mgment Cte		C
‑nna Fail	Political Party	P, B
‑e Gael	Political Party	P, B
‑bour		P
‑amber of Comm.	Economic Development	B
‑velopment Assn	Economic Development	B
‑ior Chamber	Service	
‑mmunity Centre	Amenity	C
‑ Vincent de Paul		C, B
‑e for the Aged	Charity	C, B
‑mes for the Aged	Charity	C, B
‑ Disabled Children		C
‑dit Union		C
‑ormation Centre	Welfare	C, B
‑ Pioneers		C
‑ion of Mary	Religious/ Charity	C
‑ildren of Mary	Religious/ Charity	C
‑tners Assn		B
‑hermen & Boat Owners' Assn		
‑h Farmers' Association	Trade	
‑urist Assn/ ‑iesta Cte		B

Organization	Type	Leadership
FCA	Civilian Militia	
Macra ne Feirme	Farm Youth	
ITGWU	Trade Union	(P)
WUI	Trade Union	
Other Trade Unions		
Shalom Singers		C
Youth Centre		C
Musical Society		
Bridge Club		B
Comhaltas Ceoltoiri	Recreational	
Gurty Cloona Theatre		
Phoenix Players		
High St Club		
Sea Scouts		
Girl Guides		
GAA		(P)
Bantry Golf Club		B
Glengarriff Golf Club		B
Race Committee		B
Regatta Committee		
Sailing Club		
Rowing Club	Sporting	
Badminton Club		
Badminton (Protestant) Club		
Athletics Club		
Basketball Club		
Deep Sea Anglers		
Salmon & Sea Trout Association		
Gun Club		

Key: B ... Business people
C ... Clergy
P ... Politicians
(P) .. Politicians influential rather than having leadership as such

Development Association in its heyday (see chapters 3 and 7) and Regional Chairman of Muintir na Tire (see chapters 3, 5 and 7). He was also a President of the first Chamber of Commerce, and remained an important but less active member of the revived Chamber (see chapter 7). This reflected his declining influence. The Motor Dealer was another man whose influence was on the wane. He owed his prominence to the fact that he was Chairman of the last Development Association, but he was neither active in, nor a member of the executive of the revived Chamber of Commerce. The Draper had also been an important figure for a short time. Although he was a Vice-President of the revived Chamber, he was not particularly active in it. This contrasted with his participation in the first Chamber, of which he was Secretary and President at different times (see chapter 7). As an executive member of the Bantry Fine Gael cumann, he was still active in party politics. The Solicitor wielded much of his real influence behind the scenes. Yet he was widely presumed to be an influential man because his conspicuous use of his wealth (see chapter 7) rightly led people to presume he wielded concomitant influence. He was not a member of the Chamber of Commerce, but took an active part in its affairs. Otherwise, he was most notable for his Presidency of the Golf Club, which he helped found. The Rowa Manager also wielded influence behind the scenes. But unlike the Solicitor he was not widely regarded as an important figure; he was a man growing in stature, whose place amongst the influentials was more secure than was widely recognized. This reflected his status as an upwardly mobile local, and the fact that as a key committee man on the Chamber executive, his work did not attract public attention. He was Secretary of the Chamber, and had been both a President and Secretary of the first Chamber. He was also a member of the Cork Chamber.

If they wanted to be, men without vested interests could became leading figures in local organizations. In the charity sphere, the Chemist had such a reputation. An anomaly in the development sphere was the School Principal. He was neither a key administrator (his activities in this respect were confined to educational matters), nor in business himself. Moreover, he was a Labour

Table 6:6 The structure and institutionalization of social power

The ruling bloc	Authority holders
business	owners and managers
the state	politicians and civil servants
the church	clergy and lay associates
Spheres of influence	*Local influentials*
development	business people/politicians/clergy
governmental	business people/politicians & civil servants
charity	business people/clergy and lay associates

Party supporter and active in the Teachers' Union. It would seem he owed his position to the fact that he was well-born, well-connected and very capable. In fact, he gave the impression of being a detached observer without vested interests or problematic ambitions: part of the scene but not entirely of it. But the man who had done most for himself in this respect was another development influential, the Dentist. His reputed integrity, persuasive personality and organizational capabilities, had made him a Secretary and President of the first Chamber of Commerce, and President of the revived one. Before that he had been a Treasurer and Area Council representative of the Bantry guild of Muintir na Tire. He was also a leading figure in the Development Association. His most recent success had been his election as one of the Chamber of Commerce's representatives to the Board of the Bantry Harbour Authority (see chapters 7 and 8). His credentials were such that only the County Councillor was reputed to have more influence within the town (see Tables 6:1 and 6:2); within the development sphere itself he was indisputably the key figure.

The governmental influentials were closely linked to the development sphere. The two most important of them were actually also development influentials. In fact, they were both executive members of the revived Chamber of Commerce. The County Councillor's importance in the development sphere largely derived from the fact that he was these people's political representative, their spokesman in the County Council (see also chapter 4). He was not only on the Executive of the Chamber of Commerce, but was elected as one of its representatives onto the Board of the Bantry Harbour Authority (see chapters 7 and 8). He had also participated in the first Chamber, been a Vice-Chairman of the Development Association and a joint-Secretary of Muintir na Tire. He was also active in the Vintner's Association and the Gaelic Athletic Association. He was elected to the Board of Management of the Convent School and was nominated to the Board of Management of the Protestant School. In addition, he was a nominal member of several recreational bodies, including the Golf Club, the Athletics Club and the Rowing Club. On a wider level, he was a member of such national organizations as the Hotels' Federation, but it was the politically-connected organizations which were most important: he was a Director of Ivernia, the Cork-Kerry Regional Tourist body, a member of numerous County Council committees, and the effective leader of most of the Fiana Fail cumainn in the Bantry area, holding a position on the Constituency Executive of the party (see also chapter 4).

I have previously indicated (see chapter 4) that 'the local man' amongst the politicians was the key figure in his home area. The other West Cork County Councillors and TDs all wielded considerable power as party-politicians in Bantry, but they had not bolstered this with any organizational base within the town. The Labour TD was influential within the leading trade union, the ITGWU, but except in relation to Gulf Oil, the unions did not act as a political lobby within the town (see chapters 7 and 8). They worked with and represented the Bantry leadership groups, but they were not members of them. That was only true of 'the local man'.

Of the other governmental influentials, the Engineer's importance in the development sphere was due to the fact that he was the most senior County official residing in the town and was responsible for implementing and advising on all decisions emanating from the County Manager's office (see chapter 7). Unlike any of the other influentials, the County Surgeon did not participate in any of the major local organizations. But as Manager of the Hospital, he controlled an enterprise which generated both business and jobs. He was a member of the Southern Health Board and, before its dissolution, Chairman of the Cork Board of Fishery Conservators. He was also reputed to be a friend of, and have influence with, the County Manager.

The remaining two governmental figures were both minor influentials who were ranked highly by one of the top influentials because of the official positions they had held. The Ex-MCC/Trade Union Official had continued to work with County Council Committees after losing her seat in the 1973 election. Further, she was nominated by the Minister for Transport and Power to the Board of the Bantry Harbour Authority (as a trade union representative) when it was established in 1976, largely because she had long been Chairwoman of the Labour party cumann in Bantry and an official of the ITGWU (see also chapters 4, 7 and 8). She had also been associated with Muintir na Tire and the Development Association, but had not been a key participant. Like a number of his colleagues, the Chairman of the Town Commissioners had also been a member of Muintir na Tire and the last Development Association.

From this profile it should be clear that the governmental influentials did not constitute a clearly defined group. Rather, the governmental sphere was occupied by a small, but disparate collection of politicians and civil servants who had strong links with the development sphere. This state of affairs was associated with the political weakness of the Town Commissioners (see chapter 7). Not only were the County Councillor and the Engineer ranked much more highly as influentials than the Chairman of the Town Commissioners, but the latter was only regarded as influential in the sense that he represented the Commissioners as a whole. That is, the Commissioners as a body had some importance, but not any particular individual on the board (see chapter 7).

Like the development influentials, and unlike the governmental influentials, the charity influentials were a fairly solidary group. They clustered around the Care for the Aged Committee and St. Vincent de Paul Society. But they also attached importance to the development sphere. Apart from the Canon, all but the Retired Draper belonged to the revived Chamber of Commerce, and he had been a founding member of the original Chamber. In striking contrast, none of the development influentials belonged to one of the major organizations in the charity sphere. A corollary of this was that the charity influentials tended to rank the development influentials highly, but the development influentials did not rank them highly. That is, whereas seven of the ten development people were top influentials only two of the five charity influentials were, while three of the five charity were assumed influentials, i.e. ordinary influentials generally presumed to wield more influence than was actually the case.

The strength of the charity sphere was primarily due to two factors. The three ordinary influentials were extremely effective activists; one of them, the Retired Draper, was formerly a top influential and one of the town's leading business men (see chapters 3 and 7). He had been a key figure in the West Cork Development Association, in Muintir na Tire, and also the first Chamber of Commerce. He was also a Town Commissioner for a time, but lost his seat in the 1973 election (see chapter 7). His activities now centred on the St. Vincent de Paul, the Homes and Care for the Aged Committees, and the Information Centre. It is worth noting too that of all the influentials, he alone at one time or another had been active in all three spheres. The Chemist was Joint-Secretary of the Homes and Care for the Aged Committees, and arguably the leading figure on the latter. The Business Woman was Public Relations Officer for both these organizations, as well as holding executive positions in a number of other organizations. The second factor contributing to the strength of the charity sphere was that the Biggs group's Manager and the Canon were both highly placed behind-the-scenes influentials.

Parish Priests were universally spoken of as powerful men, but they were also known for their covert methods. The Bantry Canon adopted a low public profile and exerted most of his influence through his curates. In fact, his public reticence was premised on the activism of his curates. The other top influentials recognized that the Canon's quietism was not the same thing as a lack of power: they knew how many organizations he could control if he wanted to do so; they knew his strengths were their weaknesses. This assessment was confirmed by his Chairmanship of the Homes for the Aged Committee (see chapter 7). His other activities included positions as Chairman of the Old Aged Pensioners Association, Honorary Director of the Community Centre, and Spiritual Director of the St. Vincent de Paul Society, the Legion of Mary, and the Church Co-Fraternities. In addition, one or other of his curates was Chairman of the Care for the Aged Committee, Chairman of the Boys Club Committee, Chairman of the Community Centre, Vice-Chairman of the Homes for the Aged Committee, Director of the Shalom Singers, and Spiritual Director of the Children of Mary, the GAA, the Society for the Blind, and the Youth Club. Members of the clergy had also been influential in the foundation of the Credit Union, and the Information Centre (see chapters 5 and 7).

Given the relatively informal way in which public affairs were habitually conducted in Bantry (see chapters 3, 4, 5 and 7), it is not surprising that these divisions of influence were reflected in the friendship networks of the key figures. Among the top influentials, most of the activity centred on the County Councillor. He had fairly limited friendship contacts with the charity group, but strong ones with the governmental people. In the development group the Dentist was the centre of most of the activity. He too had good contacts with the governmental people, but weak ones with the charity group. In the charity group, most of the activity centred on the clergy (but on the two curates, not the Canon) and the Chemist.

The dominance of business

Twelve of the eighteen influentials were in business, including six of the nine top influentials. Some had taken over businesses, others had bought into the town. All the twelve were employers. If those who had connections with business are included, then sixteen of the eighteen could be regarded as potentially representing the interests of business or as having a business-oriented outlook. The Biggs group's Manager was gradually taking over from his father as head of the town's largest commercial enterprise. After coming to Bantry as a young man, the Company Secretary had become the key non-family executive and public representative for the group. The Motor Dealer — whose prominence in Bantry was partly due to his marriage to one of the town's most notable business women (see below and chapter 7) — managed a business in Skibbereen which operated under his own name but was tied to a larger firm. The Manager of Rowa Ltd came from a Bantry family and had worked his way up in the firm to become an executive operating under the instructions of the firm's German owner (see chapter 3). The Draper came from a notable local family and was part-owner of the town's leading clothing store. The store had been purchased from his uncle, the Retired Draper, who himself took over from his uncle and like him in turn became one of Bantry's most prominent business men (see chapter 3). The Chemist was one of three in the town owning and running their own shops, but (on appearances at least) since arriving in Bantry he had made his the most successful. In addition to a cafe-and-bar on the Square, the Restaurateur–Publican had, since coming to Bantry, bought a farm and started a diving business, while his wife shared in a hairdressing business of her own. The Business Woman was a shop owner with a Bantry background. Her deceased husband had been the Harbour Constable as well as a fishing-boat owner; her son operated the Bantry Marine Company whose service boats were under contract to Gulf Oil. The Fianna Fail County Councillor, as already indicated (see chapter 4), was Bantry born. He was the son of one of de Valera's 'Broy Harriers'[2] who became, in part because of this, a man of some influence and pull in the town. Upon his father's death the son took over the running of the family hotel with his mother, but looked to his political career as his best entrepreneurial asset. The Dentist had come to Bantry from another part of West Cork and established a flourishing private practice, subsequently investing in property. The Solicitor, who was descended from an old Bantry district family, had an extremely profitable practice, his firm servicing clients as disparate as Gulf Oil, the foreign settlers, and the farmers and fishermen (see also chapters 3, 7 and 8). As Manager of the Hospital the County Surgeon was a state official who since taking up his appointment in Bantry combined the running of the hospital with a lucrative private practice. The County Engineer, another state official, had married into a wealthy Bantry business family after coming to town. Because of the positions they held both these men were major local employers of state-paid labour. The (Vocational) School Principal, another state official, came from a leading West Cork business family. Moreover, his sister was married to the Biggs group's Manager. The Canon, of necessity an outsider, also came from a business family, but of course was not personally involved in any business activities apart from those of the church itself. This leaves only the Chairman of the Town Commissioners and the former County Councillor Ex-MCC/Trade Union Official. The former was a Bantry man, the latter married one. Neither had business interests, but the Ex-MCC/Trade Union Official's husband had owned a pub when he was a Labour County Councillor many years before.

On these figures, the business people had an almost total monopoly on public leadership in Bantry. Although the working class had enlarged its voice in town politics because of the Gulf Oil intervention (see chapters 7 and 8), it still did not have any stable, independent leadership. The Town Commissioners took some part in a number of projects and controversies, but the Ex-MCC/Trade Union Official had a very low level of involvement in such things. Most of the time class alignments among the Commissioners were expressed through, and complicated by, party-political divisions. This was also true of the unions. Their representative was influential because of party-political affiliations. As she became less important in party-politics, her influence declined, in spite of the fact that she remained the leading official representative of organized labour within the town.

A simple if predictable conclusion can be drawn from this. If as the most visible and vocal representatives of business, the influentials at their core constituted an economic leadership, they thereby also constituted a political leadership.

The influentials in the social structure

This study is premised on the argument that as a lived experience localized class relations can be examined in terms of the status forms which express them. Given the theme of this book it would not be appropriate (and space would not permit) a comprehensive discussion of status configurations in Bantry (for this see Eipper, forthcoming). But in order to show how the influentials were placed in the local social structure I will now briefly describe the major ideological cleavages differentiating groupings within the community and show how these related to changes in property ownership and the division of labour.

Prestige and esteem as indices of status

The status vested in a social position derives from the prestige accorded the manner of production of wealth and privilege, their distribution throughout society and what they can be exchanged for in it, and so too the manner of their consumption. It is, then, the attribution of prestige to the hallmarks of social position which, as it were, *positions* people in society, and designates the standards by which they are judged. We can thus in status terms distinguish between a given social position and the incumbents of such a position. And also between the analysis of positions and the analysis of the relations between people occupying those positions. Following from this, we can distinguish two attributes of status attainment: prestige and esteem. The distinction is a simple one. Prestige is honour derived from simple incumbency of a position; esteem is honour derived from actual performance — i.e. what you do gets you prestige; how you do it gets you esteem. For example, in armies officers are accorded more prestige than privates, but heroes of any rank are esteemed more than cowards (cf. Oxley, 1973: 30–1). The distinction is important: it denotes, in my terms, the relation between the structural and institutional configurations of status (see chapter 1). In a local community where persons and events are known and scrutinized with a special intimacy, the complex relationship of esteem to prestige is an especially important feature of the lived experience of class. In large part, a person or group's *reputation* is a function of the way the prestige due to them is qualified by the esteem accorded to them. The vividness and immediacy which comes from this intimacy encourages a preoccupation with personalities which can often occlude other elements of consciousness. Of course, when power enters the picture the interplay of prestige and esteem is likely to become particularly noteworthy. Now there is a sense in which as an index of social position, status is thereby also an index of social power. This is so to the extent that a person's social position confers upon them a capacity to realize objectives which determine the conditions under which they and other people live. But individuals and collectivities do not wield power merely as a reflex of their social position. A reputation for power thus becomes an attribute of status as well as a form of power itself. As such it is perhaps one of the most important examples of the way consciousness actually enters into and becomes part of power relations.

Consideration of this aspect of the relationship between power and status brings to the fore the methodological problem of how to determine status. It is important here to recognize that, understood in these terms, status is not merely a matter of the differential distribution of such objective attributes as occupation, income, education, etc. throughout society. It is also a matter of how those differentiated by such criteria relate to one another as social agents functioning as the occupants of given social positions, and as acting subjects interacting with one another in a multiplicity of ways in everyday life.

Localized status relations are expressed as expectations, conventions and customs which are organized as informal or formal rules that determine the criteria, context and relativities of prestige accorded to disparities of privilege and wealth. Enshrined as codes of conduct, these relations comprise the distinctive styles of life of people in different social positions. By definition, then, social prestige rests on subjective evaluation of objective inequalities, for example, expressions of condescension or deference, admiration or contempt, honour or shame, respect or disrespect, reverence or irreverence, dignity or indignity. Status relations, therefore, are irretrievably qualitative in character. For this reason their analysis can only be accomplished using the various techniques of participant-observation, though these may be buttressed by other methods. In my case, this consisted of in-depth interviews combined with a random sample questionnaire-survey of 20% of the town.[3]

A profile of social stratification

The major ideological cleavages culturally differentiating various groupings within the community both marked off distinguishable social strata from one another, and either segmented these strata or delimited them. Whereas the cleavages delineating the different strata were based upon an *amalgam* of *diffuse* ideological principles and invoked a consciousness of rank and interest (without necessarily implying a rank order), the cleavages segmenting these strata divided Bantry people into complementary groupings according to a *specific* ideological principle of one kind or another. The intersection of these cleavages resulted in the formation of a number of overlapping social *milieux* whose ways of life were habitually identified, stereotyped and stigmatized by a complex of cultural symbols. The different strata were fuzzy at the edges due to them being defined by a variable deposition of ideological elements. However this blurring of strata was tempered by their being segmented. By clarifying the definition of various strata, the significance of the segmentary cleavages was thereby also enhanced. The major ideological cleavages in terms of which status relations were lived out in Bantry can be represented diagrammatically, albeit in an historically frozen, schematized form (see Figure 6:1). All but two of the major cleavages can be depicted in this way, the two exceptions being the biologically-based ones of sex and age, which, of course, intersect with all other cleavages. In spite of its artifice, the diagram makes it clear that the segmentary cleavages marked off a core of people who were catholic natives deriving from the old-stock of the town. In their different ways, the cleavages of religion and local ancestry embraced more inclusive and overlapping categories of people, namely the catholic natives and the native old-stock. The cleavage distinguishing nationality, being more inclusive, embraced the native Irish as a whole to the detriment of foreign nationals. Amongst the native Irish, protestants were marginalized by their religion, though members of the old-stock. By contrast, since the blow-ins were almost without exception catholics, they were centrally placed in that respect, but were marginalized by their lack of local ancestry. The native Irish, then, were segmented into three groupings, namely a tiny minority of protestants, a much larger proportion of blow-ins, and a kernel comprising the town's catholic old-stock.

Taken together, the cleavages of age and sex funtioned to preserve the status and power of adult males to the detriment of females. Patriarchal familism found ideological support in the pronouncements of the churches on the position of the family as the fundamental unit of society. While the gerontocratic authority apparently typical of farm families in an earlier generation had been eroded with increasing dependence of the elderly on state welfare, and also the financial independence of young adults, males still remained the head of the household. Deference to the husband and father might often have now been more limited and formal but wives — especially if they were mothers — were actively discouraged from working. Women's marital status was still first and foremost, then, the criterion fixing their social position and determining the nature of their social action. Although women were expected to give priority to home and family, their growing involvement in voluntary organizations signalled more thorough incursions into public affairs. Even so, this involvement tended to be confined to recreational and welfare organizations, the latter usually under the auspices of the church and thus the leadership of the (male) clergy. If women were not quite as marginal to organizations wielding power within the community as were the youth and the elderly of either sex, they were still, with the notable odd exception, apparently unable to surmount the barriers inhibiting them from being influential in their own right.

Figure 6:1 Stylized 'snapshot' of the major cleavages

The major segmentary divisions

Natives and Foreigners
Catholics and Protestants
Old-Stock and Blow-Ins
Business people, Professionals, Farmers and Workers
Men and Women
The Adult, the Youth and the Elderly

The major strata

The Native Irish   The Foreign Nationals
The Top Business & Professionals   The Anglo-Irish   The Settlers
The Old-Established   The Hippies
The New-Rich
The Well-Off
The Ordinary-Working
The Poor

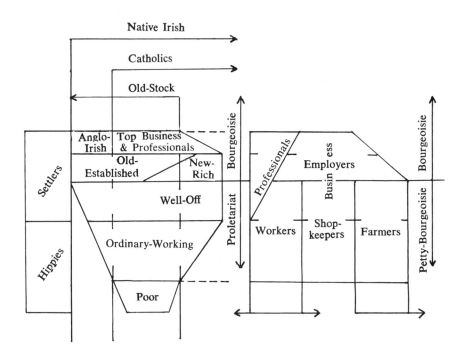

The foreign nationals and their lifestyle was alien to the Irish. Although the 'foreigners' included Germans and other continentals, most — and these were the more visible — were English. The country's colonial history, including Britain's continued occupation of Ulster, gave an enduring ideological potency to nationalist sentiments. This was reflected in the use of the term 'settlers', or, less often, 'planters' to refer to them. These labels evoked and expressed a virulent antagonism which reached its peak when the settlers organized to oppose the siting of an oil refinery on Whiddy Island adjacent to the Gulf Oil terminal (see chapter 8 and Eipper, forthcoming). Because of their historical associations and their social intermixing, the settlers were often 'lumped together' with the Anglo-Irish by the natives, and stigmatized as 'West Brits'. They were alike not only in that they were from business and professional backgrounds who had often fallen on hard times, but also in that many were ex-colonials who had resided most of their lives in Africa or other parts of 'the Empire'. Foreignness and protestantism were thus equated, as were Irishness and catholicism. Those who did not accept the equation nevertheless testified to its presumptive persuasiveness. The symbiotic relationship of nationality and religion acquired an even more astringent tang by being expressed in the language of race in that cultural attributes were taken as sympomatic of blood and breeding, particularly when old colonial antagonisms between 'the Saxon' and 'the Celt' surfaced. The foreigners were, in addition to their cultural distinctiveness, formally excluded from political life because of their alien citizenship. Moreover, they were by and large financially independent of the area or only coincidentally committed to it. In other words, they did not 'belong' but had merely 'settled' for a greater or lesser length of time. They were, then, at least in this respect if not in any other, the examplar of the 'blow-in'.

Whereas the social isolation of the settlers from the native population was bridged to some extent by the interaction of some of them with the Anglo-Irish, this was not true of the hippies. Certain individuals — usually those associated with arts and crafts — fraternized to a limited extent with some similarly inclined settlers and Anglo-Irish. But their personal as against their business contacts with the native population were limited to their immediate neighbours. They were, if not deviant, certainly marginal in everyone's eyes, including their own.

The protestants numbered less than 5% of the local population, and were further marginalized by the way the social complexion of the most notable of them, the former gentry or Anglo-Irish, was stigmatized by the historical link between religion and nationality. They were, though Irish by birth, English in their breeding — i.e. as the descendants of an alien colonial ruling class whose cultural model was England and who, in their names, their dress, their behaviour, education and upbringing, emulated the English gentry. To the catholics, the Anglo-Irish were 'West Brits' or *Seaneens,* 'little John Bulls'.

The latter rejected the imputation, though, that they were 'English' and not 'Irish', whether the suggestion came from the catholic Irish or the foreign settlers with whom they fraternized. They did not repudiate the English connection and its effect on their outlook, but their historical roots, experiences and allegiances were in the first instance Irish. The Anglo-Irish families living in the immediate vicinity of Bantry were all connected in one way or another by kinship and marriage. Their declining fortunes and personal eccentricities exacerbated the social irrelevance of an aristocracy deprived of its class basis and unable to maintain the standards of the past. With the loss of the status and power their class prerogatives as landlords gave them in the colonial era, they became interstitial figures who had acquired a new visibility in Bantry because of the links made between them and the foreign settlers.

Meanwhile, 'the ordinary protestants' had become less and less distinguishable from their catholic neighbours, particularly those of them who were small farmers and/or had intermarried with catholics. Protestants in business had been 'accepted' by the gentry — unlike 'the small-farmer protestant' who 'was merely tolerated' — but they had not socialized with them unless a marriage connection was established, and with time were also more and more coming to resemble and interact with their catholic neighbours. Although protestants could be stereotyped as being 'very straight' in their dealings, as 'keeping to themselves' and 'sticking together', religion was becoming more and more a matter of simple denominational differences than a badge of social distinctiveness. Sectarian sentiments and enmity were neither virulent nor habitual in Bantry, and remained salient only because of the colonial hangover of the continuing 'troubles in the North'. In a sense, then, the significance of the religious cleavage was less that it marked off two potentially antagonistic segments of the population, than that it established the limits of the pervasive catholicity of the community.

A synonym for local immigrants, the blow-in label was used whenever differences of lifestyle or other behaviour called for a distinction being made between 'the interlopers' and the 'Bantry born and bred'. As such it was used not only to refer to the foreign nationals, but also native Irish immigrants. But because of their nationality the former group were more than just blow-ins, whereas for the latter the only thing that distinguished them from the rest of the native population was their lack of local ancestry.

Local ancestry conferred a sense of belonging: Bantry belonged to its people, and its people belonged to Bantry. They had a stake in the place the immigrants lacked. Bantry was theirs as kin were theirs, whereas the immigrants were 'strangers'.

The new generation of blow-ins who gave the term its special salience came to Bantry in the wake of Gulf Oil. In certain circumstances the term assumed class connotations. The immigrants were generally better off than the majority of the local population and their conspicuously consumption-oriented behaviour meant resentment of them paralleled their social visibility. Members of the town's old-stock were keen to charge them with trying to 'take-over' organizations, committees and amenities. Whereas the locals charged the immigrants with self-interest when they broached the traditions, customs, loyalties and obligations of the old-stock, the immigrants retorted with charges of narrow-minded parochialism. To them Bantry people were 'backward', 'old-fashioned'.

The 'strangers' could 'get away' with assuming a 'grand' style of life because no one knew 'who they were' or 'what they came from'. Used as a device for class levelling, the blow-in label helped rein them in. Their presence had transformed the basis upon which a person's worth was assessed, according to Bantry people. They claimed that in the past the poor were respected and wealth did not buy 'quality', 'a person's name was once part of their wealth', 'you knew what someone was and what they'd been', 'you were who you were because of what you were, not because of what you had'. Such claims of course ignored the fact that for many of the old elite just as with the new, if the important thing was now the name behind the money this was only because a generation or so ago it was the money that had made the name.

The intersection of the various cleavages delineating different forms of livelihood intersected with the other segmentary cleavages and with the various strata into which the native Irish population was divided, so qualifying their class character. The cleavages dividing the business people, the professionals, the farmers and the workers defined the way they procured their livelihood and built a way of life around it. Different ways of making a living were imbued with different kinds of moral worth. The initiative and enterprise proclaimed by the business people and the certified meritocratic skills of the professionals, won out over the farmers' championing of the outdoors life, even if this retained a rustic appeal for many. Meanwhile the workers laid claim to the indispensability of their labour, a claim which few others saw as warranting social recognition.

The poor were almost exclusively members of the town's old-stock, but as well as poor workers there were also poor shopkeepers and farmers. A large proportion of the poor were elderly retired people no longer able to secure their own livelihood and with few savings carried over from the economically depressed times of the past. These people were, then, 'the ones who'd been passed over' or 'fallen by the wayside', or were 'old and unwanted'. Although blighted by poverty, such people were nevertheless 'respectable'. In this they contrasted both with 'the sad cases' who had 'lost their self-respect' and the 'riff-raff', 'the roughs', 'the layabouts' and 'dossers', who were beyond conventional respectability. In such cases the poor were sometimes even denied their poverty, they were 'not really poor', but 'wasters'. This was particularly true of 'the chronic cases' among the unemployed, those who were 'unemployable' or 'unwilling to work'.

The 'ordinary-working people' as they were called, comprised the odd protestant and a few blow-ins, but mainly they were members of the old-stock. They lived modestly on a basic wage either in small terraces in the old part of town, in one of the Council Estates, or in a basic project-built bungalow on the outskirts. The people in the Council Estates had been taken out of 'the worst areas' and relocated, and a certain opprobrium still attached itself to living in a Council house. Those who had built their own home had usually only been able to do so because of the higher wages and employment generated by the coming of Gulf Oil and the other industry to the town. Gulf's presence showed that even the poor could make money and do well, but a corollary of this was that those who had not done so were held responsible for their fate.

Although how a person procured their livelihood affected their prestige, the effects of this in some cases could be mitigated. Often reference was made to a person's background, yet in a way which itself confirmed the differential prestige accorded different livelihoods. The links made between kinship and property were particularly important in this regard. Unless they rose in the world, the children of fishermen or manual labourers were still 'lower class' whereas some from 'old farming stock' or a shopkeeping family carried their respectability with them for having been 'got well'. But such connections did not modify the status of wage labour itself. In the end, it was the job, the income it brought, and the education it required, that was important. The changing ratio of returns to different kinds of labour reworked accepted relativities between white and blue collar work, mental and manual labour, between 'middle class' and 'lower class' jobs. This became particularly important with Gulf's intervention and the new job and wage profiles it helped introduce. There was thus a major reworking of distinctions between a job and the lifestyle it purchased, which helped create important disjunctions between class consciousness at the point of production and the point of consumption. Hence as the relativities between different forms of work changed, highly paid jobs acquired a 'name' of their own if only because they purchased a style of life equivalent to or better than anything trade, clerical or even some professional skills could provide. In spite of these changes, the discrepancies between the market men found for their labour power as against that women found for theirs persisted, as did therefore the gap between male and female earnings. It remained the case that working women could not make themselves affluent by their labour but only by 'marrying well'.

Shopkeepers, publicans and small farmers were often no better off than wage workers and regarded themselves and were regarded by others as among 'the ordinary people' even if they salvaged some prestige from being 'in business', because a shopfront or few acres bore the family name. The prestige of the small farmer was in decline as their living standards deteriorated relative to the working class. As a result, they were increasingly seen as relics of the past, stereotyped as uneducated, backward, old, etc. The country in a sense was increasingly the reservoir of the real old-stock and the town increasingly an island of blow-ins within it, the most striking indicators of these polarizing tendencies being the dress style and accept of 'the cosmopolitans' as against those of 'the mountainy men' and their families who invaded the streets on fair days

The changing relativities between different kinds of occupations, associated as it was with the prosperity of these years and the growth of wage levels caused by the coming of Gulf Oil, made those who were 'well-off' a rather heterogeneous category dubbed by a priest the 'licorice-all-sorts'. They were people who were 'comfortable', having 'a bit of money' though not 'wealthy'. The lower ranking salaried professionals and white collar workers, skilled technicians and the highly paid manual workers — including the tugboat crews and terminal operatives employed by Gulf Oil and its ancillary companies — lived either in the new housing estates or in the more modest of the bungalows dotting the surrounding hills. Like the farmers, self-employed shopkeepers, publicans and tradesmen often preferred their wealth to remain inconspicuous. Such people tended to live on the premises, identifying themselves with 'the ordinary' people of the town. But if they lived more modestly than they could afford or on the memory of 'old money', these external appearances helped mitigate the prestige they might otherwise have been accorded.

A person's personal worth, their esteem, was very much tied up with their ability to 'handle money', which was seen as a mark of character. Nowhere was 'social climbing' impugned more than if a person had 'no breeding behind them'. Ostentatious consumption behaviour in such cases was taken as indicative of the inability to handle money of people without a good family behind them. The snobbery which was often a corollary of conspicuous consumption was equally cause for comment. As with the new-rich it was often said of the well-off that 'tuppence was looking down on a penny ha'penny'. Many were aspirants to higher status and this was revealed as much as anything by their leisure activities, e.g. their joining the Golf Club, their entertaining at home, or their dining out. Actually it was their desire to join the Golf Club which helped make it a success, while at the same time destroying any ambience of exclusivity it might otherwise have had (see chapter 7).

For the affluent workers Gulf Oil had brought a prosperity which enabled them to take for granted things which they had once regarded as luxuries. Before Gulf's arrival they had been 'kept down', but this was no longer possible. Just as they had organized on the job to get themselves paid more so they now used this money to buy themselves certain kinds of freedom and enjoyment off the job. For these people, then, there was no contradiction between labour militancy and status aspirations; in their eyes the one buttressed the other. For some, the idea was to improve their social position as

136

workers, for others the aim was to move into business.

Because definite limits to personal wealth and privilege were set by demarcations of livelihood, these helped decide how the less prestigious new-rich and old-established families were distinguished from those well-off families who were securely prosperous, or even clamorous concerning the warrant their fresh affluence gave them in making a claim for social recognition.

The term 'business people', for example, embraced both larger employers and small shopkeepers and publicans, the 'merchant princes' and the 'small traders', but there was a point where the self-employed traders dependent on family labour for the running of the business supplemented to one degree or another by hired labour, were distinguished from the business people proper. That is, the major employers, the merchants, hoteliers, builders, etc. who to one degree or another worked alongside their employees, but for whom family labour (when it was used) merely supplemented hired labour and supervised its performance. This was also the case with the wealthier farmers with large holdings who became, in effect, farmer-business men.

An increasingly important trend in business was the growth of managerial/administrative positions. This trend reinforced the link between business and the professions in both the private and public sectors. Historically, there was a connection too in that without free education only the children of people of means were recruited into the professions, though this had now changed. Increasingly, those who laid claim to being 'professionals' were differentiated not simply by the prestige of their certified skills but by the kind of livelihood secured by the use of them. Those who were merely white collar workers, whether in public or private employment, were thus distinguished from manager-administrators, as well as owners of private practices charging a fee-for-service.

No clear-cut boundary line divided those who were merely well-off from the new-rich professionals and business people. Yet the agitated nature of the status relations in the vicinity of this cleavage was indicative of something significant. The translation of personal wealth and privilege into prestige was here accompanied by resonant proclamations and counter-proclamations as to one's social worth. In the penumbra surrounding this cleavage the mass of the people of the town were firmly distinguished from those claiming social eminence, that is, those who had the means and desire to be numbered amongst the town's elite. The intense status competition associated with this cleavage, then, reflected the attempts of the upwardly mobile to culturally negotiate their way into the bourgeoisie.

The presence of Gulf Oil had been what brought the new-rich to prominence; in this sense they represented 'a new element'. They were 'the millionaires', the 'jumped-up ones', 'the small town big shots', whose conspicuous consumption symbolized 'a new consumerism'. They epitomized the way the assessment of social worth had changed. They built ostentatious bungalows scattered across the hills surrounding the town. The luxury of these houses, the 'flash' cars, the opulent dinner parties and their cliquishness — especially on festive occasions such as the 'dress dances' held each winter in the West Lodge Hotel — all constituted a statement, a proclamation of social success. Within their ranks, finer discriminations were maintained. The 'in-crowd' or 'the jet set', as they were known, hosted the most lavish parties with invitations restricted to a select circle. Meanwhile the 'would-be's' or 'triers' imitated their example and strove for their recognition.

As parvenues the new-rich had to justify themselves to protect their social standing. Competition for prestige was their way of demonstrating their worth, of legitimating their claim, in effect, to cultural membership of the bourgeoisie. They were a new generation with wealth, but without the cultural supports that wealth required. Some were from bourgeois families, but in the local context they were not culturally entrenched members of the established bourgeoisie. Like the upwardly mobile well-off, the new-rich called into question the immutability of class relations and the differences of lifestyle built upon them. The mere pretensions of property were not enough, nor was it enough to imitate the lifestyle of the propertied. A stronger claim could only be made with the benefit of time: cultural as well as economic solvency had to be demonstrated.

In the hierarchy of prestige the differences between the new-rich and the old-established families were compounded and symbolized by the notorious clamour for recognition of the one, and the complacent confidence in the family name of the other. Class distinctions assumed a new poignancy because of the transformation wrought after Gulf's arrival. Snobbery increasingly based itself on the insignia of wealth, with breeding no longer automatically being accorded deference. The new-rich, then, were not necessarily old-established families in the making, for their emergence meant that the cultural foundations of the old elite had been irretrievably changed. Some members of the new-rich were able to mix with the top business and professional people, and one or two of them would perhaps even one day manage to do so as social equals. In other words, under exceptional circumstances, some members of the new-rich could translate a conspicuous lifestyle into high prestige by concurrently 'establishing' their name, i.e. by the time they were regarded as old-established figures, they were already near or at the top — where they then had to consolidate their position over time. For less luminous figures, upward mobility meant simply establishing one's name. For the old-established families to be upwardly mobile was to become one of the top few families, whereas to be downwardly mobile was simply to become well-off with time, the family name continuing to carry its reputation some while after the means to support it had diminished. By contrast, the social demise of any of the newly rich merely left an after-glow of brash extravagance. It was the stark visibility of the oscillating fortunes and relative standing of the old-established, new-rich and even well-off families that invoked the much-loved proverbial comment that 'castles were falling and dung-hills rising'. The volatility of status relations expressed by such aphorisms was the most evocative indicator of the transformation wrought by the prosperity which coincided with Gulf's presence.

The prestige of the old-established families rested less on the conspicuousness of their lifestyle than on the security of their capital, the returns it had brought them, and the name the family had been able to buy with it. As this suggests, it was the character of wealth as much as wealth itself which was important. Wealth had to be respectable. Theirs was 'old money' as against the 'new money' of the interlopers, and they could be complacent in the knowledge that they had 'the name of money', and with this went a presumed 'quality' of family and breeding, a quality of 'respectability'. For the fact that a family had made money and held on to it for more than one generation itself testified to a certain 'quality'. That is to say, the heirs of such a family inherited not only money, but 'the name of money' — a bequest which if things went wrong might well outlast their wealth.

The old-established were thought of as 'minding the money', though in the high spending years following Gulf's arrival some felt it necessary to demonstrate they still possessed means to match that which made their name, even if they did so with money made more recently, in the 'boom years'. If the name of money was sufficiently well established, lifestyle did not necessarily matter and many of the less affluent old-established lived quietly and modestly. The wealthier among them, like the new-rich and the top people drove expensive cars, took holidays abroad, owned a pleasure-boat of some kind, educated their children at private schools and university, employed some domestic help, and so on. Whereas some preferred to live in the older part of the town in a less than ostentatious manner, others joined with the new-rich in building large bungalows in the surrounding hills or renovating two-storey mansions.

At the apex of the social structure were the top business and professional families. Here the important thing was the size of the business or the eminence of the profession and whether these were burnished by a 'name'. The top people were really only the cream floating on the surface of the old-established families. The distinction was a hazy one, with more people clustering around the cleavage than having crossed it. That is, those rising to prominence, who were publicly associated with other strata, who did not maintain the appropriate demeanour, who had made their money in one generation, or were blow-ins — none of these were unequivocally able to claim top status. There were, in other words, a number of families *at* the top but very few *of* the top. For these reasons the top people assumed an aura of exclusivity, of being above things. They tended to participate in town affairs on their own terms, and were impatient with democratic processes which in their view allowed divisiveness and petty rivalry to cripple leadership and jeopardize organizational initiatives.

To sum up, generally speaking there was no unambiguous cut-off point, no unequivocal 'boundary' between classes as these were generated at Bantry by the translation of commodity relations into the lived form of status relations. Instead there was a complex field of force in which simple class polarities were compromised and qualified by intervening and mediating elements which meant not only that there were numerous contradictory class locations, but the polarity itself was characterized by its contradictions. There was no all-embracing consensus in the assessment of status, but conflicting evaluations of one's own or other's worth were nevertheless mediated by a common grounding in the same inter-related sets of categorical distinctions and the same ideological vocabulary — in effect, the same status paradigm.

In status terms hegemony was culturally manifested to the extent that people remained subservient to standards with which they could not hope to conform. The structure of status relations reflected the success of some in imposing on others their own evaluations of social worth. Because social change did not create or dissolve single classes, but to one degree or another, reconstituted the whole class structure, conflicts between alternative ways of life were fought out within classes as well as between them. Cleavages which crossed class lines, then, were often as important as, and sometimes more important than, ones which distinguished one class from another. Hence class relations were culturally realigned by the way old divisions entered into a dialogue with new ones.

Status struggles were in large part a consequence of some people trying to translate material advantage into cultural pre-eminence while others sought to prevent or subvert such attempts, or to remain indifferent to them, while others still sought to stave off the loss of prestige associated with the loss of material advantage. In such ways people tried to influence the way economic forces acquired a cultural imperative by negotiating and re-negotiating the value assigned to material differences. These struggles were particularly virulent wherever the newly affluent's social position was based upon pure economic advantage and their cultural claims were correspondingly weak and consequently de-mystified.

The influentials' status characteristics

Since power had passed completely from the hands of protestants in Bantry a generation before, it was to be expected that all the influentials would be practising catholics. Equally predictable was the strongly patriarchal character of public leadership. Women were active in the charity sphere, but were not important in the development sphere. Only two of the influentials were women. Another business woman activist also figured prominently in the business life of the town and the charity sphere (see chapter 7). If she had been a man, instead of the wife of an influential (the Motor Dealer), she would undoubtedly have carried more sway than she did. The charity sphere was dominated by men in their fifties and sixties. By contrast, the development influentials were relatively youthful men. With the exception of the Company Secretary, their ages ranged from the early thirties to the early forties. Because they were more youthful they were also more highly educated. Five of the development influentials had university degrees: the Dentist, the Solicitor, the Engineer, the School Principal and the Draper. The County Councillor had begun but not completed a degree. The only charity influential with a degree was the Canon; the Chemist had received his qualifications from a Pharmacy College. The most highly qualified man overall was the County Surgeon. Overall, six of the nine top influentials were tertiary educated, but only three of the nine ordinary influentials. Significantly, immigrants to the town amongst the influentials, the blow-in influentials, were more highly educated overall than those from the town's old stock, whom they outnumbered. Nearly two-thirds of the blow-in influentials were tertiary educated, as against less than a third of the old-stock influentials. A somewhat similar pattern emerges from the party-political allegiances of the influentials. Taken as a whole, half were Fine Gael supporters, a third Fianna Fail, the remainder Labour. But Fianna Fail was better represented amongst the top influentials than amongst the ordinary influentials, matching Fine Gael's strength there. It was stronger than Fine Gael in the development sphere and weakest in the charity sphere where the traditional allegiance of the old-established and top strata to Fine Gael held true. In the governmental sphere, Labour had the numbers, but Fianna Fail packed more muscle (see Table 6:7).[4]

With the exception of the Ex-MCC/Trade Union Official and the Chairman of the Town Commissioners, who lived modestly in the style of the ordinary working people, all the influentials belonged to one of the top three social

Table 6:7 The influentials' party political affiliations

	Fianna Fail	Fine Gael	Labour	Total
All influentials	6	9	3	18
Top influentials	4	4	1	9
Ordinary influentials	2	5	2	9
Development influentials	5	4	1	10
Charity influentials	1	4	0	5
Governmental influentials	2*	1	2	5

*NB Double counting: see also Table 6:4

strata. That is to say, they were, in one way or another, members of the local bourgeoisie. One or two lived in the more sedate manner of an earlier generation, but most lived at a level which denoted conspicuous prosperity. Whereas eight of the influentials (almost half) were born in the Bantry district, amongst the top influentials those from other parts outnumbered the locals six to three. These figures have to be somewhat qualified, however, by the fact that four of the blow-ins had married into the old-stock of the town, and this included three of the top influentials. Whereas the charity influentials were predominantly top and old-established members of the old-stock of the town, the development influentials were popularly typecast as new-rich blow-ins. In fact, only six of the ten were blow-ins. It was the identification of the blow-ins with the new-rich that made the difference. Not all were unequivocally new-rich either: six of the ten were from, or had married into, top or old-established families. But they had all (excepting the Company Secretary who was older) adopted the lifestyle which characterized the new-rich: indeed they comprised its leadership. Amongst the top influentials, the people who were blow-ins and/or were linked with the new-rich outnumbered the others, primarily because of the predominance of the development influentials.

Although the core of the influentials comprising the development sphere did not constitute a homogeneous group, when they socialized it tended to be with some or all of the others. Some, for example, would not have invited others to dine at home with them, but they might perhaps meet as guests at the home of a mutual friend. Even more predictably, they could be expected to attend the same social functions.

In their different ways, the County Surgeon and the Solicitor stood out from the others in the public acknowledgement of the trappings of status and their use of the reputation this gave them for wielding influence in a variety of ways. The County Surgeon could make a claim to being the town's top professional if only by, as townspeople put it, emphasizing he was a 'Mr' not a 'Dr'. But if his reputation relied upon demarcations of this sort, it also depended upon the authority conferred by his management of the Hospital and that emanating from his private practice as a specialist. Some might assert that he was 'a self-made man' who had only acquired his money after coming to Bantry, but such assertions could do little to diminish the haughty indifference or disdain with which he secured the ambience of exclusiveness which surrounded him. He was, for example, reputed to be highly selective in his socializing, even where the other influentials were concerned. His most salient social foray each year was the Hospital Dinner Dance at which he was the chief luminary. But this reluctance to become part of the social whirl was also a matter of age. And in this he was no different from his brother-in-law the Chemist, the Biggs group's Manager or the Retired Draper, all of whom were several years older than the 'jet set crowd' whose foremost figure was the Solicitor. He came from one of the district's old business and farming families. But his reputation as Bantry's most conspicuously wealthy man derived from his lavish exhibition of the personal 'fortune' acquired in the Gulf Oil period. Following a late marriage to a young woman from a prominent Cork professional family, he began to entertain ostentatiously. The parties and the dinners he hosted and the frequent trips abroad were the talk of the town, as was the money he spent in connection with the Golf Club. Partly because of this, the Golf Club came to be the venue for dances and other social occasions, patronized by the town's socialites.

Amongst the others, the County Councillor, the Dentist, the Motor Dealer, the Restaurateur–Publican, the Draper, and their wives, were conspicuous at social gatherings such as the more prestigeous formal-dress Dinner Dances where they tended to fraternize with one another and a few favoured friends, restricting their interactions with others to the exchange of pleasantries. Even when they disliked one another they still preferred mixing with their own kind. The result of this was that they were seen as a 'set' or 'clique' by townspeople. They and their associates (i.e. other socialites who were not, however, influentials) constituted the social vanguard, the 'in' crowd or 'jet set' who were emulated by 'the would-be's' and criticized by others for being 'snobs' and 'small town big shots'. Such attitudes were a component part of the individual and collective reputation of the influentials. They thus provide a revealing illustration of the complex interplay of prestige and esteem in the evaluation of social conduct. Despite the general prestige of the social strata to which they belonged and the milieu in which they moved, as figureheads of a clique or set these people were not highly esteemed. Indeed, some were widely held, and sometimes held one another, in low personal esteem. That is, their social honour was qualified by their personal worth being morally impugned in some way, e.g. because of shrewd or unscrupulous business dealings, public indiscretions or private peccadilloes, or certain unprepossessing traits of character for which they could not be forgiven.

Because there was a certain ambivalence shown by the mass of the population to the self-aggrandizement of local notables, anyone who gave the impression that they were 'that much better' due to their prominence in town affairs soon became a subject for ridicule. Nevertheless, public prominence could be a most persuasive indicator of a name either in the making or already made. And the influentials undoubtedly made a public claim to prestige through their reputation as leading figures in town affairs.

On the basis of this profile of the position of the influentials in the social structure, the conclusion can be drawn, then, that at their core the influentials constituted not only an economic and political leadership but a cultural one as well, particularly for the more affluent of the younger generation who came to maturity in the Gulf Oil period. As with their prominence in the political sphere, their cultural prominence initially derived from, but then augmented, their economic influence.

Final remarks

Overwhelmingly, the influentials were catholic businessmen and their professional counterparts from the top three strata of Bantry society, half of them from the old-stock of the town and half blow-ins from other parts of the country. Between them they controlled the key organizations in the three major spheres of influence in town affairs. Indeed, as the case studies in the next chapter will show, they also exerted an influence, albeit a less pervasive one, in matters ostensibly independent of church, state and business, for example sporting ventures (see Table 6:5).

Taken together, these results indicate that there was, coincidentally, a shift in power in Bantry in the period which followed the Gulf Oil intervention. A new leadership group had emerged. It was catholic, still male-dominated, but younger, better educated, and centred on the upwardly mobile and immigrant sections of the bourgeoisie. A brief look at the pre-Gulf era will show how much things had changed.

The business people held power in all three organizational spheres in the pre-Gulf period, just as they did afterwards. In the 1960s the key organization co-ordinating their activities was Muintir na Tire. The three spheres of influence were all represented on one executive, with most of the other organizations of the town providing the rank and file. For Bantry, this was an organizational watershed: Muintir na Tire gave birth to most of the organizations wielding influence in subsequent years. The business people constituted the core of the organization, the town's politicians and civil servants were active supporters of it, but in its heyday the leadership was provided by an authoritative capable and energetic priest. While he took responsibility for the development projects, another curate handled the charity projects. Unity on this level could probably not have been sustained. In any case, the organization broke up when a new priest with different ideas stepped in. Nevertheless, its offspring continued, albeit in a more fitful and fragmented fashion, to direct events within the town (see chapter 7). The curates who followed were, in spite of their activism, far less influential personalities. However, they were operating in a social environment fundamentally changed by Gulf Oil. Bantry might still have been clamouring for industry, but it was no longer the poor and economically precarious rural village it had been. It was not so necessary for the clergy to rally the spirits of the people as cadres of progress. Instead, they could devote themselves to 'the people progress had left behind'.

More of the influentials seem to have been involved in both governmental and development organizations in the pre-Gulf period. However, the trend seems to have been that as local political issues were subordinated to county and national considerations, the leading influentials moved out of the formal organs of town government. It is noteworthy, then, that after years of dormancy, the Town Commissioners suddenly came to life again, enlivened by a working class component whose assertiveness was in part due to the presence of Gulf Oil. For the previous nineteen years the Commissioners had been led by a business man who had been active in the Development sphere. Once a man with some influence, he had virtually no say at all once he lost his position as Chairman of the Commissioners and became part of the Fine Gael minority.

A man whose power had declined even more dramatically was the Managing-Director of the Biggs group. The son had nothing like the power his father had wielded, nor his father's style, ambition or capabilities. In his day, the Managing-Director was the single most powerful man in the town, and when it suited him he made good use of the authority his capital gave him (see chapter 3).

As a young man the Managing-Director was, for a short time, himself a Town Commissioner. In subsequent years he seldom ever publicly participated in local organizations. He did not need to do so. His Company Secretary and one or more of his other Managers were always active in the main organizations. If they did not always serve as 'mouthpieces' for him, as his critics claimed, they certainly did so when it counted. As his friend and fellow influential, the now Retired Draper put it, 'when he couldn't do it himself he allocated one of his staff and then later another of his staff' to do his bidding. These two men always worked closely together, co-ordinating their initiatives with those of the Skibbereen solicitor responsible for the West Cork Development Association (see chapter 3).

According to his Bantry friend, the Managing-Director was 'the driving force' behind the push for industrial development in Bantry.

> [He was] there as benevolent adviser and financial helper. [Moreover] he was available to discuss local conditions with any promoter [and was] best equipped to give the information required by these people.

Others confirmed how important the man was, but described his power in different terms. According to one of the Town Commissioners he was the

> director of the largest company in town, employing the largest number of people. But to suggest that he lent himself to the town is absolute rot. He stayed aloof. He employed a lot of people but they worked hard and [were] often paid measly wages. What he did for the town he did for himself. The town did progress because of expansions of the business, but don't suggest he caused it.

An incoming County official was equally emphatic: 'It was the Mafia here. He controlled everything . . . '. These views were shared by one of the top influentials, who described the Managing-Director as 'a bit of a godfather and still that way'. He commented that industries which might have come to the town were stopped by these men. 'So what kind of Development Association was that?' Like most big businessmen in provincial towns they were primarily interested in 'holding on to their money and keeping the working class down'. From these descriptions, before he became less active in the late 1960s, the Managing-Director was highly visible as Bantry's leading businessman, but worked as a concealed influential in organizational activities. His reputation for power brought a power of its own and he became known as a man with plenty of pull (see chapters 3, 7 and 8). The remarks of the county official indicate how big that reputation was: '[He was] the Lord Mayor of Bantry. Most people were working for him and no one dared say a word against him'. Bantry, he said, was 'one of the few towns where one man owned the town, controlled the business'. The town accepted 'what he said was law'. These were exaggerations, but telling ones nevertheless.

With the coming of foreign factories and Gulf Oil, the Biggs group lost its virtual monopoly on economic power in the town (see chapters 3 and 8). The major shift which occurred in the character and staffing of Bantry's development organizations following the arrival of Gulf Oil, was related to this fact. The dilution of the personal power of a few key individuals did not have much effect on the participatory capacity of the majority of people. Some encroachments were made (see chapter 7), but a small number of people continued to possess and exercise a preponderant amount of influence. Business interests were now represented by a new and younger generation who commanded less respect, less legitimacy, and who — individually and collectively — did not have the same exclusive control over the prosperity of the town. But they seem to have been no less effective for that.

7 The mobilization of influence in town projects and controversies

Leadership and domination are intimately related aspects of class. Although leadership obviously depends upon the agency of specific people to be realized, it is always vested in some form of social organization. Particular organizations may require the participation of key individuals and groups to become effective, but specific individuals and groups must also have an organizational base before they can become powerful. The emergence of leadership groups within a class can be regarded as an index of that class's organizational power, of its state of mobilization. Such a group does not necessarily constitute an elite with respect to the class from which it springs, though it may do so. This all depends upon how the leadership actually represents the class which supports it. For example, sometimes a class is able to install its representatives in formally defined positions of authority at the head of important organizations. But these representatives may or may not then function as an elite with respect to their own class as well as to other classes. In Bantry, the business influentials did not function as an elite with respect to their own class. As the participation pattern of many of the ordinary influentials demonstrates (other things being equal), any business-man (or even woman) or professional with a modicum of ability and an activist disposition, could soon find themselves numbered amongst the influentials. This would even have been true, I imagine, of farmers of means, though their concerns in the town were habitually voiced by men who engaged in trade with them, or who themselves combined farming and trade. But the same could not be said of someone who was neither a business person nor a professional who acknowledged the prerogatives of business. This suggests, and the weight of evidence confirms, the imputation that the influentials did function as an elite leadership with respect to other classes.

This becomes even more apparent if we examine the major projects and controversies which dominated town affairs in the period under review. Detailed case studies of the mobilization of different groups in the town around these issues reveal the decisive, if limited, organizational power of the influentials as representatives of business interests. They show how the influentials individually and collectively actually secured and deployed their power within their respective spheres of interest. This is done by charting the extent to which they were able to direct projects and constrain controversy by their leadership of key organizations. A few projects and controversies of major import were not concerned with development matters, local government, or charity. In the period under review the main ones (leaving aside those matters which centred on Gulf Oil) concerned recreational ventures and fishing disputes. I have analysed these to show how power was wielded in areas nominally independent of the influentials.

There was a certain fluidity about local organizations in Bantry which influenced the way people mobilized for concerted action. This fluidity can be understood as a dialectic between the urge for consensus and the persistence of conflict: people were both mobilized for a common purpose, and around opposed objectives or interests. A number of the more important projects and controversies revolved around the formation or revival of other committees and associations; one or two organizations were noteworthy because they were responsible for the formation of many others. Conflictual mechanisms led to the dissolution of certain organizations and consensual ones to re-grouping, but it worked the other way too. Consensual devices were used to stave off conflict and often led to the effective dissolution of an organization, subsequent controversy in a related area then led to a re-grouping of forces.

The appeal to a wider community interest was usually made when implacable divisions threatened to divide the population. The desire for consensus was thus a product of social divisiveness. The fact that it was so difficult to achieve consensus was a frequently voiced complaint at public meetings. One of the results of this was that by creating an illusion of consensus, i.e. a false gloss of shared objectives and interests, a veneer of legitimacy was obtained for otherwise unpopular decisions. Large, unwieldy committees were elected at public meetings in the certain knowledge that the actual working committee would end up consisting of only a handful of those elected. By co-opting additional members to the committee and by only notifying a few people about subsequent meetings, it was easy to alter the composition of a committee (especially since a fair proportion of those elected usually dropped out

148

anyway). Most ongoing committees thus ended up bearing little resemblance to the one originally elected. The compromising and steam-rolling was done out of the public gaze and private decision-making was given a democratic gloss.

Such manoeuvres highlight the kind of questions addressed by the case studies which follow, for example: how were the major projects and controversies around which the town mobilized in the 1966–77 decade initiated, developed and resolved; how did local organizations express their objectives as demands and act upon them; what connections existed between the bases of their actions, the strategies and tactics they adopted, the institutions they addressed, and the people most active in them; what was the response to these initiatives, what procedures were adopted for dealing with them?

The charity sphere

I previously suggested (see chapter 5) that influentials wanting to play a part in organizations linked to the church were required to fall in behind the clergy's leadership. Not all influentials were prepared to do this, but those who were, found that charity and business went well together.

The St. Vincent de Paul Society and the Information Centre

Bantry's St. Vincent de Paul Society was reputed to have long borne an air of exclusiveness and social condescension, but some attention was given in the 1970s to remedying its traditional image. To begin with, it had begun to broaden its membership. The Canon was still Chairman, and two other high status influentials, the Retired Draper and the Biggs group's Manager, were the dominant figures; the other members included a Teacher, a Town Commissioner who was a self-employed insurance-broker, a Deputy-Manager of one of the banks, a young Gulf Oil Engineer, and a Nun.

In the past, the Society always concentrated on aiding cases of immediate distress, attempting to provide temporary support in times of crisis. It now moved to provide help on a more permanent and substantial basis — and not just for the down-and-outs. An instance of this was the Society's decision to establish an Information Centre in the town. To get it started, the Society broke with tradition and admitted its first woman member, a Nun. She became responsible for establishing the Centre, which was based on the idea that 'we may not have all the answers, but we know how to get them'. The intention was to cut out the County Councillors who, as 'a favour', got people benefits to which they were already entitled.

The Centre was staffed by voluntary workers. Two influentials were involved in this capacity, the Retired Draper and the Business Woman; the wife of another influential, the Company Secretary, was also active. However, most of the work was done by teachers and housewives. Although originally financed by the St. Vincent de Paul, the Centre began to repay that money upon receiving a Social Service Council grant; it continued to operate under the aegis of the Society, but independent of it.

The Care for the Aged Committee and Meals-on-Wheels

This organization — really a disparate association of people grouped around a central committee — was begun in 1967 as an offshoot of Muintir na Tire by a curate who the charity influentials came to regard as 'one of the greatest men who ever came to town'. Initially the Committee was composed, in the Muintir fashion, of one member from each of the interested organizations in town.

The first major activity undertaken by the Committee was the setting up and running of the Meals-on-Wheels program. This required a considerable public relations effort: old attitudes to charity had to be broken down. People did not like to be thought of as poor, let alone in need of charity; they wanted to remain independent and keep their dignity. For some the program resembled a mobile soup kitchen, with all the attendant connotations of famine degradation and the work house. In spite of these sentiments, the program proved successful. Whether this was because of necessity or amelioration of the stigma is not clear.

Nearly half of the meals were delivered to rural areas where the isolation of the elderly was a particularly serious problem. The Committee also ran a chiropody service, arranged parties and outings, provided a laundry service, and purchased and renovated houses. The work was done by voluntary labour. Kitchen facilities were provided by the Convent; the Secondary School, student cooks and helpers. The Musical Society contributed the bulk of the entertainment. Others volunteered their cars for the delivery of meals.

The Committee prepared an annual report for and received a grant from the Southern Health Board. The members of the Committee were well connected in this respect. The Chemist was a brother-in-law of the County Surgeon, who was a member of the Board. The Committee saw its work as vindicating the policy of channelling state funds through private organizations: 'We don't look on it as charity from the Health Board, but their duty. It keeps people out of institutions and is saving state money'.

Like most church-led affairs, the Care for the Aged was run as a closed-shop. The Committee was disciplined, and all on it had to be active. In fact, only those people with a record of dependability, a willingness to work, or special expertise, were invited onto the Committee. As one of its members put it to me: '[We are] a kind of dictatorship in that we keep it closed. But we find it works better that way'. The Committee was chaired by one of the curates, the other key figures on it were all business people. They were the Chemist (Secretary), the Retired Draper and his wife (Treasurer), the Business Woman (PR Officer), and two other women with commercial interests. Other activists were the wife of a deceased influential, a school teacher, two young nuns, and a disabled working woman — a sister of the Company Secretary's wife, who was also active in a number of other organizations.

The Care for the Aged staged numerous functions throughout the years — dinners, suppers, concerts, entertainment evenings, and so on. The influentials on the Committee pitched in with their colleagues and all the voluntary workers, preparing the food, dancing with the old people, joining in the singing, and so on. The lead was given by the two curates, who participated with a gusto and sincerity which could be equalled by few of the other key organizers.

Although more than one of the old people regretted having need of such consideration, and such an organization, they admitted they benefited from the company, the music, the cameraderie and the evident concern for their welfare. Some danced and sang and talked avidly with their friends; others remained quieter and more subdued. Most praised the priests and the Committee — sometimes deferentially, often as a matter of course. These were occasions, then, when power spoke in a popular idiom. The whole town acknowledged that it was indebted to the charity organizers. They, in turn, dispelled any suggestion of snobbery (and demonstrated their personal worth) by mixing with anybody and everybody as if they were equals. By assuming an egalitarian style, the charity influentials simultaneously burnished their souls, their name and their authority.

The Homes for the Aged project

On the instigation of the St. Vincent de Paul Society, the Care for the Aged Committee in 1976 agreed to form a joint body to be known as the Bantry Homes for the Aged. The St. Vincent de Paul had had £20 000 left to it in trust to begin the project, but they felt they needed help to get it going. Their co-operation on this venture grew out of previous joint action in the purchase and renovation of houses for the accommodation of needy cases. The link-up was made possible by the clergy's leadership of both organizations.

The Canon became Chairman of the new Committee, a significant move given his usual low profile. By assuming direct leadership of the project he signalled his and his Bishop's commitment to it. The clergy's control was further reinforced by the curate from the Care of the Aged becoming Vice-Chairman. The other positions were divided between the two organizations and included both influentials and activists as office-holders.

The original initiative had been the Canon's. After consultation with the Bishop, he had offered a plot of ground near his residence known as 'The

Canon's Field' as the site for the construction of eight houses which would whithin a year accommodate 32 senior citizens. Following the formation of the joint-committee, a remarkable mobilization took place. The venture received considerable publicity in the press; numerous local organizations (and not only church-led ones) rallied to the cause; a wide range of people contributed their voluntary labour. Local firms, the County Council and the relevant departments of state also contributed. Even more remarkably, Bantry emigrees in Cork, Dublin, England, America and Australia were written to for support and responded with donations and good wishes. Donations of all sizes poured in. A widow contributed a week from her pension. One local firm gave £1000. A further £1000 was raised from the sale of home-made bread and cakes. The newly formed Junior Chamber held a handicraft exhibition and sale and with the Shalom Singers staged a series of Variety Shows in the West Lodge Hotel, raising £700. Two large Social Evenings were held in Cork City and raised £1000 between them. All this was achieved before the building had even begun. The clergy was clearly pleased with the response, which embraced virtually every section of the community. Once construction had started, it was soon ahead of schedule.

A mobilization on this scale could not have been achieved by the development influentials for one of their projects. In fact, it was this capacity to mobilize the whole community which made the clergy so useful to the business influentials. Among the business leaders, the charity influentials preferred to achieve their objectives by helping the priests achieve theirs, whereas the development influentials wanted to run things their own way, i.e. they preferred the clergy to work with them. It was an important difference (see below), and the clergy knew it. When they wanted to make absolutely sure of the results of a project they took direct control themselves, and drew whatever support they could wherever they could — preferably with the business influentials but, if need be, without them.

The governmental sphere

Acting under the auspices of the Minister for Local Government and the County Council, the Town Commissioners were the formal governing authority within the urban limits. This situation resulted in a three-way division of authority between the County Councillors, County Council officials and the Town Commissioners, with the TDs and officials of the national government also often having a say. Such was the case for example, in an acrimonious dispute over the routing of traffic through the town. Before giving an account of this controversy, it is first necessary to indicate the Commissioners' standing as a town council.

152

The Bantry Town Commissioners came into being in 1896. It is not possible to trace their history here, but probably the most decisive point in their evolution as a council occurred in the 1940s when, under the re-organization of local government, they lost (among other things) the power to strike a rate (see also chapter 4). Up until that time the Commissioners were primarily concerned with rates, rents and lighting. In later years their main task was to ratify the estimate of expenditure prepared by the County Manager's staff and oversee the work of the County Council within the town limits. This entailed scrutinizing such things as the condition of the streets, footpaths, road signs, and the provision of such services as sewerage and the garbage collection. A part of each monthly meeting was taken up with these and related matters. Invariably, the Secretary was directed to write to the Assistant County Engineer (the senior County official resident in the town) requesting information or asking that something be done about a particular matter. When it was thought necessary, the Engineer was invited to attend a meeting. He would make a report and be questioned by the Commissioners on any matter of concern. This was also the case with the Assistant County Manager (the senior official in charge of West Cork), the head of the West Cork Development team and the West Cork politicians.

The Commissioners had no power to enforce their decisions if the Engineer chose to ignore them. Council employees in the Bantry area answered directly to him, and in consultation with his superiors, he both implemented Council policy and made the day to day decisions which helped set the context for future policy initiatives. He was responsible, for example, for advising whether planning permission should be granted or not.[1] The Commissioners had virtually no say in such matters.

The Engineer's attitude to the Commissioners was one of impatient condescension. As one influential commented, 'His say is bigger than he pretends himself'. His posture was intended to keep the public at a distance. He did not regret having influence and pull, he merely wanted to maximize his discretion in using it. He was frequently being asked to have work done here or there, to support a planning application, to give someone a job, to do a favour, and to answer complaints. To him, the Commissioners were just an additional bother. He heeded them when he had to and used them when it suited him (see below), but most of the time he ignored them.

Because of the Commissioners' legal authority as the town's elected representatives, other bodies were also forced to take some account of them. The Commissioners mostly used their authority to lobby higher organs of government. They had been especially vociferous for instance, in trying to get the town sewerage system improved and extended, but to no avail. With equal vehemence, they continuously lobbied the County Council, the

Industrial Development Authority and the relevant Minister to set up an industrial estate in the town, but again without success. Over the years they provided support for most major local projects, aiding the efforts of the various Development Associations and co-operating with Muintir na Tire in its many activities (see chapters 3, 5, 6 and below). They supported the Community Centre in its early years; they also looked with favour on the Homes for the Aged venture (see above).

As an organ of the state (albeit a lowly one), the Commissioners were in a unique position to have a decisive say in town affairs. They had the authority of being the only organization in town with a popular mandate: they were the people's choice, and they could speak in the town's name. The individual Commissioners tended to construe this as a personal obligation and as a stamp of legitimacy. In a sense they were right. There were very few among the influentials who would have been prepared to run the risk of presenting themselves at an election. Decrying the Commissioners was one way of minimizing the significance of that fact. The Commissioners were jealous of their limited authority and offended by the condescension of the influentials, and resented it when other bodies failed to consult with them. They were sceptical about their own significance, but they did not like to see the status of the Commissioners demeaned and they all took pride in holding office. The Chairmanship was prized, for example, although it only brought a modicum of prestige to the incumbent, and virtually no power.

The Commissioners were popularly regarded as at best unimportant and at worst a poor joke. The carnival atmosphere of the most recent election had something to do with this, but so did the strong working class flavour of the new council (see below); because they had little social prestige, the success of some of the candidates was widely taken to be a measure of the irrelevance of the Commissioners. The low regard in which they were held was both a comment upon the Commissioners as a body and upon the men who had been elected to it. But this judgement underestimated some of these men, and the influence the Commissioners commanded as a council. Although they actually wielded little power, and potentially commanded little more, they were not devoid of all authority.

The Commissioners preferred a consensual style of decision-making. This desire for consensus reflected the pervasive feeling in the town that everyone should 'pull together', that the benefit of one should be the benefit of all. To lobby outside interests and the authorities, the town had to present a unified and vocal front. Because they saw themselves as representing the town to the state and other parts of the country, the Commissioners tended to respond to events in a parochial manner. But this was not so much a narrow-minded provincial chauvinism, as a defensive parish patriotism. They were motivated by a dramatic awareness that if they did not look after their own interests no one else would. As one Commissioner put it, 'we've got to shout and never be done shouting while all those other blackguards are screeching away'. They were fearful that Bantry was going to get left behind and forgotten. The rest of the country thought that because of Gulf Oil, the town had got all that was due to it and it was the turn of others now. But like the rest of Bantry, the Commissioners were fearful that Gulf Oil would go 'without a thank you or kiss my arse', and Bantry would slip back to be as badly off as it ever was. The pressures associated with the drive for economic development thus reinforced the consensual tendencies affecting all local organizations.

Yet the preference for consensus was seldom allowed to interfere with party-political priorities. It was a feature of the history of Bantry Town Commissioners that every so often an election would produce a dramatic change in the stautus quo. The newly elected representatives then set the pace for the other Commissioners (even when they did not control the majority) and consensual considerations temporarily became relatively less important. In this tradition, the 1973 local government elections produced a dramatically different council from the outgoing one. As one person put it: 'the crowd that is in now is a different bunch altogether'. All the new men had been elected with one or another kind of reformist zeal fueling their intentions. The two main causes of this were Gulf's influence on the working ·class (see chapter 8) and disenchantment within the Gaelic Athletic Association over its treatment by the Commissioners (see below). The re-elected incumbents had neither a grievance to satisfy nor a desire to make the Commissioners take a more active part in town affairs; they saw the assertiveness of the new men as misplaced and wrong-headed. It was not that the remnants of this 'old guard' were any more cynical about what the Comissioners could do than were 'the new blood'. The difference was that the new men were not yet resigned to this situation and were impatient with it whereas the others seemed almost glad of it.

In party-political terms, the balance of power was now held by the Inde-dependents. They made the running, but were able to do so only because of an informal understanding with Fianna Fail. Three of the Independents had Labour leanings, but came from Fianna Fail family backgrounds.[2] At the county and national level Fine Gael and Labour held power as a coalition government, but in the Commissioners, Fine Gael remained in a permanent minority of two.

For a brief period in the mid-1970s, the Independents made the Commissioners a new force in town affairs. Their effectiveness then had a lot to do with the way they lobbied in alliance with other interest groups, and depended upon the fact that other state functionaries still felt the need to deal with them, and were even required by law to do so. An example of the way the Commissioners aligned with local interests against higher organs of state, including the Minister for Transport and Power, the County Council, and the West Cork Councillors and TDs, was a dispute over local control of the

Harbour Authority (see chapter 8). An example of the way they aligned with state officials against powerful local interests, including the West Cork County Councillors and TDs, was the controversy over the town traffic plan. The Commissioners were at their most assertive in the latter controversy, hence it is particularly revealing of the limits and ambiguities of their power.

The town traffic controversy

Periodically over many years the Commissioners had tried to regulate traffic in Wolfe Tone Square. A new attempt to do so erupted in controversy early in 1976. This followed an approach made to the Engineer and Garda Superintendent late in 1974 asking them to present proposals which could improve traffic flow and parking facilities and reduce the increasing risk of accident.

The townspeople first heard that something was being done to re-route through-traffic when a couple of the traders confronted the Engineer who was supervising the marking-out of a new thoroughfare for the Square. The traders' response was to quickly organize a protest meeting. The prime movers in this were a publican–farmer and an activist business woman (see chapter 6). They argued that their businesses were directly threatened by the new arrangements. They mobilized the traders to attend the protest meeting, and 'stacked' it with farmers and 'tanglers' (cattle dealers) from the country. As a result of the meeting, a 'Bantry Protection Association' was formed.

The West Cork politicians attended the meeting, gave their support to the traders, and stressed that they had been no better informed than anyone else. However, the politicians' names were not seconded when a committee was proposed, reflecting a common feeling that it was better to keep them off such committees if you wanted to achieve something. But, significantly, the local man was later co-opted by the Protection Association (see below).

The Engineer and his superior stressed that the arrangements were temporary and subject to further change. They also pointed out that the scheme currently in operation was not the one they planned to lay down because they had modified it as a result of representations from the traders. They also assured the farmers at the meeting that there would be no disruption to the livestock fairs, which were protected by law. They were in turn criticized for not consulting with the people of the town or with the County Councillors. A motion was passed to remove the 'bollards' (kerbstones) that had been laid down to mark out the new thoroughfare.

A rapid succession of meetings followed. In the meantime the Commissioners and Engineers had decided at one of their own meetings to convert the two-way traffic scheme (which had only been given a trial because of the traders' protests) to a one-way scheme for a trial period (which was the official's original intention).

In the early stages of the dispute the Commissioners did not look as though they would act in concert. One of them had attended the protest meeting and even became a Secretary of the Protection Association. A businessman himself, he shared the traders' views about the traffic plans. He was heavily criticized by a number of the other Commissioners for trying to ride two horses at once, and was eventually persuaded (as were the other waverers) to fall into line. A decisive factor here was the determination of the Garda Superintendent and the Engineers to proceed regardless of opposition. To strengthen their case, the officials argued that the choice was really only between one-way traffic with minor parking restrictions and two-way traffic with severe parking restrictions.

The Commissioners who were leading the fight took a strong stand in favour of the one-way scheme. The key figure was a young tug-boat shop-steward. He skilfully led the attack on the traders and the County Councillors, and pressured his fellow Commissioners into supporting his stand. He was forcefully backed up by the Chairman and two others, a fisherman and tug-boatman. That is, the battle was being led and fought by the working class representatives on the Commissioners.

The local County Councillor was co-opted onto the Protection Association to become the traders' spokesman. Yet he was responsible for an extraordinary compromise. At one of the Special Meetings of the Commissioners he was instrumental in committing a delegation from the Protection Association to a three-week trial of the one-way plan in spite of the fact that the traders were implacably opposed to such an idea. On the basis of this meeting, the Engineers the next day began to convert the Square for a trial of the one-way system (which turned it into a kind of giant roundabout with a large parking space in the middle). The delegation was not due to report back until that night, and so the traders did not have a clear idea of what was going on. Feelings were running high and a confrontation took place in the roadway. That night, as planned, the delegation reported back to the Protection Association. The County Councillor explained that their delegation had been 'heavied' into accepting the trial of the one-way system by the Garda Superintendent and the Engineers who had the support of the Commissioners. Neither of the other members of the delegation questioned this account of the proceedings of the night before, or suggested that the County Councillor had agreed to the compromise too quickly, even though the idea of the one-way scheme remained repugnant to them. It seemed as though things had happened too quickly for them to realize exactly what had taken place. Although he always maintained otherwise, the County Councillor gave the impression that his heart was not in the dispute, that he was not particularly concerned which way the issue was decided so long as it was resolved as quickly as possible. His agreement to a trial of the one-way scheme, has to be seen in this light. Because the traders remained unconvinced by the trial of the one-way scheme, he found it expedient to continue to espouse their cause, claiming his business had suffered as much as anyone's. In this context it is worth noting that the Development Association had some time earlier unanimously agreed on a proposal by him to issue a statement that the alterations were satisfactory.

When the traders found the Commissioners would neither agree to leaving the Square as it had been, nor to the two-way system, they decided to petition all the business people and canvass public opinion. They also arranged to lobby each of the Commissioners in person. At this stage they were still confident that they could get the one-way decision reversed. This was not to be. At a further Special Meeting, the Commissioners went beyond their plans for the Square and unanimously agreed to a one-way system for the top part of the town as well. In the meantime, the traders had organized a deputation to the County Council's Western Roads Advisory Committee. Its members agreed to meet with three of the traders and three of the Commissioners. The Commissioners were given very short notice of this proposal and were forced to call an additional Special Meeting on a Saturday to discuss it. They were incensed by the terms of the invitation and what they saw as interference by the County Councillors.

They refused to send a deputation and attended as a body. Led by the tugboat shop-steward, they contested the arguments of the traders and alleged that the County Councillors were trying to 'take over'. Their stand was underwritten by the Superintendent and the Engineers who claimed that they only had authority to deal with the Commissioners on this matter. The Superintendent took a consistently hard line against the traders. He doubted that they had actually lost business due to the new arrangements, and argued that in any case, his job was not to be concerned with the loss of a little bit of business when human life was at stake. He showed that he was impatient to get things finalized and was not going to be deterred by the traders whom, he said, represented only themselves. The Engineers adopted a more conciliatory tone, but were equally intransigent. They emphasized how they had met and consulted with the traders and pointed out the technical problems associated with the different schemes. They had given 'gentle advice', listened to suggestions, and made modifications; they had done all they could to meet the objections and all they were willing to do.

The County Councillors disputed the officials' interpretation of who had the authority. They argued that the Engineers were responsible to the County Council and by implication, the Western Roads Advisory Committee, not the Town Commissioners, who, in any case, got their money from the County Council. The Chairman of the meeting, the Fine Gael TD, quickly summed up its mood and realized that the Commissioners were not going to buckle under pressure. His most critical remarks were addressed to the County officials for their indifferent attitude to his Committee and their arrogant assertion of authority. But, like his colleague the Fianna Fail County Councillor, his manner suggested that he really only opposed the changes because the traders opposed them.

The traders reiterated their objections and continued to insist that they had not been properly consulted. The Biggs group's Manager made an ineffectual speech, but none of the other business influentials bought into the issue. The battle was mainly being fought by a garage proprietor whose petrol sales were going to be affected, and the publicans and shopkeepers on the Square and Quay who were concerned about the loss of tourist trade they would suffer. They wanted to give the motorists for Cork a 'choice' between going up-town or out the Glengariff Road. In fact, rather than having a choice when they entered town, motorists were usually confused, for it was quite ambiguous which was the way through the town. Once anything was done to the Square this ambiguity was destroyed. In the opinion of the traders, traffic arrangements worked best when they served as a tourist-trap. Their idea was to lure tourists into the town, not help them get through it. They hoped that by obstructing potential customers, some would stop, look and buy.[3]

Their most effective spokesperson was a woman from a wealthy farming and business family with a record of activism in both trade-related matters and charity organizations (see chapter 6). Her newsagency was directly affected by the new traffic arrangements. She claimed that the town rested on the shoulders of the business people. There would be no town at all without the business people. Is it fair, she asked, that a few people can take away a person's business when they have worked hard to build it up? The workers on the Commissioners responded sharply to these remarks. The tug-boat shop-steward replied that everyone made their living in the town, not only the business people. What kept a business in operation was its consumers, and most of the town's consumers were ordinary wage-earners. There were, he said, a lot more people walking the streets who made their living in the town than were 'inside in the business houses'. The traders, he said, were attempting to dictate to the town, to the ordinary working man and the consumer.

The meeting produced plenty of barbed exchanges and ended without resolving any of the differences. The Commissioners felt they had won a considerable victory. They were to meet a delegation of traders the following night; when they did they were in no mood to moderate their stand. The one-way system remained in force.

After six weeks of frenetic activity and rancour the traders accepted that all that was left to them was to lobby behind the scenes. The one-way 'trial' scheme, to all intents and purposes, became a permanent fixture, although no final decision was made by the time of the summer tourist season. In fact, twelve months eventually passed and still nothing happened. Meanwhile, the Bantry Protection Association had 'withered away'. A spontaneous, one-issue organization, its formation helped get the traders mobilized. After the first flurry of activity, its leaders returned to their businesses and let the County Councillors and the Chamber of Commerce represent their interests. Since he was a member of the Chamber, the Engineer was party to all its discussions of the issue. He usually remained silent, except to point out that it was still open to the Chamber to suggest alternatives. At their own meetings, the Commissioners constantly claimed that 'certain sections' were still trying to sabotage the permanent implementation of the new arrangements. In all probability, covert pressure was being applied at higher levels, for the authorities were particularly concerned about a legal difficulty associated with a Charter to the Square originally granted to Bantry House. Another tourist season approached, the one-way system was still in operation, and there seemed no imminent prospect of a final decision on the matter. The plans for the rest of the town centre were still in existence on paper, but were even further away from being put into effect.

This controversy raises a number of points for discussion. I have suggested that as managerial administrators of a capitalist state, senior civil servants functioned as auxiliary members of the bourgeoisie (see chapter 4). The Garda Superintendent and the Engineer buttressed this relation with business interests of their own. Culturally speaking, both men were also prominent members of the local bourgeoisie, being core members of the so-called 'jet-set' milieu (see chapter 6).

Given these characteristics, the dispute between the state officials and the traders can be seen as an institutionalized clash between the objectives of the governmental leaders of the local bourgeoisie and those of the business leaders, i.e. as a contradiction arising from the bureaucratized specialization of leadership functions within the locally dominant class. The state officials did not believe their plans were threatening the profits of the traders on the Square; they saw themselves as combating a group of shopkeepers who were notoriously short-sighted and provincial in outlook. In their view, the traders were so jealous of their profits that they were inclined to see a threat even when there was not one. They argued that something would have to be done to the town's traffic before Bantry could industrialize further, and that the one-way system would eventually have to be introduced as traffic levels increased. They saw themselves as servicing economic development, as agents of progress introducing the necessary and the inevitable, and their methods were adapted to promote these ends.

The officials were impatient of democratic processes. In the Superintendent's view, if you asked people what they wanted you would never get anything accepted. They had to be given something, and once it was seen to work they tended to accept it. This thinking lay behind the way the various schemes were put on trial. A scheme in operation created its own inevitability; it became the reality, the thing that had to be argued against. Acting on this assumption, the officials tried to 'fix' the result. They had tried to put down a one-way system in the beginning but the traders had prevented this. So they went ahead with a technically temporary plan and then declared it unsatisfactory. By this time there was no question of the Square being returned to its former state (that proposal was rejected out of hand), and, according to the officials (as 'experts'), the best alternative was the one-way system.

From this perspective, there was a pungent irony in the alliance between the Town Commissioners and the officials. The Commissioners saw themselves as the voice of 'the ordinary people of the town', but the officials' administrative procedures were designed to remove decision-making from effective democratic control. The Commissioners were aware of this problem, but there was little they could do about it. The traders were trying to dictate to them how the town should be run, that was the real issue as far as they were concerned.

It was the working class Commissioners who felt most strongly about the issue, and they saw it in class terms. According to the tug-boat shop-steward, 'the top dog's' power was not as important as it had been in the past, this type of issue was new to them and they did not know how to react. The traders identified the interests of the town with their interests, but he would not accept it. The dispute thus took on a class character even though it was not itself a class dispute.

The Town Commissioners were dominated by the working class because workers had found it easiest to capture control of local government where it was weakest and least effective. The business people had seen little need to hold onto power at this level, in fact it probably suited the bigger business houses to have a weak town council. But with assertive leadership and strong solidarity, the Commissioners were not as weak as they seemed. Given the pressures applied, it was a considerable achievement for them to maintain unanimity. That they were able to do so was related to the fact that, except where party-political considerations became involved, they habitually adopted a consensual style of decision-making. Consensual decision-making tends to have a conservative bias, but it need not always do so, hence the tug-boat shop-steward was able to use his fellow Commissioners' consensual inclinations to push through a proposal that a number of them were initially cautious about supporting. He made such an issue of the matter, took such a strong stand, that any opposition would have been particularly divisive.

The controversy saw the Commissioners at their most assertive. They seldom ever attempted to make or implement policy without sooner or later seeking the imprimatur of a higher authority, usually the County Manager or the Minister for Local Government. Otherwise they acted at the behest of the County officials and under their guidance. They had no sanctions which they could invoke, and if they had had any they would have been reluctant to use them. They had been notoriously cautious in exploring their powers, continuing to operate within the prevailing hegemony without ever seriously questioning it. Because of their statutory authority, they remained a force in town affairs, albeit a weak one when their power was compared to the substantive dominance of the business influentials. But for once the working class's representatives on the Commissioners refused to bow to the directives of business. The controversy showed that, led by one or two politically astute individuals, the Commissioners could take a stand and influence the direction of events — at least if they had powerful allies.

The development sphere

There was only one organization concerned with progress and prosperity for Bantry that was not dominated by the leading development influentials. That was the Fiesta Committee, and it proved to be none too successful.

The Fiesta

In the spring of 1975 Bantry hosted a festival designed to promote the tourist potential of the Bay; called a 'fiesta', it was dubbed a 'fiasco'. If it had been a success it would have done wonders for the reputations of its organizers; as a failure it encouraged ridicule.

The idea for the Fiesta originated with the owner of the Bantry Marine Company. He saw it as a way of combating the bad publicity of the spillages (see chapter 8). He was elected Chairman of a committee dominated by business people, but seeing itself as representative of the town. In fact, it mainly represented tourist interests. The Committee's treasurer was a guest-house proprietor, one member was the wife of a hotelier from neighbouring Ballylickey, another was concerned with farmhouse accommodation. Three ordinary influentials were active on the committee, the Business Woman (the Chairman's mother), the Restaurateur–Publican and the Draper. A former Chairman of the Town Commissioners and one other Commissioner were also involved. The Chairman, the Business Woman, Restaurateur–Publican and the former Chairman of the Commissioners all had an interest in the tourist trade.

To get things moving, the Committee called a public meeting, which got a big response. At this stage there were 'very few knockers'. A door to door collection was taken up among the business houses and other organizations were invited to join in. The Committee's Chairman had discussed the project with Gulf's management, and received an undertaking that the company would support the project. There were others, however, who had their reservations about the Committee's plans. Neither the organizers of the annual Regatta, nor the Gaelic Athletic Association, were happy about the Fiesta being held in August in competition with their activities. Because of this opposition, the Fiesta organizers changed their date to May, though this was not the best time of year from the tourist point of view.

The plans for the Fiesta were ambitious. It had originally been hoped that Gulf Oil would sponsor the hire of a hovercraft for the ten days, an extremely costly undertaking which the company decided against. Meanwhile an expensive, formal-dress banquet was held in Bantry House. Caterers were brought down from Cork City, and hot punch and mead was served, but only a limited number of tickets were sold. An RTE newsreader was brought down to help open the festivities, a tenor singer came from Wales, and a Garda band from Dublin gave a free concert in the Square. Costs mounted, the response was not what was expected, and twelve months later there were still large outstanding debts.

There was undoubtedly strong local support for the idea of a publicity program to counter the bad image given to Bantry Bay by the spillages. But as one of the participants (who thought they had made 'a great effort in a slack period') said, they 'ran for things too high . . . miles too high for the man in the street'. Popular doubts about the Committee were also an important factor. One man, who was active for a while, thought that people felt they were 'being manipulated'. 'What's he getting out of it?' they asked of different ones on the Committee. 'He's not in it for the good of his health — or our health.' One of the influentials, who could easily have been linked in the popular mind with the Fiesta, categorically stated that he had nothing to do with it, didn't know anything about it and didn't want to know. Another businessman who *was* associated with it, sardonically commented that the 'Fiesta people were regarded as mini-plutocrats — they couldn't be anything more than mini in the Bantry context'. In sum, the consensus of opinion was that the organizers had too many grand ideas, foolishly going for the big splash rather than the small profit.

The organizers in turn blamed the public for not supporting them. They were willing enough to admit they had made mistakes, but not to admit that these mistakes had caused the failure. Undeterred, they wanted to organize another fiesta, but they were not even able to get former committee members to attend meetings. It was suggested that a notice should be placed in the paper saying there would be no festival this year because of lack of public support. However, this was not done.

The Committee still had the problem of its debts. To help pay these, it was counting on the money Gulf Oil had promised to donate to the area as compensation for the damage done to the tourist industry by the spillages. The multinational had donated £15 000 to be divided between various local organizations concerned with tourism. The company stipulated that the division of the money be handled by Ivernia, the Cork-Kerry Tourist body. It had been agreed that Ivernia itself would receive £1000, with £7000 going to Bantry and £7000 to Glengarriff. Of the £7000 going to Bantry, £1000 was said to have been already pledged by Gulf to the 'Bantry Tourist Association'.

Since there was no 'Bantry Tourist Association' as such, the Fiesta Committee drafted a letter inviting business people to come to a meeting to form one. The letters were delivered by hand. There was immediate criticism of these methods, which were seen as a deliberate attempt by the Fiesta Committee to get hold of the Gulf Oil money to pay off its debts. The Fiesta organizers replied that the money was, in fact, intended for them. They maintained that they were the ones who had originally approached Gulf Oil for the money, and maintained that the company had at that time earmarked £1000 for the Fiesta.

The Ivernia Chairman described it as 'an invidious task' trying to divide the money between the various local organizations seeking a share. One member of the Fiesta Committee later declared that 'Solomon in all his wisdom couldn't have done it'.[4] Yet the most salient feature of the public meeting called to announce the division of the Gulf money was the way it was used to attack the Fiesta Committee. It was established that Gulf Oil had, in fact, given the Fiesta people an undertaking, but there was still some scepticism about the claim that the organizers had always realized there would be a deficit and had calculated for one in the vicinity of £1000. One speaker from the floor of the meeting asked if the Bantry Tourist Association and the Fiesta Committee was 'an umbrella with two handles'. Such remarks were intended to entertain the meeting and embarrass the Fiesta Committee's Chairman.

Organizers of the Fiesta were not particularly popular before their attempted extravaganza, but they were even less popular afterwards. It should be emphasized that none of the leading development influentials was involved in this project. In fact, once they saw where it was heading, they stayed well clear of it. At the time this probably suited the organizers, who wanted to run things their own way and reap the credit. Only when it came to dividing up the Gulf Oil money did one of the key influentials get implicated. As a member of the Ivernia board, the County Councillor had an important say in the decisions that were made about which organizations should benefit. It is also worth noting that once the Fiesta became controversial, Gulf Oil kept as far away from the dispute as it could. The scramble for the money it had donated further tarnished the publicity value it hoped to get from its 'voluntary compensation' payment.

The Community Centre

Bantry's development organizations all grew out of Muintir na Tire (see chapters 3, 5 and 6). It got the inner harbour dredged, a tourist office established, encouraged a farm-guesthouse scheme, began a Beach project to create a sandy strand that would attract tourists, and lobbied hard to get more industry for Bantry. By contrast, the Town Commissioners of the time were 'a dead duck' according to the priest who became Muintir's driving force:

> The only power we had that they hadn't was we were prepared to stick our necks out and keep pressuring those with the power to give, and [we were able] to convince people.

In spite of its record, Muintir fell apart after its leader was transferred in 1970. The cause of the break-up was a dispute about the organization's future. National policy encouraged the formation of Community Councils which would replace the existing guilds. The new curate, who was immediately invited to become Chairman of the Bantry guild, wanted to implement this policy. The question at issue was whether the Community Council should be formed under the auspices of the existing body, or whether an entirely new organization should be set up. In the new curate's opinion, the popular view in the town was that Muintir was run by a clique, and other organizations were not prepared to be dominated by it. He called a public meeting to discuss the matter.

A lot was riding on the outcome of this meeting. A project to establish a Community Centre had been initiated by Muintir na Tire five years before. After protracted negotiations with the County Manager, the old railway station which had recently been vacated by King's Shoes (see chapter 3) was purchased for the establishment of such a Centre. Gulf Oil had promised money for the project provided it had community-wide support and did not represent a sectional interest. This stipulation was one of the reasons why the curate was concerned to have a truly representative Community Council run the Centre. He was also sensitive to the criticisms levelled at the church because of its control of another public amenity, the Boys' Club (see below). If Muintir ran the new Centre, then the church would again be criticized for its undemocratic methods. In any case, the public meeting howled down the suggestion that the Community Centre should be run under the auspices of Muintir na Tire.

It was decided that the Centre would be run by a Council composed of representatives from 11 town areas and every local organization, its Trustees being the Canon, the protestant Rector and the Chairman of the Town Commissioners. At the time morale was high. For example, one pamphlet exclaimed:

> IT COULDN'T HAPPEN? That ALL organizations, ALL sections, ALL interests of this town and district take down the old barricades and get together in a spirit of friendly co-operation for the good of all, young and old . . . IT'S HAPPENING! BANTRY COMMUNITY CENTRE — the first result of just that kind of co-operation. It could not exist without it. Its future depends on it . . .

Gulf Oil subsequently donated £5000 in 'two moieties' towards the Centre, which included a function room and meeting rooms, a children's playground and tennis and basketball courts. It also staged a reception and got press publicity for what it had done. At least one of the leading figures in the Centre later wondered whether he had been used by Gulf Oil. But shrewd as it was, the multinational was not able to gain permanent advantage from the Centre. In spite of the early optimism, popular support for the Council had been variable. The business houses were particularly unco-operative, responding to a fund-raising drive with a 'see how you go and if you get stuck' attitude.

The Muintir influentials bitterly resented the curate's handling of the issue. In their view, by wrong-headedly trying to democratize a successful organization, all he had done was sabotage it. They predicted the Community Council idea would be a flop, and by gradually withdrawing their support from it, they helped turn their criticisms into self-fulfilling prophecies. The Centre came to be run by a committee which had neither the organizational resources nor the funds to improve the premises and make the Centre work as it was intended. The facilities were occasionally used for meetings and for card games and other recreational activities, but the better equipped rooms in the Boys' Club were preferred by most organizations. Meanwhile, the development influentials who had previously been active in Muintir organized themselves into a Development Association.

The Development Association

Around the time of the Community Centre controversy, the development influentials were trying to get Bantry's first Chamber of Commerce off the ground, but without a great deal of success (see below). By 1973, they had a new rationale for getting organized . The stringent opposition by the foreign settlers to the proposal for an oil refinery in the Bantry area (see chapter 8) had to be countered, and industry encouraged to come to Bantry. It was also felt that the Bay would not be developed unless a Harbour Authority was established and in 1974 the Association prepared a submission to this effect which was presented to the government.[5]

The Association was run by an 'ad hoc committee' for some time before a public meeting was called to elect another. At this meeting a resume of what had been achieved to date was given and it was stressed that the existing committee wanted to make the Association representative of all sections of the community, notably professional, commercial and trade union interests. This way of proceeding was typical of a core group who wished to give their actions a democratic gloss and get public support. By demonstrating their initiative in getting the organization going, by being able to point to work already successfully completed, and by occupying the executive positions at the election of new office-holders, the key figures were able to make sure they would be elected and retain control of the organization. New members of the committee could then be incorporated into the core group or, if necessary, eased out. These tactics were not necessarily worked out in a self-conscious manner, but the key figures were quite aware of what they were doing. They simply took it for granted that this was the way to get things done.

The leading figure in the Development Association was its Chairman, the Motor Dealer, but most of the development influentials were either active in the Association or linked themselves to it at one time or another. A number of other activists also participated. These included businessmen, the Ex-MCC/Trade Union official, and at least three Town Commissioners, among them the Chairman. By and large, though, these people remained peripheral figures. One of the Commissioners, a working class activist who was not easily deterred from having his say, went along to a couple of meetings, but said it wasn't a case of standing up and making a point from the floor. 'It was "What do you think [he named a business activist]? You had a point, so-and-so".'

The Association flourished for a couple of years, then became less active as the prospect of imminent industrial development receded. When the Chamber of Commerce was revitalized in 1976 a number of those who were members of both bodies assumed that the Development Association would dissolve itself. As Chairman, the Motor Dealer wanted to keep it going, but once the Chamber proved itself viable, the Development Association never met again. Within the Chamber, the Motor Dealer was neither on the executive nor particularly influential. He had always divided his energies between Bantry and Skibbereen (where he had his business) and he now became less involved in affairs in Bantry. In fact, his only attempt to recoup his ground was a faint-hearted bid to become one of the Chamber's nominees to the Harbour Authority (see below and chapter 8).

The original Chamber of Commerce

The possibility of forming a Chamber of Commerce in Bantry was first investigated by a Muintir na Tire committee. Once it was agreed to go ahead with the project, a caretaker committee was appointed to draw up the articles of association and draft a 'monograph' on the town for presentation to prospective industrialists. A key figure in getting the Chamber started was the (not yet) Retired Draper, but except for the Company Secretary, it was younger men who ran the caretaker committee. The key figures were the Dentist, the Rowa Manager, the young Draper and the County Councillor (who had been co-opted). The committee met throughout 1968, drafting a constitution for the new Chamber. Eventually it handed over to the Chamber's first executive. In early 1959 a successful public meeting was addressed

167

by a member of the Cork Chamber. The scene was now set for the holding of the first annual general meeting (AGM). In the light of subsequent events it is worth noting here that the question was raised that the Chamber had been got going by a group working behind closed doors before any public meeting had been held. This issue was apparently then discussed. Another complaint was made after the public meeting and AGM that decisions were being made outside Chamber meetings. However, the matter was let drop when specific instances were asked for.

The young Chamber prepared its booklet promoting the town, surveyed all the business houses, combated bad publicity in the press, and investigated the feasibility of a town festival. Meetings were held regularly but by the 1970 AGM it was noted with disappointment that the attendance was far from satisfactory. Although there were only 18 paid-up members, an election of officers was held. Meetings ceased a short time after and the 1971 AGM had to be adjourned. A new executive was elected at the adjourned AGM but no more meetings were held until December 1975. The minutes were not signed until March 1976.

The Chamber went into hibernation partly because of a lack of substantive projects and partly because of conflict between the key figures. In spite of the quasi-consensual rotation of executive positions,[6] the Chamber's leading figures were deeply divided on one issue: what its attitude to Gulf Oil should be (see also chapter 8). The Dentist was extremely assertive in his criticisms of the multinational. He wanted the Chamber to agitate for the establishment of a Harbour Authority. Few in the Chamber wholeheartedly shared his convictions; in any case, they were not likely to act on whatever criticisms they did have. Some were even hostile to the Dentist's stance. The Biggs group's Company Secretary not only did not share the Dentist's attitude to Gulf Oil, he was implacably opposed to the idea of a Harbour Authority. It was during his Presidency that the Chamber ceased to meet regularly. He thought it should be 'a talking shop' not the kind of pressure group the Dentist wanted it to become. It was because of these divisions that the Development Association, not the Chamber, was the organization championing the development cause in the early 1970s. Significantly, one of the major platforms of the Association was the demand for a Harbour Authority.

The revival of the Chamber of Commerce

Gulf Oil was not only responsible for the Chamber going into hibernation, it was also the cause of its revival, and again the issue was the Harbour Authority. The Minister for Transport and Power had announced that the Bantry Chamber of Commerce would have the right to elect two members to the board of the Authority that his government had agreed to establish following the outcry over the Gulf Oil spillages of late 1974 and early 1975 (see chapter 8). Significantly, the Chairman of Gulf Oil found it sufficiently interesting to attend the AGM of the reconvened Chamber.

The manner of the Chamber's revival was, to say the least, unconventional. The then President of the Chamber, the young Draper, sent out notices for an AGM without notifying the executive. This was done at the instigation of the Solicitor, who had never been a member of the Chamber and had no intention of becoming one. The executive was extremely critical of both men's behaviour. At a meeting held immediately prior to the advertised AGM, it was pointed out that a proper AGM could not be held since the executive had not been correctly consulted and because notices had been sent to non-members. All the meeting could do was agree to revive the Chamber and arrange to convene a properly constituted AGM. In due course this was done and the Dentist and the Rowa Manager were once again elected President and Secretary. The partnership which had got the first Chamber going was once again in command.

The common view in the town even within the Chamber, was that 'When the Chamber has nothing to do it will fade away. It was only formed to get two men on the Harbour Authority'. One leading influential of the past declared that it had already 'flopped — a great disappointment to me'. 'They can't get the message to the ordinary labourer, the shopkeeper or the house-wife'. Another was less certain: 'We're waiting to see,' he said. '[They] may be a virile young group wanting to do something. But what can they do?'

According to its critics the Chamber's deficiencies had been highlighted by the establishment of a Junior Chamber in 1975 by a young bank official. It was an immediate success, undertaking fund raising activities such as craft exhibitions, concerts and ventures which included putting up a Christmas tree in the Square. The organization drew its support from the banks, other young professionally-oriented clerical staff, teachers, and young business people (mainly prospective heirs). Most were under 30 and slightly more females than males were involved, and apart from the young business people, the majority were temporary residents. Some people argued it had done more for the town in its time than the Chamber in all its time, and hence was an equally important organization. However, its durability was still to be tested and it had no financial or political clout.

To show that the Chamber was not just revived to get two of its members elected to the Harbour Authority, the executive was keen to organize new projects. Hence in late 1976 and early 1977 it staged three major seminars concerned with Mariculture, Social Development and Tourism. The Mari-culture seminar was the one that interested the organizers most. It could potentially lead to the development of fish-farming as a new industry for Bantry. The future of the Chamber was riding on this seminar, and the executive was anxious that it be a success. It was made one by the organi-zational efforts of the Dentist and the Rowa Manager and the sponsorship of the Solicitor. The whole West Cork seaboard was circularized by poster. Parish priests were asked to read notices from the pulpit, and personal invitations were issued to any businessman, politician or civil servant who was likely to be interested or influential. The Solicitor also saw to it that the seminars were advertised extensively in the local, county and national media. Fishermen, farmers and businessmen were all welcomed:

> An effort is to be made to encourage fishermen, businessmen and farmers on the seacoast to think again, and think freshly about new ways of getting money and jobs from the sea on our door steps. (*Star*: 9.10.76)

The motto for the Economic and Social Development seminar was 'Our People and Our Potential'. One of the advertisements for this seminar reflects the thinking behind all three. Under the title of 'West Cork How Do We Stand?' it read in part:

> we are a small rural community becoming more and more influenced, for better or for worse, by the powerful emergence of the new European Community, by world political and financial crises and by difficult times nearer home.
> How are we doing? Are we doing enough? Can we say we are doing our best for own people, by creating conditions where our people can work and live in proper social and economic conditions? Should we be doing more to create jobs for new generations? If we cannot provide them with jobs are we training them the right way to get jobs available elsewhere?
> How do others see us? Have we a good community spirit or are we a community of hurlers on the ditch? (*Star*: 27.11.76)

Because he met the cost of all the advertising (which was worth around £1500), the Solicitor was given prominent billing, he had a place on the official podium, his name headed the list of sponsors, he gave the summing-up address and entertained and lobbied the luminaries in attendance. Consequently, both the public and the press assumed he was a member of the Chamber or a co-organizer with it of the seminars. And yet up until a week or so before the first seminar, the Chamber's executive was not sure whether he would give them his full support.

An estimated 300 people attended the Mariculture seminar. The expert opinion was that Bantry Bay seemed suitable for a mariculture project; the difficulties which stood in its way were not technical ones. This put the Chamber members in a buoyant and optimistic mood, but a latent ideological conflict now surfaced. This conflict centred on whether the project should be run on private enterprise lines or as a co-operative. The Chamber was going to provide a co-ordinating committee to get viable production started, but it would not itself become involved in any subsequent commercial activity. To whom, then, did it intend handing over the project?

This was a potentially explosive issue. The local fishermen had already challenged Gulf Oil's encroachment upon their fishing grounds and incursions into their field of production by 'outside' fishermen (see below). This was one of the reasons they refused to participate in the Mariculture seminar.

When the Dentist spoke to the fishermen's representative about participating, he replied angrily, 'I told you before, we're not going to sit down inside with those fellows [i.e. the outsiders from other West Cork ports]. They've stolen our livelihood for the past two years. What have we got to talk about? What good is fish-farming or anything else to us? This was not the only reason they had for being wary of the mariculture project. They saw the Chamber as an exclusive body looking after the interests of business. Its involvement in mariculture was liable to be at the expense of the traditional fishermen. In fact, they had already seen that other interested groups had been vigorously encouraged to participate in the mariculture project, while little or no effort had been made to overcome their own objections and allay their particular fears. And they knew that if they were to be given a chance to participate it would only be in a decidedly qualified way. The accuracy of this perception is illustrated by the Chamber executive's attempt to simultaneously restrict the number of invitations issued for its cocktail reception preceding the seminar while inviting other guests who were not members of the Chamber. A woman whose husband was a fishing agent and herself a shrewd observer of the local scene, maintained that the cocktail party was held before and not after the seminar to ensure that no fishermen would get to go. It was, she said, a function 'for some few and their friends'. In her view the seminar was purely for the self-aggrandizement of the organizers. The fishermen remained firmly convinced that the 'outsiders' and the business people would control and benefit from any fish-farming project and this would be to their detriment. A few of them might get jobs, but the rest would lose out. Articulated as a struggle between 'the big shots' and 'the ordinary fishermen', they saw the issue in class terms.

So did the Chamber's executive and the Solicitor. They thought the benefits of any venture should accrue to them as businessmen, the function of the Chamber being to promote business in the town and advantage its members. They also thought of themselves as natural leaders, maintaining that the only way the project would be successful would be if it was run by businessmen as a private enterprise. The Dentist was the only dissenter, being an advocate of a co-operative venture. His colleagues thought he was motivated by mis-placed idealism, but recognized that only with his leadership did they stand any chance of escaping the wrath of the fishermen. He prepared a memo-randum which stated that the aim was to establish a mariculture industry which would be 'owned and operated by the people of the area'. Pilot projects were

> to be undertaken only where participation is open to all members of a local community. The committee will ensure this by convening, in co-operation with local organizations or individuals, previously announced public meetings, in the various centres, to elect local committees.

The Dentist remarked that someone implied he should be buying a ticket to Red China. But what he was concerned about was keeping the money local rather than just having local fellows employed for a little money while the bulk of it went into the hands of industrialists from away. Most of the executive, however, thought that money would come to the area by virtue of investment providing employment. The Solicitor insisted that the local fishermen would never do anything until some businessman or outsider came and showed them it could be done — 'how to do it by doing it'. The Restaurateur–Publican argued that the initiative would always come from individuals and it was the individuals who showed the initiative who should be rewarded. He was against public meetings where a lot of talking would be done and very little accomplished. He too had a low opinion of the fishermen and what they could achieve; they were, in his view, only a divisive and negative force. In this connection, it is significant that his activities as a diver had already got the fishermen offside. They claimed he was clearing out the sea-urchins rather than farming them and was not training other young men to learn diving. According to this latter argument he should 'spread it around a little bit' — a common complaint against local capitalists, particularly blow-ins who made money for themselves but did not provide jobs.

To the Chamber executive, getting involved with the fishermen meant getting involved with other disputes, i.e. the dispute with the 'outside' fishermen (see below). They believed the fishermen had no rights over and beyond anyone else, but that was what they would claim if the project went ahead. The Solicitor summed it up when he said that the days of the small traditional fisherman were finished and the sooner they woke up to it the better. The Chamber President persisted in his view, pointing out that the local fishermen had no capital and would need help. However, he knew that the Solicitor and the Restaurateur–Publican intended branching out on their own once the pilot project proved the security of the investment.

The organization of the seminars showed that the real work of the Chamber was done by its executive. It made the decisions, implemented Chamber policy and prepared new initiatives. This is not to say that all the key decisions were made at meetings of the executive, often they were not. People who were not on the executive, but were influential useful or sympathetic, were often party to deliberations that strictly speaking were no concern of theirs. The Solicitor was not even a Chamber member, but took part in several of its executive's meetings. In fact, a number of key decisions taken by the executive grew out of meetings in his house to which a select few were invited. The executive did not like the situation it was in, but while the Solicitor was prepared to use the Chamber for his ends, it was prepared to use him for its ends. The methods the Solicitor used to get the Chamber revived foreshadowed his later behaviour. Typically, he combined public self-promotion with behind-the-scenes manipulation of issues and personalities, intervening in the business of the Chamber in an irregular and unpredictable manner, using his wealth to bring him power. Following the seminars he invited a few key figures to his house to discuss the mariculture project, but not all the members of the Chamber's sub-committee were invited. The following night there was a sub-committee meeting which started late because everyone was waiting for the Solicitor. He was downstairs but had not come up, so someone went down to get him. There was then discussion of an outlay of £15 000 for a period of three years and he declared that there was no problem, he would cover that amount. Unilateral action by him more than once put the executive in an awkward position. For instance, he wrote a personal letter of thanks to some, but not all, of the speakers at the Mariculture seminar. He also travelled to Brussels and acted in the name of the Chamber without its authority. He then made an 'eyes only' report to the Chamber President, the Dentist, who ignored this and reported back to the executive. 'What is the man's motive?' one Chamber member asked. 'It is resented, this business of buying influence or prestige, power or whatever'. 'What is his game? It is resented. [The Dentist] resents it, [these attempts] to influence or dominate events'. By contrast, the Dentist was himself widely respected and trusted both in and outside the Chamber as a public spirited organizer. The high esteem in which he was held was especially significant given the fact that he diverged ideologically from his business colleagues.

Recreational ventures

Few sporting and recreational groups were class-specific in their social composition. In order to remain viable in such a small town, special-interest groups had to draw recruits from wherever they could. The Bantry Musical Society and the Gurtycloona Theatre, for example, both tried to embrace a broad cross-section of the community. Football, hurling, handball and basketball may have been played mainly by working class youth, and tennis, badminton, sailing, rowing, shooting and angling by 'middle class' youth, but these were fluid distinctions. Since golf was nowadays played by all and sundry, bridge was the only leisure activity which unequivocably retained its reputation for elitism. The leadership of recreational and sporting bodies tended to reflect the social composition of the membership. Most were fairly loose groupings of people who had got together to arrange matches and competitions, etc. Three major bodies were more organized than this, the Boys' Club, the Golf Club and the Gaelic Athletic Association (GAA). Coincidentally, these bodies grew out of, and in that sense represented, the influence in town affairs of, respectively, religion, business and nationalist politics.

Owned by the Parish, the Club was vested in the Parish Priest. It had a committee of six, one of the curates being its Chairman. For its time it was, if not a charity venture, certainly a youth welfare project. As its name implies, it was originally designed to cater for the male youth of the town, but over the years this changed. 'If built today, it would be called the Youth Centre', remarked its Chairman. But really it was more a general entertainment centre, in fact a surrogate town hall. Built in 1950 with voluntary labour, it was the town's most impressive monument to the clergy's leadership efforts. The curate who was responsible for its construction was still renowned for toiling for long hours 'with his bare hands' beside the other workmen. The voluntary workers remained proud of their efforts, but a number were critical of the way the Club had been run since.

The basic criticism was that a building put up by voluntary labour was not being run democratically, but was controlled by the clergy and its appointees, and run as a closed shop, 'like a secret society', a money-making venture for the church. These sentiments became entangled with other emotions when particular decisions caused controversy, e.g. when youths whose fathers had worked on the Club were banned from the premises because of their behaviour. Other bannings were resented because they reflected the influence of conservative, church thinking on social issues. These had included bans on women wearing slacks, men with long hair and rock and roll. Said one former committee member, 'We thought they were mad . . . We didn't know what we were banning'. Present and past members of the committee admitted that some of their decisions now looked quaint or narrow-minded. They also acknowledged that they were not elected democratically, but co-opted. They defended this by saying that all members of the committee were proven workers, and that everyone had to agree that the Club was run efficiently to a high standard. Nevertheless, in their view, someone with 'a crib' against the parish priest would be likely to cite the Club as an example of the clergy's dictatorial method of doing things. In a sense, then, criticism was less directed against the committee — which in the period under review was comprised of men who were personally quite popular — than against the church.

The administration of the Club reflected the clergy's ability to control key local organizations in spite of the erosion of its influence by pervasive cultural changes affecting the whole of Irish society. In this case, it had found it best to rely upon a group of men who had wide contacts amongst the youth of the town and were dedicated organizers, men with modest aspirations from working class and small farming backgrounds. For the task they had to perform, personal popularity was more important than personal power.

Golf was traditionally the main sporting activity of the Bantry elite and their associates. Their club was at Glengarriff, a good small course, but unplayable in winter and without a clubhouse. It is not exactly clear what the precise motivations were for starting another club, particularly since relations between the new and old one remained cordial. Undoubtedly the optimism of the times was a factor: Gulf Oil had just opened its terminal and tourism was booming.

In early 1969 a circular which declared that it was 'not addressed to any section or persons' but to 'all interested in Bantry, in golf, in tourism', was sent to potential subscribers asking them to support a proposal to build a new golf course nearer Bantry. The circular resulted from a meeting in late 1968, which had been called by the instigators of the project — the Solicitor, the Biggs group's Manager, the Vocational School Principal's predecessor, an Engineer with the P & T, and a clerk in the Post Office.

The opportunity for building a new course had arisen when an English millionaire who had retired to Bantry in the early 1950s decided to sell his home, Donemark House (subsequently purchased by the Biggs group's Manager) and the land accompanying it. He offered the project's sponsors 57 acres for the same price as he had paid 15 years before. The land was in a beautiful setting between the Glengariff Road and the sea, and had a private beach. A golf architect surveyed the site and thought it would make an excellent course of high scenic quality. The cost of development, including £12 000 for land purchase, was predicted to be about £30 000.

Approaches were made to Ivernia, the Cork-Kerry Tourist Board and to Bord Failte, the Tourist Board, for aid. However, a government grant could not be obtained for one individual sport. To get around this problem, the project's organizers formed a company, Bantry Park Ltd. The idea behind this move was that the organizers had now gone beyond their original concept, and planned to build not merely a golf course but a sporting complex. The virtue of this scheme was not just that it would qualify for a sizeable grant, but that it would appeal to a wider cross-section of the community.

Impatient with the tardiness of the government funding agencies, the sponsors decided not to wait for their decision, resolving that the project should 'go ahead anyhow: that the land should be bought'. The Solicitor, the Biggs group's Manager and the School Principal's predecessor, were authorized to find ways and means of raising the purchase price of the land. Hence the circular. In it the sponsors expressed confidence that

> Bantry and district has private individuals, business concerns and friends of sport who are prepared to finance the land purchase. We are looking for contributions of £100 and upwards, and in return each contributor will be a member of the Club for 10 years without further contribution and additionally will have his or her

name inscribed on a plaque in the Clubhouse listing the founder members of the Club.

Confidence there may have been, but it was fringed with doubt. The sponsors were concerned that the request for financial aid would be seen as an imposition, and emphasized that donors would be providing 'Bantry with a major sporting centre', that the course would be 'a very scenic one, and will be highly thought of . . . at home and abroad', and that further developments would be forthcoming: 'a first class swimming pool is envisaged by the sponsors'.

The fears about how the circular would be received were justified. There were still recriminations about it eight years later. It confirmed many people's suspicions that the real intention of the sponsors was to set up 'a rich man's club', a Country Club for the few. Sponsors who had contributed £100 or more were written to personally and now asked to choose to take out an option on debenture stock in Bantry Park Ltd, to opt for ten years free Club membership, or to decide that their donations conferred no special privileges. As it turned out, the majority chose the last alternative.

A wide variety of fund-raising activities was undertaken. A festival was staged in the early 1970s featuring, at the instigation of the Solicitor, a national entertaining star; races and a car rally were were staged; and each year a bazaar was held in the Boys' Club. People were approached personally for donations, as were firms — including Gulf Oil, which gave £500.

In spite of these efforts, Bantry Park Ltd remained over £14 000 in debt. Moreover, since the sporting complex never materialized, the exact relation of the Bantry Golf Club to Bantry Park Ltd was not clearly specified. A dispute developed within the Club about what should be done concerning the debt. The Golf Club had opened its own working account with the bank but a strong body of feeling existed among some that the debt should be paid off. One of the main reasons for this was public opinion. As one man put it, he wanted to make sure 'that people can't say we codded them to get the Golf Club'.

There were other dealings which some people were not entirely happy about either. Land adjacent to the course had become available for sale. A large Bantry land holder and businessman had offered to loan the Golf Club money to purchase it. Instead of interest, he asked for the grazing of it. The critics thought that if the Club had negotiated a bank loan and had the grazing for itself, it would have been much better off.

To its critics the Golf Club project represented an attempt by a few key business influentials to establish a leisure centre for the town's elite. Those involved denied this charge, claiming that they wanted 'to break down' this kind of thing. Whatever their intentions, the financial requirements of the project and the size of the town meant that exclusiveness was not viable. As one man put it, they 'got in the brains and the brawn' and 'squeezed local organizations for money' so as 'to make the thing a success'. They made membership accessible to everybody, they opened a Clubhouse bar, and held social occasions. The result was that financial necessity had prevented an exclusive social haven from becoming anything more than 'a Municipal Golf Club' where, as one of the influentials put it, you could find an ordinary sort of person 'asserting superiority over people who normally [would] be their social superior'. In spite of such nuisances, the status-conscious still found ways to mark themselves off. For instance, those who could afford it retained joint-membership of the Bantry and Glengarriff Clubs.

Because 'anyone' could join, it was often claimed that there was no snobbery in the Golf Club. Certainly anyone could join, and there were working class people on the Club's committee, but the committee was itself effectively controlled by a few key figures who had their own way of doing things: 'decisions are made and then other decisions are made later', commented one influential. The Biggs group's Manager remained important in the Club but the key man was the Club's President, the Solicitor. He performed like a true impresario. He used his wealth to make sure he had the final say, and to enhance the Club's reputation by inviting international golfers to special exhibition matches. The Golf Club project was one of the most notably successful undertaken in Bantry for many years. Its success demonstrates well the naked power of money.

The GAA and Wolfe Tone Park

The Gaelic Athletic Association (GAA) was historically Bantry's most important sporting club, the football competition being the main event on its sporting calendar. The whole town rallied behind the 'Blues', especially when they were playing an old rival. Spirits ran high, the beer and porter flowed freely, and the post mortems went on for weeks.

The Bantry Club was run by a mixture of workers and businessmen. Neither group really dominated the organization, but it was, if not working class in character, decidedly populist in style due to its nationalist origins. For the same reasons, Fianna Fail was strongly represented within the Club. The County Councillor was an active and enthusiastic member and his hotel was the GAA watering-hole. A number of the other key figures also had Fianna Fail sympathies.

The Club's problem was not its ability to win matches, but its lack of a usable home ground. Wolfe Tone Park, the town's oval had been built by one of the early Development Associations on land that was also used to provide sites for the Rowa and Flately factories (see chapter 3). It was a major undertaking carried out under the direction of the town's Engineer of the time, and the Rate Collector, an influential who was active in Fianna Fail, the Development Association, and many other projects. But they made a calamitous mistake by removing the topsoil from the football pitch, turning it into a quagmire. Just as it seemed within their grasp, the members of the GAA were deprived of their much-needed home ground.

The Club came to resent its predicament. It lobbied the Town Commissioners (in whom the ground was vested) and the County Council (who funded and advised the Commissioners) to do something to make the pitch playable. Eventually the Club applied to the Commissioners to grant it a long lease so it could rectify the situation itself. The answer was that only a one-year lease could be granted. With the backing of its Central Board, the Club then tried to buy the ground. They were again rebuffed, being told that the ground could not be sold; it had been vested in the Commissioners as a town park for the use of all groups, not just the GAA. The Club's response was that it was the only real user of the oval, for it had been designed as a football pitch and it was the only football club in town.

Because of this stalemate, the GAA got permission to use an open field for its pitch and Wolfe Tone Park was left virtually unused. The Club then tried to buy the field it was using, but a businessman bid against them, 'puffing the price' above the maximum the Club was prepared to pay. He subsequently offered it to the Club at the same price he paid, but the offer was refused as a matter of principle. Subsequently, when prices had inflated further, the field was again offered to the Club by a new owner, but the members again felt the price was beyond their reach.

The GAA felt it had been arbitrarily denied the use of an otherwise wasted amenity. It became convinced that the legal difficulties could be overcome if there was a will to do so on the part of the Town Commissioners. The Club therefore decided to run its own candidates at the next election. It was successful in the election, but not in achieving its objective. The men elected were the P & T technician who was to become Chairman and a man who was to become a spokesman for the small fishermen (see below) as well as the GAA. These men were both belligerent and intelligent representatives, but their fire and bluster failed to achieve the result they wanted. Wolfe Tone Park may have been vested in the Commissioners on behalf of the ratepayers, but it was the County Manager who had the final say, and he was not prepared to hand over the publicly-owned amenity to a private club. The GAA remained powerless to do anything except to pressure for a new grass-seeding program. In the meantime it instigated a search for the title to the Park, hoping to find a legal loophole it could turn against the authorities.

The Club remained unsure about how it should proceed. Its members were cautious about spending large sums of money. They were also reluctant to raise revenue by raising membership fees. One informed observer attributed the GAA's problems to the inexperience, youth and working class origins of the majority of the Club's members. The Club was not without the support of key influentials, but they had not been able to help it out of its predicament.

The County Councillor was an active member, but it was wary of giving him too much leeway. Nevertheless, he used his influence on its behalf wherever he could, pulling for the GAA because of his love of football and also because the GAA pulled votes for him. The only other influential having a close connection with the GAA was the Solicitor. In his younger days he had been its Chairman for a time. He remained the Club's legal adviser, but he no longer had any influence within it. His interests now lay elsewhere — with the Golf Club.

Whereas a few wealthy businessmen catering to the town's 'jet set' succeeded in getting a Golf Club established in spite of legal and other problems, a popularly supported football team was stymied in its efforts to get its pitch playable again. No one wanted to deny the GAA a playing field, but it was a poorly financed village club (even if part of a national organization). It did not have any power because it did not have any money. Golf might no longer have been exclusively a rich man's game, but it was still the game into which the rich put their money.

Fishing rights

A series of intermeshed conflicts broke out in Bantry Bay in the 1970s over the question of fishing rights, culminating in a 'fishing war' between local boats and 'outsiders'. Gulf's presence had added an important new element to a developing situation. Gulf Oil made fishing rights an issue in two ways. Firstly, it tried to introduce by-laws regulating fishing between its jetty and Whiddy Island. Secondly, its spillages upset the seasonal pattern of fishing in the Bay.

The Gulf Oil by-laws

In 1972 Gulf Oil announced its intention to introduce by-laws regulating shipping (and hence fishing) in the vicinity of its Whiddy Island terminal. It stated that it was required to do so by law to ensure safety and pollution control. The company maintained that it was obligatory to have such regulations in the absence of a Harbour Authority (see chapter 8 and Eipper, forthcoming). According to Gulf's Manager the latest joke was 'to touch the side of tankers from small boats, often while smoking. I wouldn't mind if only they were blown up, but explosions do not discriminate'.

The fishermen accused the company of encroaching upon, and denying them access to, one of their traditional fishing grounds. It was accused of exceeding its jurisdiction and of seeking to become a law unto itself in regulating the use of the Bay. For example, the company had already sent out boats to prevent fishing in the disputed area. The fishermen pointed out that in Ireland there was a long standing principle of compensation rather than appropriation by the state, but there had been no compensation paid to fishermen in this case. In the opinion of the fishermen the company should have put up a bond when it came into the area so that when people had a legitimate grievance against the company they could make claims against this bond.

At a meeting of the Cork Board of Fishery Conservators it was stated that 'the consensus of opinion in Bantry' was that there was a secret deal between the Minister for Transport and Power and Gulf Oil, and according to the Board's Chairman, the Bantry County Surgeon, this was a situation which did not exist anywhere else in the world.

To combat the multinational, the fishermen formed the Bantry Bay Boat Owners' and Fishermen's Association and received support at a public meeting which was attended by over 100 people, including the West Cork politicians and Gulf Oil officials. The initiative for organizing the fishermen had come from the Dentist. He had no personal stake in the fishing industry, but was critical of Gulf Oil on nationalist grounds. Acting as spokesman for the fishermen, he pointed out that Gulf Oil had been subject to no interference from local users of the Bay. In fact, the company failed to appreciate how much co-operation it had been given from small users who had been severely penalized in their lawful pursuits by the multinational's presence. He put it to the company that if it was 'really sincere' it could 'withdraw the present proposals, publicly request the establishment of a democratic [Harbour] Authority and then seek the required safeguards'. This pressure contributed to the by-laws being withdrawn. But the fishermen were subsequently prevented from fishing between the Gulf Oil jetty and the Whiddy Island shore by the Minister for Transport and Power using a Marine Order originally made in 1968 when the terminal commenced operations.

It is doubtful that the fishermen seriously thought they would get their way. What they were trying to do was enforce their claim to traditional rights, i.e. they were attempting to prevent the privatization of collectively regulated property. The Dentist, for example, made a point of landing his pleasure boat on Whiddy Island in defiance of Gulf's *No Trespassing* signs: the beaches were regarded as public property by Bantry people just as the fishing berths were thought by Bantry fishermen to belong to them.

The effect of the oil spillages

When Gulf Oil introduced its by-laws, the fishermen were already dissatisfied by its response to the early oil spills, which they maintained had ruined the sea-urchin beds. These beds were damaged again in 1974 when the first of the two big spills occurred. The 1973 and 1974 seasons had not been good for the fishermen; they feared their fate was now permanently sealed.

The Department of Agriculture and Fisheries sent in experts to investigate and report on the oil and detergent damage, and the amount of compensation to be paid. The fishermen were still contesting these conclusions years later, insisting that permanent damage had been done and time would prove them right. As a result of the spillages, they lost a full season of fishing and had to wait well over a year for compensation (see also chapter 8).

The Solicitor was an important figure in the negotiations about compensation. His and another firm represented most of the fishermen who had lodged a claim against Gulf Oil. He had already demonstrated a certain interest in the fishing industry by preparing his own report on the effect of the EEC regulations on Irish fishermen. But he also had a history of legal dealings with Gulf Oil going back to the original purchase of the terminal site on Whiddy Island. These links must have played a part when he and his colleagues helped thrash out the final figure to be paid by the company in compensation. The Dentist tried to organize the fishermen, but the Solicitor probably had a greater influence on their actual fate.

Developing tensions between the fishermen

After it was formed the Bantry Bay Boat Owners' and Fishermen's Association decided to set limitations on the size of nets to be used by members and the number of nets to be used by any one boat. The owners of bigger boats were not happy with these limitations. When a vote was taken at the beginning of the 1974 season, the owners of the half-deck trawlers refused to accept the majority decision. The result was the organization broke into two.[7]

The 'big fellows' kept the old title while the 'small fellows' symbolically reversed the relationship between owners and men, calling their organization The Bantry Bay Fishermen's and Boat Owners' Association. The only large owner to join the small men was the proprietor of the Bantry Marine Company, who had converted some of his boats for fishing after they and their crews had been laid off by Gulf Oil. The key figures among the owners were two publicans from Bantry and a businessman from Dunmanus Bay.

The two publicans had already caused some dissatisfaction in another way. In 1974, just before the first major spillage, they had started an auction. Until then the Bantry fishermen had been selling their fish to a single buyer who was paying them £8.30 a cran. The auction had the immediate result of raising the price to over £16 a cran, but this did not last long. The three buyers involved soon boycotted the auction, holding the fishermen to ransom. Faced with the prospect of having to dump 50 cran of harvest herrings, the fishermen were forced to rely upon one of the auctioneers making a telephone sale at the much reduced price of £10 a cran. In Castletownbere, where the catch of a single trawler equalled the total haul at Bantry, herrings were at that time making £18 or more a cran. The fishermen became unhappy about the running of the auction and the use being made of it by the buyers and the auctioneers.

The 'small men' and the 'big fellows': the locals and the outsiders

The tensions between the men with motor-powered punts and the owners of the half-deck trawlers developed into a conflict between 'the locals' and 'outsiders' in 1975, the first fishing season following the spillages. In the past only a few boats had come to Bantry to fish; because of the impact deep sea trawlers were having, it was now expected that more than two dozen half-deck trawlers from ports all along the south-west coast would be coming. The Bantry fishermen spoke out. According to their spokesman, who was also a member of the Town Commissioners, there was

> not enough fish in Bantry Bay for everybody; many of our 35 members are nearly broke and we will not stand for anymore.
> We have not been able to earn any money since the oil spills in the Bay last October and now the very people who caught all the salmon want to come in here for the shell fishing and the herring season. It is just not on.
> We must accept that the salmon are gone from us forever and that the herring are the only thing we have left. If they are taken from us we are finished.

As a measure of the damage done to them, they pointed out that there had been seven Bantry seine boats (with four men to each boat) in 1969 as against one in 1975. They wanted the government to rezone for fishing those beds from which they had been excluded because of the Gulf Oil terminal, to guarantee them a market for fish landed, and they wanted a quota imposed on nets and catches 'so that everyone will have a chance of making a living'. They recognized that the half-deck trawlers had themselves been squeezed by the big trawlers in the deep sea, but they feared the herring season would be a poor one because of the spillages, and they were worried that the 'outsiders' would then turn to the shellfish and clean out the Bay leaving them with nothing for future years.

The 'outsiders' maintained that there were enough fish in the Bay for everyone. They pointed out that they had not been alone in reaping the salmon harvest off the coast. They argued that their economic survival was now based on the Bantry Bay salmon and herring, estimating that the 16 week season was worth about £1000 per week to each boat. With some 25 half-deck trawlers planning to fish the Bay, that put the total value of the season to them at about £40 000.[8] To circumvent the hostility of the locals, they now agreed to a limit being placed on the number of nets used by any one boat. But such things were no longer negotiable.

On the eve of the arrival of the herring shoals, the Bantry fishermen blockaded the Bay.[9] They intended enforcing the blockade until assurances were given that portions of the inner Bay would be reserved for them. They rejected offers of talks, a truce or an interim settlement. Their spokesman said they would fight to the bitter end:

> This is our last stand because we realize that if we are beaten now we will be beaten forever. Even if it means that we cannot fish ourselves, neither will anyone else.[10]

The dispute climaxed a little over a month later when about a dozen half-deck trawlers sailed into the disputed fishing grounds from Glengarriff Harbour. They were met by about a dozen small Bantry craft, plus one or two larger boats, including a steel-hulled vessel owned by the Bantry Marine Company. Groups of people watched the bobbing lights from shore as the boats manoeuvred to swamp and ram one another. All police leave for the area was cancelled for the next morning when the boats were due to dock, and members of the Gardai were stationed at the Bantry and Glengarriff piers.

Other physical clashes occurred between the two groups, both onshore and at sea. Eventually the 'outsiders' got a High Court injunction placed on the Bantry fishermen, restraining them from intimidating or interfering with the business of the trawler owners, from harassing or interfering with their vessels, from damaging them or their equipment, from unlawfully interfering with the unloading or auctioning of fish, and from attacking, assaulting or interfering with the plaintiffs themselves. The Bantry men responded by tying their boats up at the pier to prevent their opponents docking. Injunction and counter-injunction followed,[11] but the final result was that the Bantry men were forced to allow the 'outsiders' to fish the Bay for the rest of the season.

As tensions mounted and the distance between the two sides grew greater, the auctioneers' pubs were boycotted by the Bantry fishermen; they in turn tried to get a petition started condemning the actions of the Bantry men. They only managed to get one businessman to sign it. No one else wanted to buy into the dispute: they did not approve of the dispute, but they did not want to suffer the fishermen's wrath either. The business influentials were critical of the Bantry fishermen but were not prepared to take a stand on the issue: they would not have been listened to, and they might have been victimized. When populist sentiments were as strong as this, their power found its limits.

The outside trawlers accused the small Bantry fishermen of lacking initiative, pointing out that they had made no attempt to acquire boats (e.g. with the help of a government loan) which could compete. They had thus shown themselves unwilling to risk investing in the development of the Bantry fisheries. Now that they were satisfied with the potential of the Bay, they had suddenly decided to seal it off, leaving the trawlers 'with a fleet of white elephants'. But the Bantry fishermen's ancestors had been fishing these berths for centuries, and to them the claim that they had only just realized the potential of the Bay was nonsense. Their problem was that they lacked capital. It was the 'outsiders', who had only appeared that season, who were guilty of opportunism. The Bantry men maintained that all that they were trying to do was preserve for themselves fishing grounds that they had traditionally taken to be theirs.[12]

The Bantry Bay fisheries had always been controlled by capitalists, but the actual fishing had been done collectively. That was all changing now. Gulf Oil was fencing-in the waters of the Bay, and the only room for the small man on the water was as a wage-labourer. Few of the Bantry fishermen could expect permanent work on the trawlers replacing them. They were being thoroughly proletarianized, but they were not being given jobs. Seen in this light, the struggles described here constituted the tail-end of one complex set of class processes, just as the struggles of the newly industrialized workers (Eipper, forthcoming) constituted the beginnings of another. The connection between the two sets of processes was Gulf Oil. Because of this, it is worth noting that whereas business influentials such as the Dentist and the Solicitor were still able to play some limited part in organizing and representing these proletarianized remnants of the peasantry, they had no such part to play in the struggles of the town's nascent industrial proletariat (see also chapter 8).

Final remarks

The aim of this and the previous chapter has been to relate activism and influence to the individual and collective possession and exercise of power. From this it has emerged that those people reputed to have influence within Bantry actually tended to be the key participants in major projects and controversies; they also held the major positions of authority in the town. In fact, it was because of the use they made of their control of these authoritative positions that the influentials dominated the organized life of the town. They were the ones who had most say in initiating, making and implementing policies of potential consequence for the population as a whole. By contrast, the influence of other groups, e.g. working class activists, tended to be more intermittent and oriented to a particular range of issues, i.e. their say in how the town was run was related to specific issues and was circumstantial.

This picture would not be complete without some mention of the part played by the influentials in the various issues arising out of Gulf's presence in the Bay. Some indication of this has already been given whenever Gulf's presence was integral to the evolution of a given issue. Further evidence of the prominence of the key personalities and organizations will emerge in the course of the analysis of the power wielded by the multinational itself. Suffice it to say at this point that the evidence provides further confirmation of the importance of the top influentials, most notably, the Solicitor, the Dentist, and the County Councillor — as well as the other West Cork politicians — and the organizations through which they worked.

The influentials putatively possessed more power than they exercised, i.e. they had more potential power than their actual circumstances allowed them to use. They did not achieve very much more than other groups in the town, but they had the edge on them. If and when bigger and better things proved possible, they were in a position to step in and take control. The business people were the key figures in all three spheres of influence. They controlled the development sphere directly. They were also dominant in the charity sphere, except that here they worked under the direction of the clergy. Similarly, in the governmental sphere, they took their lead from key politicians (usually themselves businessmen) and civil servants. These people sometimes came into conflict in those grey areas where jurisdictions overlapped, i.e. where more than one category of influential was concerned about the outcome of a project or controversy, but such disputes were about the use of power rather than examples of competition for a greater share of power.

As a measure of the working class's subordination by business interests, the virtual exclusion of its representatives from key sites of influence in town affairs deserves further comment. This situation did not result from quiescence on the part of the workers (see chapters 6 and 8, and Eipper, forthcoming). For if they were not influential in town affairs, a number of individual workers were certainly active, and within their ambit quite effective activists at that. And even if they seldom achieved unequivocal victories when pursuing their objectives in the face of opposition from business, the problems that could be caused by their use of their latent collective power in town affairs meant that the workers were always a force to be taken into account by the business influentials and their associates. An important institutional obstacle confronting any worker influence in town affairs was the limited number of existing avenues open to their representatives for pursuing their objectives and the limited autonomy of their organizational base.

Individual workers who wished to have a say in town affairs had tended to try and participate in whatever development organization was currently active. But they inevitably remained marginal figures in such bodies, forced to fit in with and follow the dictates of business, applying whatever pressure they could by aligning themselves with individuals sympathetic to their arguments and by supporting initiatives which promised to provide employment or otherwise improve things for the ordinary townspeople.

There was also a tradition of individual workers getting themselves elected to the Town Commissioners. But the depreciated power of the Commissioners as a formal organ of local government and — at least until the Gulf Oil period — the paralysis associated with the Commissioners' substantive use of what power they did have, meant that participation in this arena bestowed little influence.

Any concerted campaign by workers which encroached on the governmental sphere was invariably going to be hampered by split party-political allegiances, notably between Fianna Fail and Labour. Even in its early years Fianna Fail had claimed to speak for the small farmer rather than the worker; its drift towards business further diminished the influence of workers in its ranks, even in local branches such as the Bantry cumann. For its part Labour remained a minority party which in a bid to exert some influence on national policy formation was predisposed to entering, as the junior partner, a coalition with the more conservative of the two parties, Fine Gael.

The predicament of Bantry's labour-aligned workers was further exacerbated by the subordination of party branches in West Cork to the TD's electoral machine. As already indicated (see chapter 4), this man was known for his pronouncements on behalf of business interests and farmers, not for his espousal of policies advocated by the Labour movement. His rise to power and the consolidation of his position by the elevation of his brother at the expense, first of his Bantry colleague and then this man's widow, had caused bitter splits in the Bantry branch and left it organizationally paralysed — for a long time unable even to hold a meeting.

From a broader perspective, the problems the widowed Ex-MCC/Trade Union official faced can be taken as a measure of the problems of organized labour itself. As the local official of the largest union, the ITGWU, she was the key representative of organized labour in Bantry. Yet she lacked personal experience of industrial work, took a conciliatory stance towards business, and had no liking for the ruthless cut and thrust of electoral politics. Moreover, given the patriarchal disposition of business management, the union membership and party colleagues, she was restricted in what she could achieve even with loyal supporters behind her.

The coming of Gulf Oil created the conditions for a new assertiveness on the part of workers, especially the tug-boatmen servicing the Whiddy Island Terminal which extended to their wanting to have a say in town affairs. But the more assertive workers had to cope with the fact that their industrial militancy and the aspirations which went with it, met with the scorn, ridicule and resentment of much of the rest of the population. Even so, they were still able to mount an impressive campaign of protest around a package of issues concerning Gulf Oil and industrial development (see chapter 8 and Eipper, forthcoming) which secured virtually the unanimous support of the townspeople. It is significant that this campaign was organized, on the initiative of two key tug-boat shop-stewards, one of whom was for a time the key figure on the Town Commissioners (see above), by an ad hoc all-union shop-steward committee. Although a one-off achievement, this mobilization is nevertheless notable both for the fact that its leadership was provided by militant rank and file workers rather than union officials, and for being completely independent of the influentials and the organizations they commanded.

The survey of influentials was limited to people *from* the town who exerted influence *within* the town. Quite obviously this ruled out of consideration those individuals and groups who had an effect *on* the town but wielded their power outside it. Given that 'outside' social forces made major interventions in town affairs on a regular basis, it should be obvious that some of these people had power overshadowing that of all the town's influentials. This was commonly recognized in Bantry. The influentials were 'community decision-makers', but in the opinion of many people, including the influentials themselves, this was an impoverished or even paltry form of power. The attitude was most colourfully expressed by the Chairman of the Town Commissioners:

> Making decisions — you are bordering on the ridiculous? Individuals making decisions — are there any individuals making decisions? Have we got an industry in the past five years? Who are the leaders? [It's] natural to expect the politically appointed people are the leaders, but we got nothing [from them]. We have three TDs, but we might as well have three bonnafs [piglets].

The political power of the business leaders was not tangentially related to their economic power, but directly and obviously based upon it. They participated in town affairs as business people rather than as private citizens. Even when they did participate as private citizens, it was their position in business which determined the character of their involvement. It was widely regarded as natural and necessary that the 'interests of business' should have the major voice in the town, if only because (in general) what was good for business was good for others too.

The instability of the organizations upon which the influentials depended was one of their strengths, not just one of their weaknesses. When they lacked substantive objectives or were internally divided, they abandoned an existing organization and subsequently re-grouped in another on a slightly different basis.

Their lack of a firm basis of popular support was probably their greatest problem. A working class activist attributed their lack of popularity to the fact that they had lost touch with the common people, with the ordinary view of things. Because they found it difficult to accept that they were not regarded as natural leaders, the influentials attributed the equivocal support they received to the apathy and traditionalism of the population, and to the tendency to 'knock' anyone trying to achieve something. They constantly had to guard against the charge that they were selfishly pursuing their own private interests rather than the public good, and they had problems trying to mobilize popular support for their projects. Of course, they usually did not have to moblize the whole town, and could often rely on the politicians and the clergy to do it for them. But unlike their predecessors, who controlled the town's main employment outlets (see chapter 3), they had little they could use to encourage people to rally behind them. They did not even have the whole-hearted support of many of the town's traders who regarded them as young, untried blow-ins full of big ideas and their own self-importance.

This was not the only measure of the poverty of the business influentials' power. The other is that most of their major initiatives were a response to the turbulence caused by Gulf Oil. In this context, it is worth pointing out that the multinational scarcely ever found it necessary to have its executives take part in town affairs. It even changed its Terminal Manager every couple of years, hence preventing him from becoming an important figure in his own right. This seems to have been a policy calculated to prevent complications that would affect the operation of the terminal. In fact, the only time senior executives became involved on a regular basis in one of the business organizations was when the Terminal Manager and one of his aides joined the Chamber after the Harbour Authority was established. For the first time since it arrived, the company felt it needed a personal voice within a Bantry business organization.

Because they wielded power within a restricted domain, and because their power was dwarfed by that of outside influentials, it would be a distortion to describe the Bantry influentials as a power elite and leave it as that. Also, given the overwhelming dominance of town affairs by business interests, it is clear that the power of the influentials had a class basis. And it was because of *this* that they constituted an elite with respect to the majority of the population. But their relationship to the members of their own class differed from this. For as the political representatives of their class, theirs was a leadership function, not a hierarchical one.

These two chapters have traced how the specific configuration of power relations in Bantry corresponded with the configuration of economic, political and cultural power nationally. The Bantry influentials were the local representatives of a nationally dominant class whose power was socially effective precisely because it controlled the major institutional structures through and around which society was organized. The key thing here is that at both the so-called local and national 'levels', the reproduction of capitalist enterprise, government and religion was interlocked. This does not mean that these institutions were held together by some kind of functionalist fixity, only that their evolution and their futures were *functionally coupled,* and that because of *this,* changes *within* and *between* them were extremely important for the cohesion of the ruling bloc locally.

The influentials who locally comprised this ruling bloc constituted the political leadership not only of the town's bourgeoisie, but the town itself. Their class hegemony was such that as its leaders they could posit their interests and objectives as the interests and objectives of everybody. Their concerns, their terms of reference, were thus made the dominant ones, the ones that mattered. They were able to use their leadership position to mobilize people in support of projects while denying them a say in the running of these projects. One of the effects of this use of power was that people were ideologically pressured into taking stances on issues without always being able to decide what the issues were. They were asked to acquiesce to proffered policies, and their consciousness of alternatives was thereby occluded.

There were, of course, definite limits to this hegemony. The influentials did not control the course of events, nor was their leadership always accepted. In fact, they were often ignored and widely resented. At times, they found it difficult to mobilize support for their objectives. Occasionally they were resisted. Limits had been imposed from below on their use of their power. These controls rendered the influentials vulnerable to the challenge of democratic procedures. Yet in spite of some evidence of anti-clericism, disenchantment with party politics, and populist constraints on the profit motive, opposition to the influentials' leadership had not been particularly frequent or demonstrably effective. Only by turning the ruling ideas back upon the ruling bloc could the powerful easily be made accountable to the mass of people. Which is why catholic or nationalist principles, and even notions of progress and development, were so readily used to criticize the powerful.

Far more important in the end than these challenges was the Gulf Oil intervention. It demonstrated that the type of power wielded by the influentials, namely, power deployed individually and collectively through the medium of inter-personal relations — i.e. power wielded by known personalities and constrained by the effects their actions had on specific persons and groups — was not to be compared with the power wielded impersonally through a corporate structure, in this case by one of the world's largest companies.

8 Corporate persuasion, state compliance and community impotence

A comprehensive analysis of Gulf's intervention in Bantry Bay raises diverse issues.[1] Central to all of these is the nature of the power wielded by the multinational and the types of consciousness associated with this power.

From the first announcement of its interest in Bantry Bay, Gulf Oil effectively colonized the consciousness of local people and was a constant source of controversy. The town's preoccupation with the multinational reached its tragic climax when the dilapidated tanker, the *Betelgeuse,* caught fire and exploded while discharging its cargo at Whiddy in January, 1979. For not only did this accident cause the loss of fifty lives, it also closed the terminal because of the destruction of the offshore jetty. Although there is a sense in which Gulf Oil and its activities became *the* issue in Bantry, certain events stand out because they raise questions of wider significance. The most obvious feature of Gulf's influence should already be clear from the controversies associated with its donation of money to the Community Centre and the Fiesta, the payment of compensation to the town for the spillages, the demise and revival of the Chamber of Commerce over the Harbour Authority question, and the effect by-laws and spillages had on the local fishermen. These controversies indicate the extent to which Gulf Oil 'recontextualized' local events. It would be wrong, however, to see this as simply due to its size rather than the use of power, for as each of these controversies shows, Gulf Oil — as a corporate body — was an actor, one conscious of its power, and conscious in its use of it. In terms of the themes of this study this is an important point to stress. A central feature of this 'recontextualization' was the way the state was hegemonized by the multinational. This hegemonization was effected through a complex interplay between the impersonal corporate power of each of these institutions, and the individual and collective personal power of their officials, and the local influentials.

Patterns of dependency and deference

By definition both local communities and nation states are bounded geographic entities. This mundane fact acquires poignancy, though, when these entities come to deal with that most modern of phenomena, the multinational corporation. For as an example of the most thorough concentration and centralization of capital, multinationals are geographically promiscuous. Capital by its nature is nomadic, and its *raison d'être* lies neither in community loyalties nor national allegiances, but only in its ever-expanding, ever more extensive reinvestment. Of course these companies may be the instruments of the imperialism of one or more states, and may align themselves with and remain dependent upon, as well as seek to control, given states. But such allegiances are contingent arrangements whose viability and durability remain hostage to the dictates of capital accumulation through profit-making.

A consequence of this is that even though local communities and nation states may be characterized by a pattern of class domination which finds its ultimate expression in the power wielded on the world stage by the multinational corporation, they nevertheless find themselves in a tension-ridden and contradictory position when it comes to dealing with these conglomerates of capital.

The vast literature on modernization, underdevelopment and dependency suggests that if this situation creates dilemmas for the metropolitan heartlands of advanced capitalism — the headquarters from which the multinationals direct their worldwide operations — these are nothing compared to the problems of the vast hinterland of the capitalist world economy.

Community leaders and state officials in these regions habitually seem to make an initial assumption of common interests between themselves and incoming multinationals — though this is invariably tempered by a sense of anxiety when it is recognized that this commonality inheres in analogous rather than homologous interests. Such recognition tends to be publicly associated with tension-management, the need for negotiated reconciliation of discrepant priorities. It is significant, then, that awareness of a divergence of interests so often gets voiced in terms of the unavoidable commitment of community leaders and state officials (and also, of course, the people in whose name they speak) to the prosperity of specific places — which contrasts starkly with the speculative indifference of the one type of enterprise which can bring prosperity with it when it comes only to take it when it goes. In Bantry this predicament was expressed time after time whenever some

191

serious attempt was made to make Gulf Oil accountable to the nation or the local community. Again and again it was asked: 'Will Gulf pull out?' It is a question with traumatic echoes wherever multinationals create dependencies and encourage deferential consent by making it invidious for people to be anything more than ambivalent advocates of their own interests. As such it illustrates perfectly the hegemonic position of multinational corporations in dealing with those nation states and localized communities to which they export their capital.

Chronology of key events

As I have already indicated (chapter 3), the Bantry influentials had spared no effort in attempting to please the various small manufacturers who expressed interest in or actually set up factories in the town prior to Gulf's intervention. In these highly personalized dealings the influentials wanted to leave nothing to chance and were generous to a fault in their attempts to sell Bantry as a site suitable for industrial development. Although it would seem both the Cork County Council and the Industrial Development Authority were somewhat more discriminating than the local influentials when doling out concessions and subsidies, nevertheless it can be said that they were not as cautious as they might have been.

Construction of the Whiddy terminal began in 1966 and the first ship to bring oil to Bantry, the *Universe Ireland,* arrived in October, 1968. The following year Gulf Oil hosted an extravagant ceremony at which the Fianna Fail Taoiseach (Prime Minister), Jack Lynch, officially opened the terminal.

Not until 1973 did the first major controversy erupt. It concerned proposals for a refinery in the Bantry area. Gulf Oil, however, was not really a party to these moves since it declared it had nothing to do with any of the companies making the proposals. The foreign settlers together with the Irish National Trust, An Taisce, opposed the idea of a refinery for Bantry and eventually a public inquiry was instituted which recommended against a refinery being sited in the area. Bantry people were virtually unanimous at the time in their opposition to the settlers, even though they themselves had a variety of reservations about the refinery. Represented by the Dentist, the Boat Owners' and Fishermen's Association, for example, prepared a submission protesting the inadequacy of the planning permission guidelines, but stressing support for properly regulated industrial development including a refinery.

By contrast with the settlers, the Dentist's position in this regard was given considerable credibility because he was known as an active campaigner for industry. For example, he had in the past made it clear that his criticisms of Gulf Oil were motivated by his belief that Bantry was not getting the best deal from the multinational's presence. His convictions were given further legitimacy by their being based on nationalist grounds.

Because of the outcry from Bantry people and the prospect of further industrial development, all political parties supported the refinery. In some cases key political figures had a personal stake in seeing one or another of the projects go ahead. For example, a leading Fine Gael TD was made a Director of the Irish subsidiary of one of the companies interested in siting a refinery at Bantry. The Fianna Fail TD from Bandon and the Skibbereen solicitor who founded the West Cork Development Association (see chapter 3) were involved with another of the projects. Meanwhile, the company responsible for yet another proposal went so far as to take options out on land reputedly owned by the Labour TD and his brother.

All things considered, it came as no surprise, then, when the Minister for Local Government overturned the recommendations of the inquiry. By this time, however, the likelihood of a refinery being built had evaporated because of changes in the world oil situation. Bantry people blamed the settlers for holding things up until it was too late, and felt cheated of further prosperity.

The changes to the world oil market proved to be epoch-making ones. This was the period which came to be known as the 'oil crisis' when, it seemed, OPEC was holding the world to ransom. In fact, though the issue cannot be dealt with here, it was rather more complicated than that. As the upturn in traffic through the Bantry terminal suggests, the oil companies and not only OPEC stood to gain from the changes wrought at this time. It was ironically coincidental, then, that two major spillages occurred within a few months of each other in late 1974 and early 1975. For at this time Gulf Oil had an unprecedented amount of shipping in the Bay — full of oil bought at one price and waiting to be sold at another.

The furore that followed provided the settlers and An Taisce, at least in their view, with retrospective justification for their stand against the refinery. Meanwhile the local fishermen demanded compensation for their loss of a season's work.

The massive clean-up operations were carried out amidst a cross-fire of recriminations against Gulf Oil for its attempts to suppress the true dimensions of the spillages as well as for its failure to take proper precautions to prevent such calamities. It was also alleged that the fishermen had made exaggerated claims for compensation. In any case, it was said they were being doubly compensated because of the employment provided by the clean-up work. The settlers, An Taisce and the media were also criticized for what Bantry people regarded as the excessive publicity given to the spillages — publicity which threatened to damage the tourist season. The political parties were condemned too because of the failure of successive governments to establish a Harbour Authority to police Gulf's use of the Bay. And so too was the Minister for Transport and Power in the government of the day, when, following his announcement that an Authority would finally be established, he introduced interim measures strictly limiting the amount of shipping allowed in the Bay. He was accused of over-reacting, and there was an outcry that if he was not careful he would chase Gulf Oil out.

The spillage marked a turning point in the terminal's history. Whereas its profitability had previously depended on high throughput of oil for an expanding market at (given subsequent trends) a low price, it now depended on a low throughput of oil for a contracting market. This had occurred because of a combination of factors, which included the downturn in the world economy and austerity measures imposed by European governments to reduce oil consumption and the changing significance of the Bantry terminal in Gulf's European marketing strategy. These trends saw the tran-shipment of oil through Bantry Bay slashed year by year. Finally, in 1976, Gulf Oil announced a rationalization program designed to lower the cost of operating the Whiddy terminal. The tug workers opposed the retrenchments and the erosion of real wages and conditions and safety provisions entailed by this program. This resulted in a strike cum lockout which Bantry people feared Gulf Oil would use as an excuse to close the terminal down. Once work resumed throughput at the terminal continued to decline, but Gulf Oil didn't pull out.

Meanwhile the moves to get the Harbour Authority established progressed exceedingly slowly. After further delay the new Authority finally held its inaugural meeting late in 1977. As it turned out few such meetings were to follow. The question of how much Gulf Oil would henceforth be charged for the use of the Bay, or how closely its actions would be monitored, in the end never had to be confronted. The Authority was never given the go-ahead by either the government which set it up, or the one which subsequently took charge.

The struggle for control of the Bay

The struggle for control of the Bay really only began with the controversy over the refinery. At that stage it was a broadly fought issue about who had the right to determine the future use to which the Bay would be put. As such, though Gulf Oil was implicated, the main battle at this stage was between local people and the foreign settlers who found in An Taisce a body willing to fight in their name. Without the support of An Taisce the settlers would never have been given a hearing. In any case, their lack of numbers and electoral representation virtually guranteed they would eventually be defeated on this issue and make bitter enemies of the host population.

Following the spillage however, Bantry people themselves became more adamant about the need for some policing of Gulf Oil and more insistent in their demands for a Harbour Authority. Although the County Council acted with a notable alacrity in acceding to Gulf's wishes to use the Bay as a transhipment port, the Manager with the support of the Council had for some years previously been calling for some form of Harbour Authority for

Bantry, and the coming of Gulf Oil intensified that call and gave it a new rationale. Muintir na Tire had compiled a report on the Harbour Authority question in the early 1970s, and the Development Association subsequently prepared a submission of its own to the government in 1974. The Boat Owners' and Fishermen's Association also lobbied the government. The Dentist was a key figure in each of these initiatives. Meanwhile, the Town Commissioners and the West Cork TDs and County Councillors added their voice to the call for an Authority as did the Cork Board of Fishery Conservators under the Chairmanship of Bantry's County Surgeon, and, of course, tourist interests from Glengarriff. The most dramatic attempt to apply pressure came from Gulf's (direct and indirect) employees. They mounted an impressive campaign for a locally controlled Authority (see chapter 7), attacking on a number of fronts. They confronted An Taisce and the settlers for opposing industrial development, the County Council for looking to its own rather than Bantry's interests in seeking control of the Authority, the Minister for his tardiness in establishing an Authority and his apparent over-reaction to the spillages, and Bantry's business people for not having taken more vigorous action on these issues themselves. Their actions climaxed in a cavalcade of cars to Cork City, a protest endorsed by a public meeting which overflowed the Bantry Courthouse.

By this time there were few in Bantry who remained opposed to the idea of an Authority. The Solicitor had published a paper on the question the import of which was to question whether one was justified. His interests in this matter were not clear. He had consistently involved himself in matters relating to Gulf Oil — representing the farmers on Whiddy Island in the sale of their land, supporting the refinery proposal and, subsequently, attempting to mediate between Gulf Oil and the tug-men during the 1976 strike/lockout. The one or two other business people who made their opposition public had a more obvious stake in the matter. The most notable of these was the Biggs group which was fearful that it (and not only Gulf Oil) would have dues levied against it.

Once the decision was taken to establish an Authority of some kind, the struggle for control of the Bay became, in effect, a complicated contest for control of the Authority's board. Bantry people strongly lobbied for local control whereas the Cork County Council sought to have itself made the relevant Authority. Meanwhile the West Cork politicians had been forced by local feeling to change their allegiances on this question and support the call for a locally run Authority which would ensure the revenue collected would be spent on local industrial development, thus providing extra jobs and business opportunities for Bantry people. However, ignoring these pressures, the Minister retained control of the Authority, making it answerable to the Department of Transport and Power. Aside from his own appointees, elections were to be held for the remaining positions which were allocated to the County Council, the Bantry Chamber of Commerce and the Town Commissioners.

At the last moment it was announced that Gulf Oil would not have a position on the board because of a legal technicality. But, as already indicated this was not to matter for the company proved to be able to have its way quite effectively as it was.

Henceforth it was to be a party-political struggle and a battle of personalities. The outcome was a board dominated by business interests but divided along party lines. Whereas the Chamber of Commerce was given the right to elect two of its members to the board, the trade unions had no such choice. Provision was made for them only in that one of the Minister's appointees had to represent the interests of labour (by implication, then, the other two did not). The person chosen was the Ex-MCC/Trade Union Official. The other two appointees of the Minister reflected both a party and class bias. West Cork's Fine Gael TD became the Minister's personal representative on the board. The President of the Glengarriff Development Association was chosen both as a representative of the resort's tourist interests and because he was a leading local Fine Gael figure.

The County Council had a right to elect two members to the board. The issue was decided by relative party strength and the West Cork Fine Gael and Labour Councillors were elected. Having been revitalized at the beginning of the year for the sole purpose of securing two positions on the board, the Chamber of Commerce also divided on party lines (see chapter 7).

As a member of the Coalition government, the County Council Chairman had used his casting vote twice against the Fianna Fail County Councillor to prevent him being elected to the Authority's board by the County Council. The Chamber had its biggest turn-out ever on the night of its vote, largely because of the County Councillor's canvassing. He received a large sympathy vote because he could claim that though he was the man best suited to look after Bantry's interests — the only truly local elected representative — he had been denied a voice. Nevertheless, he left nothing to chance, calling in debts and favours, and seeking the support even of Fine Gael stalwarts who would otherwise have been expected to oppose him. In fact, he and the other successful contender, the Dentist, canvassed for one another. Since the Rowa Manager came in third on the vote, it is obvious that Fianna Fail had things pretty well tied up. Meanwhile among the Town Commissioners the Independents and Fianna Fail had entered into a tacit understanding which resulted in the election of a Fianna Fail man and an independent. These manouevrings proved important for the parties. For in spite of its best efforts, the Coalition government only obtained a majority of one on the board.

The struggle for control of the board came to a head at its inaugural meeting. The Coalition parties endeavoured to consolidate their position by having the Chairman and Vice-Chairman elected from their ranks. In fact, the Minister's prime nominee, the Fine Gael TD, was elected to the Chair as expected. But because of internal politicking in the Labour party the Dentist was elected as Vice-Chairman when the Ex-MCC/Trade Union Official used the argument of the need for a local man to break party ranks (see chapter 4). This was a victory both for those seeking maximum local control of the Authority and for Fianna Fail. As the town's most articulate critic of Gulf Oil, the Dentist's election meant that the Authority's executive would not become a complacent tool of government. Along with the Independent from the Town Commissioners, he could not be expected to let his Fianna Fail sympathies overwhelm his concern for the Authority's autonomy — though as it turned out, the problem was not that the Authority lacked autonomy but that it was never allowed to function.

Because it was never allowed to function, the Harbour Authority was exonerated of any blame by the Tribunal investigating the tragedy which closed the terminal. The same could not so easily be said of the various governments and government departments responsible for the Authority's still-birth. The owner of the *Betelgeuse,* Total, was condemned because its cost-cutting measures meant the ship was in a dangerous state of disrepair and because it had not been equipped with adequate safety devices. Gulf Oil was condemned, not because it had been responsible for the initiation of the disaster but because it too had resorted to cost-cutting measures which violated safety requirements and because of the negligence of one of its key personnel which in all probability helped magnify the dimensions of the tragedy. The report of the inquiry also accused central figures amongst Gulf's Bantry management and staff with instituting a cover-up and with lying to the Tribunal (Costello, 1980).

Gulf Oil and the grace of God

Having been a poor place for virtually the whole of its recorded history, Bantry seemed destined to remain one until Gulf Oil arrived on the scene. It was an omen of things to come, then, when all levels of government unreservedly welcomed the multinational to Bantry and gave cursory consideration to the kind of terms and conditions which subsequently became so obviously necessary.

Gulf Oil exuded unqualified confidence in the terminal's and Bantry's future from the very first. Because it was so unexpected and so fortuitous, this propitious event was not uncommonly spoken of almost as if Gulf Oil were a divine favour bestowed on Bantry by the grace of God. This was the case even with the company's critics who more than once made comments to the effect that 'God gave us Bantry Bay and we gave it to Gulf Oil' — the sentiment being that if the first gift was an overdue act of charity the second was one of undue recklessness.

Although there were workers who had been prepared from the outset to take on the multinational in a direct confrontation between capital and labour so long as a clash did not prejudice the viability of the terminal, support for an Authority was the closest the business people came to opposing their interests to Gulf Oil. And as is clear from the failure of the first Chamber of Commerce, this was a commitment that was in any case easily derailed (see chapter 7). The Development Association was keen to see an Authority established, but it was if anything even more keen to spring to Gulf's defence and speak on the company's behalf when it was under attack following the spillages. In fact, the business people as a whole really only mobilized when the decision to establish an Authority had already been made, and they had been given the right, through the Chamber of Commerce, to elect two of their number to the board of the Authority.

It is significant that among those who accorded least deference to Gulf Oil were people who owed their jobs, even a life in their home town, to the company. But because of this their opposition was qualified and hedged in by the fear that excessive demands would cause Gulf Oil to pull out and leave them not only without jobs but with the burden of blame for the calamity they had brought down upon the town — considerations which were a major element in the tug workers' struggle against Gulf's rationalization program in 1976. If the workers beholden to Gulf Oil for their livelihood were periodically to be accused of trying 'to kill the goose that laid the golden egg', they in the meantime had found themselves aligned with the local business people in levelling that charge at the foreign settlers who were accused of jeopardizing the dreams of further large scale industrial development.

The media moved from enthusiastic eulogies to more ambivalent expressions of doubt about Gulf Oil, adopting a more critical stance as it became more obvious how big had been the lost opportunities and how the multinational tried to manipulate publicity. Of the popularly read press, only the *Southern Star,* the regional weekly servicing West Cork, came to adopt something approaching a reasoned and critical stance towards Gulf Oil. By contrast, the major provincial paper, *The Cork Examiner,* at most oscillated in its editorial judgements and its reporting between retailing Gulf's publicity pronouncements, and making piecemeal attacks on the company — as well as the government of the day, the parties, the County Council, the settlers and the tug workers.

In such circumstances it is perhaps not surprising that Bantry people had quite an acute sense of dependency upon Gulf Oil. But it is somewhat harder to accept that this should necessarily have been the case with the politicians and civil servants representing the state. Yet it would seem to have been the size of the company and the promise its proposal held out for further industrial development that was important even for them. The fear was, of course, that instead of ensuring that Gulf Oil 'would do the right thing', the imposition of statutory controls and the appropriation of revenue would make the company 'pack its bags and go'. Given this reaction, not to mention that of Gulf Oil itself, the government of the day soon backtracked from the one bold attempt at reining Gulf Oil in. Although there could be no rescinding of the decision to establish a Harbour Authority, what could be guaranteed was that it be rendered powerless.

And here again the remarkable similarity between the Fianna Fail and Coalition governments in their treatment of Gulf Oil — for all their point-scoring off the company — is revealed. In government as well as in opposition the major parties were fastidious in looking after Gulf's interests, or at least in their concern for its goodwill. That this was so was never more apparent then when the representative from the Department of Transport and Power briefed the new board of the Harbour Authority on its duties and responsibilities, and counselled caution in its handling of matters relating to Gulf Oil.

In this connection, it is significant that the strongest and most consistent exponent of greater regulatory powers from within the state apparatus was probably the County Manager. For if the Manager had had his way, not only would there have been a Harbour Authority, but he would have had control of it. In terms of revenue, if nothing else, this would have been a most rewarding situation to have been in. It would seem, then, that the vigour with which the County Manager pursued the issue of the Harbour Authority had less to do with a foreign corporation's use of one of the finest natural deep-water harbours in the world, than with a bid for power within the state apparatus itself. This judgement finds confirmation in the fact that the Council itself did little to improve its surveillance of the company's activities until, like the national government, its hand was forced by the spillages. Until then, the Manager did no more than complain that the only way the Council had of finding out if there had been a spillage or not was if Gulf Oil (or someone else) informed him of the fact, castigating the company when it was neglectful of this obligation or tardy in fulfilling it.

The dealings of all sections of the community as well as the media and the key organs of the state, then, were marked by a chronic ambivalence deriving from doubt and uncertainty. So much of the information necessary for an accurate assessment of whether Gulf Oil would pull out, when it might and what would make it do so, was privately controlled by the company itself. No one but it knew whether it would have tolerated greater government regulation, what influence it had exerted to prevent it, and how the absence of controls profited it. In other words, the company camouflaged the constraints and contingencies shaping its options by effective use of secrecy, and this was crucial to the way it dictated the terms of public debate.

In the absence of a detailed recounting of the various events which comprise the story of Gulf's Bantry venture, it might seem possible to conclude that the company was the hapless victim of circumstance, that it was in any case not to blame for the parlous predicament and anxious perceptions of Bantry people and the Irish state. After all, it was a business corporation and, as one Gulf Oil executive remarked when commenting on the legal manoeuvres which followed the tragic destruction of its terminal, 'we have to face one fact of life — business is business'.

The point is that the business of business did not allow the multinational to carry on impassively while everyone else got the jitters: Gulf Oil did not simply enter a given situation and cope with it from then on — it continually helped create new situations from the one it entered, and then it manipulated both the situation and the actors with it. Claims of this sort about multinationals are not novel, and might even seem unduly partisan if the evidence did not so strongly suggest otherwise.

Gulf Oil from the outset embarked upon a sustained propaganda campaign designed to blitz the media with publicity handouts promoting the company's image and the prosperity which would be an inevitable outcome of its Bantry operation, and to counter adverse comment resulting from one or another aspect of its operations.

What was good for Gulf Oil was going to be good for Bantry: the celebrated flexibility of the terminal was portrayed as a bonus for Bantry as much as for Gulf Oil itself. Its adaptability was construed as safeguarding the town's future. In fact, though, this 'flexibility' had something to do with the terminal's dispensability as far as the multinational was concerned: once it had paid for itself it was liable to be destined for obsolescence.

The company spared no expense in its efforts to drum up popular support for its project, e.g. in the lavish ceremonies it hosted to celebrate the birth of the terminal. A feature of its efforts was the way it insinuated veiled threats and instilled doubt through the use of innuendo and ambiguity. The fear that the company would pull out was not without a rational foundation. For on a number of occasions the issue was raised by Gulf Oil itself. On other occasions the possibility was denied — but at times in a manner which, due to the company's lack of credibility, seemed to suggest the reverse might be true. The company's credibility was first seriously put into question when it systematically suppressed the truth about the size of the major spillages. Yet Gulf's success in capturing the terms of the debate in other circumstances had an echo in its way of dealing with this embarassment too. Criticism of the spillages was deflected by playing upon Bantry people's sense of morality and turning it to the company's own ends. The fishermen, most of whom got work on the clean-up operation, were criticized over their compensation claims and the prolongation of the clean-up work. By focusing on the morality of their behaviour the company tried to disperse the guilt and relativize its own culpability.

It also consistently managed to cloud the issue of the Harbour Authority, firstly, by alluding to its understanding with the government that no Authority would be established while it, Gulf Oil, remained the sole user of the Bay, and secondly, by subsuming the question of regulation under that of revenue. Generally speaking, Bantry people both feared and favoured the notion of 'fleecing' Gulf Oil. The company adroitly kept this question and the morality of it at the forefront of debate. Since it had supplied all its own facilities, it claimed the state had no right to turn around and charge for the use of them. This was a persuasive and effective argument, one repeated by all and sundry. It successfully painted over the fact that there were other grounds for charging Gulf Oil for the use of the Bay, ranging from access to and use of a valuable natural resource and passage through the water, through to charges on tonnage shipped, regulation and supervision of safety and pollution, etc. Yet, however important it was, the question of revenue was not the central issue at all. Regardless of the revenue collected, the demand had always been for adequate regulation and supervision of the use of the Bay by Gulf Oil to ensure safety and prevent pollution.

Business life after death

The report of the enquiry into the disaster was the first example of an arm of the state taking Gulf Oil to task in unqualified and explicitly critical terms. Because the jetty was so completely destroyed there was little chance of the terminal re-opening in the forseeable future. In the light of previous experiences one can speculate as to the public pressure the tribunal might have been under if re-opening had been an imminent possibility. It is reasonable to suppose that there would have been a clamour for it to moderate its more definitive conclusions and tone down the language in which they were expressed. Undoubtedly such pressure would have been resisted. But the government would scarcely have been happy to endorse such findings, so one might wonder at the reception the report as written would have received if it had threatened to provoke a pull out. As it was Bantry people could express their outrage at the loss of life once the full facts of the story began to emerge without any shadow of anxiety that a pull out by Gulf Oil now would do them further harm.

And so it is with tragic , if predictable irony, that we see the various actors in the drama combine as never before to investigate Gulf's activities, reach a verdict on them, and publicly declare the company culpable of so many of the charges its critics had been levelling at it for so long. Meanwhile, and in spite of the much vaunted publicity announcements the company had repeatedly made not only as regards safety provisions, but pollution control, yet another spillage fouled the Bay as the dead bodies, unburnt oil and other debris drifted out of the broken tanker. For all the claims the company had made, when they were most needed the emergency procedures no longer functioned as originally intended, so contributing to the scale and consequence of the catastrophe.

Because of these events, Gulf's use of propaganda, including what is politely known as the dissemination of misinformation, was exposed as a normal, apparently even a necessary, part of its business activities. Not only did it seek to actively suppress the truth and deceive the tribunal of inquiry, it even went so far as to impugn the honesty of the police force. Of course, such charges may sometimes have foundation, but not in this case. And in the circumstances, they were remarkable ones to make; an indication both of the company's desperation and the lengths to which it would go to protect its interests.

Final Remarks

Since this book attempts to present an analysis of key aspects of the relations between church, state and business in Eire which were of relevance to Bantry, it is appropriate to conclude by discussing some of the more salient issues raised by the Gulf Oil intervention as these relate to the major themes of the study.

Throughout I have made use of a distinction between personal and impersonal power. That is, between power which is wielded by individuals and collectivities in their own right, and that which — though it certainly relies upon the actions of specific people — is wielded by them only inasmuch as they are the representatives or agents of organizations whose functioning is independent of (though beholden to) those who contribute to the formulation and execution of its objectives.

Although emphasizing the links between the personal power of the clergy and the business people, when dealing with the impersonal power of the church as a corporate body I focused on its hierocratic legitimation of the state and the way this, together with its organizational hold upon diverse areas of civic life, mediated its relationship to business. As a counterpoint to this while emphasizing the links between the personal power of state representatives (politicians and civil servants) and business people, when dealing with the impersonal power of the state as a corporate body, I focused on the way its relationship to business was mediated by the privatization of government administration through the dispensation of party patronage. Through a discussion of Gulf Oil's Bantry venture, I have now extended this analysis of the ruling bloc to indicate how its character has begun to be modified because of the penetration of the national economy by foreign owned capital in the form of multinational corporations.

In the introduction to this study I foreshadowed the arguments of this chapter by speaking of the impersonally instituted authority of corporate property, of capital accumulated and organized on a world scale, as a more imperious version of class domination than that confronted in the analysis of the ruling bloc dominating Irish society. To say this is both to make a connection between the nationally specific configuration of class power — given its grounding in the advancing and evolving nature of capitalism — and that other configuration of class power which is institutionally structured by, and functions through, the imperialistic growth of multinational corporations and their developmental parameters. But in seeking the terms to define the connection between these two configurations of class power, we also thereby delineate the disjunctions between them.

The reciprocities which characterize their symbiosis are ones in which the duplicative aspects of the reproduction of class power are subordinated to the transformative ones and henceforth become dependent upon them. At Bantry, Gulf Oil was able to subordinate all other objectives to its pursuit of profit. If it enhanced the profits and the power of the local business people it did so only by creating an affluent and assertive industrial proletariat, and if it enhanced the wealth, privilege and prestige of the local bourgoisie, it did so only by making a vassal of it. And though, of course, it would be ridiculous to suggest Gulf Oil by itself accomplished such a metamorphosis nationally, it does seem reasonable to suggest that the growing penetration of the national economy by foreign capital will have analogous consequences.

Moreover, if we reflect on the fact that this will be accomplished not merely by direct investment, but through the mediation of the EEC, then we have good grounds for suspecting that the ruling bloc in its present form is destined for reconstruction by the very forces which consolidated its construction in the first place. With the investment of transnational capital increasingly co-ordinated by this prototype of a supra-national state, the particular configuration of material and ideological forces upon which the national ruling bloc depended already begins to appear anachronistic.

There is nothing finally settled either about the shape of the ruling bloc or even the stability of the bloc itself, and its dissolution would herald a new era. Such would be the case, for example, if there were to be a thorough incorporation of Eire into the EEC or a reuniting of the North with the South. In both cases, we could expect a profound reshaping of two of the key ideological supports of the ruling bloc: religion and nationalism.

But to say this is not to suggest that the reshaping of this bloc of power will make old habits of consciousness obsolescent. Rather, it is more likely that they too will be reincarnated as has happened before. For it is unlikely that economic development will cease to be an hegemonic motivating ideology. It is equally unlikely that nationalism will lose its capacity for ideological mobilization. Indeed, it is here that the dialectic between the duplicative and transformative aspects of the reproduction process are potentially most explosive. For while the troubles in the North persist and while a reunited Ireland remains a possibility, nationalism will continue to have a peculiarly combustible potential both for forging a new institutional structure of domination and for providing a vocabulary and a tradition to articulate conscious opposition to it. And of course while the North remains an issue the ideological potency of catholicism is secure because of its marriage to nationalism. Given these considerations, if such a metamorphosis of the ruling bloc were to eventuate, it is unlikely that there would be a divorce between catholicism and nationalism, church and state, even if the church's position within the bloc were weakened. For, as we have seen before, by aligning itself with populist causes in the name of the people the church is both able to bolster its influence with the laity and reach an accord with the parties whereby it becomes an intermediary between the state and civil society, a legitimator of the actions of both (ultimately an arbiter of what is rightful protest and what illegitimate extremism), and so a defender of the status quo.

The warrant for these speculations inheres in the concept of reproduction itself. It implies that just as we only know the past because of what we understand about the present, in order to understand the present we must hazard a guess about the future. For every theory of contemporary society has embedded within it — which is to say, presupposes — a theory of the future. For these reasons if for no other, then, there is some point — and a certain poignancy as well — to dealing with developments like Gulf's intervention at Bantry, which from the local standpoint seems gargantuan and exceptional. It is not that they present some kind of image of the future, but that so many of the processes they unleash expose in stark form how quickly major changes are rendered unexceptional, how quickly a seemingly impossible future is lived through and comes to seem like an all too predictable fate. Moreover, such developments may appear exceptional when they occur in specific places, but nevertheless represent a variant of the form of development encountered by many areas of the world.

And if an historical perspective of this sort is taken, exposure to the gargantuan and the exceptional also shows that a satisfactory explanation of social change must transcend the complacent treatment of history which in effect portrays it as composed of symbiotic currents running parallel to one another, one at the macro and one at the micro level. For, as this study shows, the realignment of class forces Gulf Oil caused at Bantry, and with which it was associated nationally, entailed a reconstruction of the relationship between macro and micro processes of social change. Inasmuch as the local situation changed, so too did the larger context. Inasmuch as the relevant larger context became ever more plastic so too did its relationship to the local situation — more plastic but no less determinate for that. In such circumstances it makes no sense at all to try to draw frames around localities or other types of community and demarcate social processes on that basis. Far better to contextualize by charting the imbrication of spatially and temporally specific processes and those which are spatially and temporally diffuse. For this allows us to define the interplay of the varying orders of determination whose actual outcomes constitute the social habitats in which we live.

Notes

1   The two books are based on a year and a half's participant-observation fieldwork
    carried out at Bantry Bay from late 1975 until early 1977. This followed a short
    stay in the area in the winter of 1974–75 which aroused my interest in the matters
    researched. The study was written up and submitted as a doctoral dissertation in
    1980. The books are a reorganized, revised and updated version of that account.
    The ethnographic techniques of anthropological research are well known and do
    not need elaboration: I lived in the community I was studying and I observed and
    participated in as wide a range of public and private activities as I could. Many of
    these activities do not figure in this study. Either they were not relevant or tran-
    scended the limits of the completed research. They were, however, essential in
    providing a proper ethnographic grounding of the actual issues discussed in it.
    Broadly speaking, my research methods while in the field can be classified as
    follows:
    (i)   Attention to casual social interactions and events in the course of daily
           life, including conversations with people on everyday matters.
    (ii)   Informal attendance at private and public gatherings and informal conver-
           sations with people on issues relevant to the research.
    (iii) Informal interviews, sometimes entailing the taking of notes, sometimes
           not — depending on the circumstances and the personalities involved.
    (iv)   Formal attendance at public and private functions. With one or two excep-
           tions, I attended every major public function that occurred in Bantry during
           the period of my fieldwork. In addition, I attended as many important
           private functions (formal meetings and informal gatherings) as possible.
    (v)   Formal interviews with public figures and private individuals. These
           included: a) a 20% random-sample survey of Bantry town's households
           (securing a response rate of more than 80%, i.e. 140 interviews); b) a
           survey of community influentials using a reputational snowball technique.
           These surveys produced important statistical and attitudinal data which was
           used to buttress data collected by other methods.

(vi)   Informal and formal interviews with relevant state officials in Cork City.

(vii)   Library research in Bantry Library, the County Library and the Cork City Library. This entailed: a) research into local history, and b) gleaning of information from newspaper accounts of events relating to Bantry in the 1966–77 decade. The local and provincial press consistently covered events in Bantry in great detail. Consequently, I have cited all pertinent reports in the *Southern Star* and the *Cork Examiner* as supporting sources for the incidents I describe and the arguments I make. I have also used the *Irish Times* where necessary in a similar way.

(viii) Viewing of RTE's (the national television network) videotaped coverage of news events relating to Bantry for the 1966–77 decade.

(ix)   Extraction of data from Gulf's public relations material — both verbal and written. Due to naivety I allowed the company's PR Officer to keep me on 'the long finger': he made himself available, but never managed to get me the promised interview with the Terminal Manager. In any case, I doubt that I would have learned anything more from him than did the press.

(x)   The empirical research conducted while in Ireland was subsequently buttressed by further library research into the oil industry and newspaper reports once I returned to Australia.

(xi)   Use of the Report of the Tribunal of Inquiry into the Disaster.

2   Although it may be regarded as linguistically improper to use the term Eire in English, it is a sociologically appropriate and convenient way of referring to the post-colonial state — and one which allows that it was a republic in spirit before it was one in law.

3   For a work which seeks to analyse the national situation from a perspective which has some affinities with the approach taken here see Peillon (1982). Of course our interpretations differ when it comes to specifics, but probably the most obvious difference in this regard is that whereas we agree about the importance of the bourgeoisie or business and the state, I attach greater weight to the continuing significance of the church. As far as theoretical orientations are concerned, though persuaded that his use of the concept of social 'projects' provides valuable insights into the nature of Irish society, I have reservations about the primacy he attaches to it, e.g. as regards the identification of 'social forces', and I am not convinced by his theorisation of the connection between 'projects', 'interests' and 'needs' (see especially chapter 19).

4   The terms 'macro' and 'micro' used as a binary opposition actually help prejudice our conceptual recognition of this interleaving, as does the simple opposition of the national and local 'levels'. However, given conventional assumptions, and for the sake of the intelligibility of the argument, I have retained this usage rather than repetitiously reiterating the mediating presence of intervening (e.g. regional, county provincial, etc.) 'levels'.

5   For a more extensive discussion of this distinction and its applicability to the analysis of social mobilizations, mobility and closure, and thereby also to social position and status, see Eipper (1982).

6   Contrast, though, for example, my approach with both those rejected and endorsed by, say, Bell and Newby (1971, 1978); Wild (1981).

Notes Chapter 2: Class in its social habitat

1   In this and subsequent chapters I use 'cf' to indicate points where my argument intersects with data or arguments presented by other authors. Since I do not discuss these authors' work (except in footnotes), and since my analysis frequently differs

from that of the authors cited, wherever 'cf.' appears readers should interpret this as evidence of agreement on the importance of the issue under discussion, but also as evidence of differences in approach to the given issue.

2 This argument presupposes an alternative conception of the relation and meaning of class and status to that associated with either Warnerian, Parsonian or Weberian models of status and class, and the use to which they have been put by stratification theorists. For a discussion of these see Eipper (1982). Especially note the contrast between my theory and method and Arensberg and Kimball's (1968) Warnerian approach to stratification in Ennis. Cf. Jackson's (1968) national analysis.

3 Thompson relates his brilliant metaphor to Marx's famous one: 'In all forms of society it is a determinate production and its relations which assign every other production and its relations their rank and influence. It is a general illumination in which all other colours are plunged and which modifies their specific tonalities. It is a special ether which defines the specific gravity of everything found in it.' (1978a: 151)

Notes Chapter 3: Business interests and economic development

1 See and cf: Arensberg, 1937; Arensberg and Kimball, 1968; Kane, 1968; 1977; 1979; Messenger, 1969; Hannan, 1970; 1972; 1974; 1982; Symes, 1972; Gibbon, 1973; Gibbon and Curtin, 1978; O'Carroll, 1973; 1976; O'Carroll, Passchier and Van der Wusten, 1978; Brody, 1974; Scheper-Hughes, 1979a, b and c; Fox, 1979; Ruane, 1979; Higgins and Gibbons, 1982; Tovey, 1982; Peillon, 1982: 11–18, 62–8; Cuddy and Curtin, 1983.

2 See and cf: Symes, 1972; Commins and Kelleher, 1973; Commins, 1982: 219–20, 222–4, 236; O'Carroll, 1973; 1976; O'Carroll, Passchier and Van der Wusten, 1978: 81, 83, 90–1, 103–4; Gibbon and Curtin, 1978: 492–6; Drudy, 1982: 193, 199–200, 202–3, 212; Hannan, 1982: 158–62; Tovey, 1982: 71–89.

3 See the *West Cork Resource Survey* (1963) for a general review of agriculture and its 'problems' in the region. See particularly: C-2, 3, C-20 (table IV). A West Cork Development Team Survey carried out in 1973 showed that 64% of the 'unemployed' had land valued at between £5 and £15 per acre. Almost 50% of farmers were under 30 years of age (see Meehan, 1974: 102). Between 1841 and 1966 the total population of the rural District decreased by 71.8%. The loss was greatest in the densest pre-famine areas of rural settlement (exceeding 80%) and least (56%) in the Glengarriff area. The decline in Bantry town was 42.6%. There was thus a major change in the relative share of population divided between the town and its hinterland. By 1966 the town population amounted to 30% of the Rural district as a whole (Census of Ireland, Hourihane, 1971: 120–2, 124, 208–9).

4 See and cf: IDA, 1972: 76, 77; Gibbon, 1973: 494; Commins and Kelleher, 1973; Commins, 1982: 221–4, 234, 236–8; Kennedy and Dowling, 1975: 286, 289; Scheper-Hughes, 1979a: 59; Crotty, 1979; Higgins and Gibbons, 1982; Tovey, 1982: 71–5, 79, 80–9; Peillon, 1982: 184–5, 191–4; Cox and Kearney, 1983: 158, 163, 177; Sheehy, 1984: 83, 90–3.

5 Note for example, these conclusions from the writers of the *West Cork Resource Survey* (C-18): 'The most important overall change which must take place in West Cork agriculture is to bring it into the market economy by the production of a much larger saleable surplus. A peasant agriculture with production on a subsistence basis is not enough to keep farm living standards in step with those of the rest of the community . . . '

6 See and cf: Arensberg, 1937: 146–80; Arensberg and Kimball, 1968: 273–98, 309–412; Gibbon and Higgins, 1974: 40; 1977; Kennedy, 1977; Higgins and Gibbons,

1982.
7   This was a valued arrangement for a butcher and cattledealer. As the tolls were collected on livestock coming into the town, the entrepreneur's men kept an eye on the quality of the stock coming into the fair and he was then able to manipulate prices and sales to the detriment of the farmer.
8   Controversy surrounded the sale of the Fastnet Fisheries fleet. The Biggs group's Managing-Director claimed that there was not room for both a shore-owner and crew and that the boats were sold to the skippers at a reasonable price. Everyone remained good friends, he said, the skippers going on to become well-to-do men based in other ports on the south coast nearer deep water. His critics claimed that the sale was prompted by his refusal to capitulate when the men were forced to strike. They argued that his action prematurely injured Bantry as a fishing port and caused hardship to the ordinary crewmen and their families.
9   Meehan calculated that tourism provided approximately 12% of the total labour force and at least 11% of the income (Meehan, 1974: 119–20). Much tourist-based employment was seasonal. For example, the hotels of Ballylickey and Glengarriff employed young girls and students for the summer months on extremely low wages, then virtually closed down for the winter months.
10   Given the growth in tourism in the Bantry area prior to the troubles in the North and of building and construction corresponding with the Gulf Oil project, it is significant that both these industries were important to the national growth profile of the 1960s. Building and construction was obviously stimulated by the establishment of industrial estates and the provision of housing for an expanded workforce. Tourism benefited from a reorganization of the responsible public bodies and the provision of incentives, the pay-off being its contribution to the balance of payments. (See Kennedy and Dowling, 1975: 145, 249, 282.)
11   See and cf: Meehan, 1970: 136–44, 318–21, 149–53, 374–80; Cullen, 1972: 183–5; IDA, 1972: 1, 43; 1978; Chubb, 1974: 242–50; Kennedy and Dowling, 1975: 113–114, 146, 200–1, 214, 231–2, 248–51; McAleese, 1977: 19, 20, 24–5, 26, 82; 1982: 277, 284–90; 1984: 165–6; Stanton, 1979; Schaffer, 1979: 239–42; Wickham, 1980; Peillon, 1982: 57–9, 156–64; Drudy, 1984: 193, 210.
12   Under the terms of entry, trade restrictions affecting industrial products were to be abolished gradually over a five-year period, as were adjustments to agricultural prices covered by the Common Agricultural Policy. Entry also entailed acceptance of provisions concerning such matters as the free movement of labour, standardization of products, financing, etc. However, the Irish Treaty of Accession included a special protocol recognizing the underdeveloped nature of the country's economy and the need for resources to reduce the disparity in living standards between Ireland and other member states. Under the treaty, industrial incentives were to be continued, with the provision that they could eventually be superseded by other EEC measures if equally effective in promoting industrial development.
13   The principal industrial incentives used by the IDA (1972: 65) were: (i) Fifteen years complete exemption from income taxation on profits from exports and partial remission for the remaining years up to 1990; (ii) Non-repayable cash grants towards the cost of fixed assets (sites, site development, buildings, new machinery and equipment), of research and development projects and industrial research facilities; (iii) Training grants; (iv) Readymade facilities on state financed industrial estates and advance sites, factories and other services at locations elsewhere; (v) Loan guarantees, interest subsidies and equity participation; (vi) Housing for key workers; (vii) After-care advisory and information service.
14   It could be misleading to describe all overseas firms operating in Ireland as 'multinationals'. Most were transnational in the sense that they were firms with manufacturing subsidiaries in more than one country, but many lacked a definite

network of overseas subsidiaries (McAleese, 1977: 84). This was the case, for example, with foreign-owned firms operating in Bantry prior to Gulf Oil. Of the overseas-sponsored firms established in Ireland after 1960 about 31% were British, 30% American, 18% German and 4% Dutch. The US firms increased their share of the total in the 1970s, while British firms came to represent a smaller proportion of the total number of establishments with foreign participation. Looked at from the point of view of capital investment, the significance of the American presence is much more striking, constituting just under 49% of the total, with British investment amounting to just under 15%, German just under 9%, Dutch just under 4%, and, notably, Japanese investment amounting to just under 13% of the total — the remaining 11% coming from a variety of countries (IDA, 1972: 24; 1978). Of new industry employment in Ireland, 60% was generated by firms employing 200 persons and over; 20% by firms employing 100 – 199; the remaining 20% were employed by firms with less than 100 employees. The latter group purportedly included many 'still in the process of increasing output and workforce to planned capacity (McAleese, 1972: 21–3). The firms which set up in Bantry were of this last type (see also below; Manpower Survey, 1976: 11).

15 Average incomes in Ireland were about half those for the EEC; incomes in the east of the country were 60% higher than those in the west (IDA, 1972: 1). When taken together average wage levels were sufficiently low to offset deficiencies in the average level of labour productivity (Kennedy and Dowling, 1975: 112).

16 The *Buchanan Report*, a government commissioned study published in 1969, stirred up a great deal of controversy and was not implemented. Instead, the IDA devised its own plans, which on paper were more politically acceptable. The Buchanan Plan proposed a limited number of growth centres and extensive internal migration of labour. The IDA's stated aims were to keep people in their own local areas and bring industry to them, while allowing the growth centres to grow of their own volition. It was recognized that the major centres would act as a vortex sucking people in even without government encouragement. To the extent that the IDA did nothing to counter this tendency and may even have covertly encouraged it, its critics claim it really implemented the Buchanan Plan by default.

17 As designated by the IDA's Regional Industrial Plan, the South West Region included Counties Cork and Kerry. It was dominated by Cork City, which produced 90% of the total output from the region. The IDA targeted for the creation of 500 jobs in the Bantry, Castletownbere, Dunmanway, Schull, Skibbereen area. The development potential of Bantry Bay as a deep-water port was well recognized by state officials. The County Manager made frequent mention of it as did the IDA and the politicians (IDA, 1972: 10, 20, 22, 62).

18 This is perhaps an exaggeration, but the argument has a certain credibility. It fits with comments made to me on related questions, with my own observations of business practices in the town, and finds a measure of confirmation in a variety of elliptical remarks, grey areas and evasions on the part of the influentials when they were interviewed about these matters.

Notes Chapter 4: Nationalist politics and patronage

1 Gibbon and Higgins, 1974: 32–3, 40; Gibbŏn, 1975: 97; Bax, 1970; 1972; 1975; 1976: 184–5; Sacks, 1976: 24, 25, 29; Garvin, 1977: 165, 166; Kennedy, 1978; Higgins and Gibbons, 1982.

2 Gibbon and Higgins (1974: 33) distinguish five basic forms of political patron-client relations operating at this time: (a) the use of ties of monopolistic personal dependence to secure support for political purposes; (b) the use of elected office

to secure favours from party and state which promoted the entrepreneur's economic ends; (c) the use of elected office to neutralise or eliminate political opponents; (d) the use of funds to secure the support of local notables for political projects and ventures; (e) the use of elected office to obtain favours for clients.

3 See and cf: Pyne, 1969–70; Manning, 1972: 18, 31–2, 54, 60, 63, 70, 80, 111, 112; Chubb, 1974: 77–82; Whyte 1974; Lyons, 1975: 524; Bax, 1975; 1976: 34, 39, 57–9, 63–7, 72, 73–8, 137; Sacks, 1976: 55, 65–6, 162, 211, 217–24; Garvin, 1974: 308–16, 324–25; 1977: 163, 175–78, 180–1; 1978: 328–30, 332–35, 336, 345, 346–47; 1981: 135–6, 137, 143, 145–51, 154–55, 157, 158–59, 161, 165–73, 174, 176, 178, 215–17; 1982: 171–75, 182–84; Gallagher, 1976; Rumpf and Hepburn, 1977: 5–6, 8–11, 72–3, 75, 81, 119–20, 122–3, 125, 134–42, 155–56, 219–21, 223; Mair, 1979: 448, 452–54, 458, 459, 464–65 (fn 57); Carty, 1981: 20, 42–4, 50–1, 61, 71–6, 78–9, 81–2, 82–4, 86–108, 140, 147–8, 151; O Tuathaigh, 1982: 172, 175, 178, 182, 183, 184, 185; Bew, 1982: 88–9; O'Connell, 1982: 191–98; Peillon, 1982: 109–20.

4 See and cf: Chubb, 1963; Pyne, 1974: 22, 25; Garvin, 1974: 324–5; 1981: 152, 167, 195–7, 202, 203; Bax, 1976: 13, 34, 41–2, 68, 72, 180–1, 183–9, 196–7; Sacks, 1976: 11–15, 35–8, 97–100, 136, 204–5, 207, 208–9, 216–25; Fanning, 1978: 416–519; Bew, Gibbon and Patterson, 1980, 162–4, 166–7; Wickham, 1980: 54–9, 62; O'Connell, 1982: 191–8; Peillon, 1982: 110–13.

5 See note 8.

6 Peillon (1982: 183) goes so far as to argue that the initiative for economic modernization formulated in the 1950s 'came from the State' being 'imposed in part on the undeveloped and reluctant bourgeoisie' which had been 'on the whole happy to stagnate behind the protection of tariff barriers'.

7 In this context it is noteworthy that Garvin (1981: 184–5, 193–5) emphasizes the extent to which the administrative machinery the state inherited from colonial times was of a highly advanced centralized and rationalized type, contrasting its modernization with the underdevelopment of society and arguing that the persistence of populist politics meant the state apparatus was vulnerable to coming under 'siege' from forces and groups less committed to bureaucratic rationalism.

8 There are two ethnographically detailed accounts of grass-roots patronage politics in the Irish Republic, Bax (1976) and Sacks (1976). There are many points of correspondence between their data and my own, but frequently my interpretation of the meaning or significance of particular phenomena differs from theirs, and in other respects our explanations diverge quite fundamentally. As studies of machine politics, these books focus on electoral mechanisms. The empirical descriptions of both writers are vivid but I am critical of their theoretical positions. Most obviously, and despite general acceptance of the distinction, I regard it as fundamentally misleading to construe transactionalism as the antithesis of an ideologically-oriented politics since it contains within itself its own ideological rationale. Rather what we are dealing with is a pragmatic morality — pragmatism as ideology. Defining politics in interactionist terms, and adopting a subjectivist perspective, these writers are primarily concerned with political behaviour in a given institutional context. Consequently they tell us a lot about the strategies and tactics of politicians, particularly the problems they encountered in building their machines and keeping them intact, but they never really come to grips with the problem of how these manoeuvres were structurally shaped. Taken overall, they give the impression that the major struggles in Irish politics were personalised, intra-party machines contests rather than impersonal inter-party ones. Carty (1980a; 1981) is less ethnographically and more quantitatively oriented. Although he pays due heed to inter- as well as intra-party struggles, to both party allegiances and brokerage ties, he advocates a one-sided emphasis on elites and a 'top-down conception of the political

system' which goes beyond what is required by his analysis (see 1981: 23–6, 109, 112–7, 129, 133, 148–52). Accordingly, he ends up unnecessarily espousing a programmatic political reductionism as a counter to what he sees as a socio-logical reductionism which treats politics as an epiphenomenon. Nevertheless, he rightly emphasizes that transactionalism and partisanship are 'not necessarily in-compatible' and that they can actually 'complement' one another, stressing that the social nexus 'does not occur in a void' but is 'shaped' by its 'institutional framework' which thereby also shapes the behaviour of those who 'inhabit' it. Bax, Sacks and Carty all treat class statically and minimise its relevance. In their accounts it remains an a-historical and loosely defined indicator of social stratifi-cation. Higgins (1982) provides a counter-weight to such approaches. Komito (1984) foreshadows a further detailed study. See also Gibbon and Higgins, 1974: 27–31, 38–44; Garvin, 1981: 197–8; O'Connell, 1982: 186–191; Peillon, 1982: 127–29.

9 Chubb, 1963: 223–5, 273–5, 276–9, 280–7; Gibbon and Higgins, 1975: 41; Bax, 1970; 1972; 1975; 1976: 33, 37–9, 45–52, 53–67, 73–9; 1982; Sacks, 1970; 1976: 7–8, 34–45, 50–3, 62, 65–71, 83–94, 145–6, 182–5, 191–5, 211–2, 216–8, 220, 221; Garvin, 1974: 317–20, 324–5; 1977: 182; 1981: 195–9, 200–6; 1982; Rumpf and Hepburn, 1977: 126; Mair, 1979; Carty, 1981: 22–3, 23–6, 129, 133, 146–7; Higgins, 1982: 114–123, 124, 133, 134, 135, 136, 137; O'Connell, 1982: 196–7; Roche, 1982; Komito, 1984: 174, 177–9, 180–92.

10 For descriptions of the day to day brokerage activities of TDs and County Councillors, their 'hearing of confessions' and their clinics, their letter-writing to constituents, their use of parliamentary question-time to get local press publicity, their badgering of civil servants, etc. see Chubb (1963), Bax (1976), Sacks (1976), and Higgins (1982).

11 These are primarily examples examples of what Garvin (1981: 195 – 9, 204 – 6) refers to as the 'undergrowth of petty patronage at local and subordinate levels'. He emphasizes the demarcation of areas in which recruitment was by 'merit', the 'majority of civil service posts' being filled on this basis. The 'core of the bureau-cracy' retained a considerable independence of party machines, nevertheless the civil service did become more sympathetic to Fianna Fail, with considerable 'penetration' of the party into the bureaucracy.

12 For further examples of pull see Chubb, 1963: 276–9; Bax, 1976: 48–9, 64, 65, 74–7; Sacks, 1976: 65–7, 83–93.

13 See also *Cork Examiner*, 17.1.1976, and Fergus O'Sullivan's account of the Labour TD's machine in *Hibernia*, 4.6.1976: 'The Baron of West Cork'.

14 Higgins (1982: 133) argues that as well as 'disorganizing' and 'disaggregating' the collectivist orientation of the poor, clientelism also worked against their representa-tives who lacked the private resources of entrepreneurs which make the latter freer 'to get on with the business of influencing state law and state administration for the benefit of their class'.

15 The use of the male gender is apposite here. There were few women in politics in Ireland, and they had usually inherited the seat from their father or husband. See also Manning, 1979; Carty, 1980b.

16 The County Council rather than the Dail was responsible for the administration of those services which most obviously and directly affected people in their daily lives, for example, health, sanitation, housing, welfare, roads and planning. In addition, the other major County Authorities, the Vocational Education Committee and the Committee of Agriculture had their members appointed by the County Council. Direct control over all local authorities was exercised by the Department of Local Government, which also controlled local appointments. Even the County Manager could only be removed by the Minister for Local Government; the Council

could at most suspend the Manager. In carrying out its functions, the County Councils were in many respects increasingly the agent of the central government departments (see Chubb, 1963; 1974: 280, 284).

[17] Higgins (182: 124, 137) argues that there was a considerable degree of understanding as to the parameters within which the rules of collision and collusion operated. If, for example, someone went 'too far' in 'pulling a stroke' this was made clear 'in the executive response' which gave 'a gentle reprimand that this was not playing the game'. He also elaborates on the democratic consequences of these arrangements. The County Manager, he says, deflected public scrutiny of government administration and created a facade of 'illusory accountability'. Enquiries by councillors into matters of routine administration were answered by the county secretariat in duplicate (one copy for the councillor's files, one for the client) thus fulfilling formal compliance with the constitutional requirements, but not providing any 'public participatory dimension'. Komito (1984: 183, 188-9) points out that inquiries by politicians 'inevitably' took priority over those of ordinary citizens, the civil service being 'primarily accountable to politicians and not the public'. Moreover, some bureaucratic responses 'merely appeased the politician without altering the end result', for 'a cosmetic reaction' fostering 'the illusion of special influence was sufficient for the politician's purposes'. Such correspondence provided the voter with 'proof' of the politician's influence as did the arrangement of 'special' interviews with officials and Ministers.

[18] According to Higgins (1982: 134, 136) the effect was a legislature ill-disposed to initiate policy, draft and scrutinize legislation, and handle public finances. Whereas Chubb (1963: 285-6) does not seem unduly perturbed by this, portraying the politician as increasingly a 'consumer representative' within a bureaucratized government, Higgins argues that the electoral recruitment of representatives to assemblies provided 'an elaborate pseudo-democratic facade to a non-accountable state'. Carty (1981: 136-9, 140, 141-2) emphasizes the 'conservative' effects, the 'incentives' which 'unduly reward' the 'suppression' of talent, 'particularism' and 'the pursuit of the status quo', thus perpetuating 'the stagnant cast' of party politics to the point where it 'stifles' competition and choice. He sees the parties as 'left impoverished, with neither the will nor the capacity to develop an effective policy-making machinery' and 'incapable of involving citizens in the issues that confront the polity'. For his part, Peillon (1982: 130-3) argues government activity develops an 'autonomy' which 'isolates' it from 'the debilitating influence of over-rigid principles and restrictive ideologies' because of being 'to some extent freed from electoral control' whilst acknowledging the ritualistic dimension which democratic elections assume when they come to serve as primarily legitimating 'integrative ceremonies'. Of course many of these complaints are ones which are, to one degree or another, symptomatic of parliamentary politics everywhere, not only the Irish version of them,.

[19] Higgins (1982: 123-4) like Bax and Sacks describes how local cadres took over positions in community associations and attempted to manipulate them for party political ends to that credit could be taken for the expeditious use of pull. In so doing they attempted to block such demands as could not be met by government when their party was in power, and brought such demands forward when their party was in opposition. In Bantry there was plenty of scope for these kinds of activities but since such cadres were, if not key influentials in their own right, small fry compared to them, their significance was diminished (see also chapters 6 and 7).

[20] See and cf: Chubb, 1963: 279, 284; Garvin, 1974: 323; 1981: 162, 197-8; Bax, 1970; 1975; 1976: 39, 40-2, 79-86, 88-93, 97-8, 129; 1982; Sacks, 1970; 1976: 62-3, 63-5, 137-9, 145-53, 164, 175-9, 233; Carty, 1980a; 1981: 27, 62-9, 112-22, 124-6, 129-31 133-9; Higgins, 1982: 119-27; Komito, 1984: 181, 190-1.

21 This had not always been the case. According to Bax (1975; 1976: 185–7; 1982) 'the brass' of the nationalist movement originally became TDs and 'the gunmen' went into the County Councils, but once they realised their position was threatened by ambitious County Councillors, TDs moved into the County Councils to take advantage of the opportunities they presented for dispensing patronage. Bax thus distinguishes between nationally oriented leaders attracting supporters on a moral (ideological) basis and parochially oriented brokers who tied their followers transactionally. This seems, though, an overly schematic account of what happened. I would venture that both elements were used to some degree at each level both by men with a 'name' because of their 'record' in the 'Troubles' and those without one — even if a lack or loss of revolutionary charisma encouraged a reliance upon transactionalism.

22 See note 13.

23 See and cf: Bax, 1970; 1972; 1975; 1976: 50–2, 68–9, 183, 189–94; 1982; Sacks, 1976: 7–15, 211–5; Carty, 1981: 1–13, 14–26, 109–12, 140, 148–9, 150–2; Higgins, 1982: 137–8. Lest my argument be misconstrued it perhaps needs to be reiterated that we are here dealing with issues of cultural economy not merely ones of political economy. This follows from the anti-economist conception of class used throughout this study, and a rejection of the all to familiar tendency to oppose class to culture which bedevils discussions of 'political', 'peasant' and 'modernizing' culture in Ireland. See and cf: chapter 3; Carty, 1981: 15–26, 129, 142–3; Garvin, 1982: 176–85; O'Connell, 1982: 187–93; Peillon, 1982: 122–33. Relevant here too, of course, is the issue of how best to conceptualise and analyse the relationship of the 'centre' to the 'periphery', and the 'domination' of the former by the latter. See and cf: Bax, 1972; 1982; Garvin, 1974; 1981; 162, 216–7; 1982; Carty, 1981: 93–8; Komito, 1984: 174, 178–9, 190, 191.

24 Higgins (1982: 134) argues that policy innovations were jeopardised and policy differences minimized as the central bureaucracies of the political parties had their influence eroded by the clientelism of the politicians, causing stagnation of policy and ideological development. The small Labour party struggling 'to achieve an ideological identity' was faced, he says, with the 'co-optation of its members into clientelism' and the adoption of 'positions completely at odds with its policies'. There may be considerable truth in this, particularly where the Labour party was concerned — as the example of the West Cork Labour TD shows. And Higgins' concern and perspective is understandable given that he was himself both a Member of Parliament and Chairman of the party and is personally opposed to clientelist practices. But it would be wrong, I believe, to suggest a simple polarity between the ideological initiatives of the centralized party bureaucracy and the clientelism of the ordinary politician or the mass of the electorate — see also Chubb (1963) and Garvin (1974: 323; 1981: 184–5, 204). Such a dichotomy under-estimates the part played by the party leaderships (at least in the major parties) in fostering patronage politics and diverts attention from the interplay of bureaucratic and personalistic modes of domination. Once again it makes clientelism seem a product simply of competing bids for personal power by individual politicians and/or a simple cultural disposition.

25 Cf Bax, 1976: 193–4; cf Sacks, 1976: 223. It is of course on this point that my analysis most starkly runs counter to their conclusions and calls into question the adequacy of their approach for dealing with such issues.

26 Note the generality of, and variance between, the definitions of, patronage and brokerage provided by Bax (1976: 50) and Sacks (1976: 81–3), and the implications raised by my argument for them. See also the distinction Komito (1984: 174, 176–7, 178–9) makes between brokerage, clientelist links and clientelism. See also note 23.

27 It needs to be emphasized that as used here the term *comprador* refers specifically to the brokerage characteristics of the relationship to foreign capital, and is not meant to imply any kind of instrumentalist relationship, but rather a more ambiguous and ambivalent one. See also Wickham (1980: 59, 69–72) and note 28. My argument goes some way toward answering questions of the sort raised by O'Connell (1982: 198). In so doing it recasts the connection Gibbon and Higgins (1974: 39–42) make between patronage, brokerage and the advance of capitalism. Patronage relations, pure and simple, certainly have a compulsory and monopolistic character. Brokerage relations, however, do not only result from the dissolution of these, nor need they entail a multiplication of brokers, although this does seem to have been important in rural Ireland. Hence, to take an extreme case, where the state becomes a local broker for monopoly capital the number of brokers is restricted to one (although competing parties may function as brokers' brokers). In this instance brokerage even loses its non-compulsory character: the citizen is formally free to choose between parties, but not states.

28 Peillon's (1982: 183, 191–4, 206) arguments are worth noting in this context. He asserts that rather than the modernizing initiative of the 1950s being a case of the bourgeoisie 'imposing its will on the State' it was the other way around. However, he says, 'the bourgeoisie can now dictate to the State' which, 'like the apprentice sorcerer, is dominated by its own creation'. This is, if anything, even more true of its conjuring with foreign capital. This latter relationship further exacerbates the complexity of the tasks confronting the state which, though it 'incorporates the particular project of the bourgeoisie into its general project, modifies it, goes beyond it, and links it to other orientations'. In so doing, it 'escapes the control of particular projects but not their influence'. For such reasons it would be wrong to regard even a clientelized state as a mere instrument of the bourgeoisie. Peillon does describe this case as 'a simple matter of interests coinciding, one using the other', nevertheless, his general point holds, namely that although 'the State takes the bourgeois project as the pivot of its own project', and though the bourgeoisie's needs may be given priority, and its demands never ignored, this is not to say it invariably receives satisfaction, nor does it prevent conflicts of interest even ones leading to open confrontation. As far as foreign capital is concerned, the most important point is that, unlike the indigenous bourgeoisie, it 'takes advantage of the State while remaining independent of it'.

Notes Chapter 5: Catholic culture and civic affairs

1 The most thorough examination of church – state relations in Eire is Whyte (1971). He uses detailed case studies to illustrate the changes that occurred following the founding of the state. Mainly preoccupied with refuting the notion that Eire is a theocratic state, he focuses on the ideological kinship of the powerful — but since he has a liberal, not a class view of the state, he does not explore the material underpinnings of this relationship. Hence, although in this Section I draw extensively upon his data, his concerns and argument differ from my own. For an account of the contemporary position of protestants, see White (1975).

2 See and cf: Whyte, 1971: 10–11, 24–61, 48, 90–3, 320–2, 375; O'Brien, 1972: 103–4, 110–22; Miller, 1973: 485–96; Larkin, 1975: 391–6; White, 1975: 108–9, 112–15, 124–81, 183–5, 190–3; Rumpf and Hepburn, 1977: 15, 95; Garvin, 1981: 154–5, 156, 167, 179–80, 185.

3 Weber (1968: 1162) in a different context, suggested that the catholic church '... makes acceptance and submission a religious duty in the face of every government that indisputably holds de facto power, as long as such a regime does not

215

despoil the church'.

4 See and cf: Whyte, 1971: 39–56, 62–3, 65–74, 80–1, 85–6, 98–100, 112–17, 119, 171–95, 300, 312–14, 330, 333, 337–41, 350, 356–60, 373–4; Manning, 1971; O'Brien, 1972: 117–27; White, 1975: 99–102, 116–24, 129–36, 137–58; Rumpf and Hepburn, 1977: 15–16, 81–7, 128–34; Garvin, 1974: 312; 1978: 336; 1981: 154–5; Peillon, 1982: 89–99, 113, 125, 150–1, 175, 190–1, 192, 198–9, 202, 206.

5 Gramsci (1975: 262) argued that to the church the state was not a class state, but an umpire, a guardian of 'fairplay' according to 'the rules of the game': 'The Catholics would like the state to be interventionist one hundred per cent in their favour; failing that, or where they are in a minority, they call for a "neutral" state, so that it should not support their adversaries'. In a similar vein, Weber (1968: 1209) distinguished between the necessity for catholics to be free to follow their own conscience against the recognition of the freedom of conscience for others: 'A fully developed church — advancing universalist claims — cannot concede freedom of conscience; wherever it pleads for this freedom, it is because it finds itself in a minority position and demands something which, in principle, it cannot grant to others'. Bishop Lucey, for instance, viewed majoritarian democracy in a manner similar to the Unionists in the North who argued for a protestant parliament for a protestant people. For Bishop Lucey, if the majority was catholic that meant catholic rule. This was an argument for undiluted ideological purity before any democratic ideals.

6 According to Whyte (1971: 158–9, 195) the integralist thrust reached its peak during the 1948–51 period of inter-party government. Hence he pays most attention to the church–state clash over the Health Act of 1947 and the Mother and Child Scheme, 1951.

7 Whyte (1971: 335) argued that the hierarchy had, according to Cardinal Conway in 1966, feared the effects of 'the increasing invasion of the state into the field of economics', but it now thought those fears exaggerated. Previously the bishops had seen 'a close connection between increased state control of the economy and totalitarianism'. Since it had not ushered in socialism, state intervention was apparently no longer seen as a danger in itself.

8 A corollary of this seems to have been that some doctors, when charging fees, did not ask for a specific figure, patients paid what they could afford or what they thought was expected of them. Some older business people still annually sent their doctor an open cheque for his services. In spite of having a medical card which entitled them to free health care, some pensioners insisted on giving the doctor money for consultation.

9 During my fieldwork, the parish priest in Dunmanway, a village not far from Bantry, became embroiled in a bitter and complicated controversy which split the parish into two antagonistic camps. To my knowledge, the Bantry clergy had never done anything to cause this kind of resentment, but given the right circumstances an irascible priest might well have done so. Peillon (1982: 91) has made the pertinent comment that 'Paradoxically, anti-clerical sentiment serves as a support mechanism for religious institutions, since it activates the religious values which serve as criteria for the criticism of clerical shortcomings'.

Notes Chapter 6: Town influentials and the basis of their influence

1 Cf. the stratificationist tendency to analyse these questions primarily in terms of a dichotomy of elites and masses, the powerful and the powerless. These theorists rightly emphasize that there is a plurality of power in capitalist society, but

stress the autonomy of economic and political elites. By contrast, I treat the emergence of different kinds of leaderships as an attribute among other things, of class mobilization. Moreover, I stress the interpenetration and interdependence of cultural as well as political and economic mobilizations.

2   These were auxiliaries recruited into the police force by de Valera to combat the threat represented by Blueshirts in the 1930s. Like this man, most were former members of the IRA (see Manning, 1971; Lyons, 1975: 523–36).

3   I have not presented a detailed statistical analysis of different people's views of the local class structure and their evaluation of their own position within it as revealed by the survey data. A thorough analysis of the relevant material requires separate treatment and is beyond the limits of this study.

Because of time, money and methodological problems I was forced to restrict my random sample to the town limits. This meant that none of the hippies or settlers were included, and only a couple of farmers. Even so, I did formally interview some hippies and settlers and informally interviewed others, as I did those Anglo-Irish who lived beyond the town limits. I did not conduct formal interviews with farmers outside the town limits. However, I lived in the country myself, in the townland of Glenlough near Gerahies, and observed and participated in the life of the people of the Muntervary peninsula for the entire period of my fieldwork.

Although a random sample survey of the countryside would have been immensely valuable, it was beyond my resources. A survey of the hippies and settlers would have been particularly useful, but to do the job properly it would have required the coverage of the whole of West Cork. This suggests that a separate study of settlement by foreign nationals would be warranted.

These deficiencies are not as great as they may at first seem. The random survey is invaluable as a pathfinding device for the fieldworker, but there are many problems associated with interpreting the results. Other fieldwork encounters (formal and informal interviews, discussions, conversations, chance incidents, etc.) provided me with information which often was more ethnographically vivid, pertinent and representative of actual reality than that revealed by the survey. Some people of particular interest escaped the net of the sample, casual conversations were habitually reservoirs of the unforseen, confidants and friends provided opportunities for exploring issues and personalities with rare candour, and so on. Some respondents to the survey showed remarkable frankness, others were tight-lipped or prone to dissimulate. A few lied and let it be known; others may have lied without my knowing. At times it was well nigh impossible to distinguish between lying, evasiveness and honest opinion. (It was easiest to be sure when people gave their income.) If we are to follow our instincts as social scientists we must assume that these variations in response (between individuals, and in regard to particular issues) follow definite patterns. The random sample questionnaire reifies these rather than illuminates them, hence the need to establish the prior claim to empirical validity of the ethnographic data over the statistical. Nowhere is this more true than in answering questionnaires where people are giving a public (if anonymous) response to contentious issues. The answer we get may have more to do with their perception not only of the interviewer's expectations and attitudes, but of public attitudes to what can be said. In other words, in principle we only get what people are *prepared to say as a matter of record,* rather than what they *happen to say,* let alone what they *actually think.* Nowhere is this more important than in the discussion of class distinction.

4   See also chapter 7, note 2.

1   Included among the Engineer's other responsibilities were road maintenance, the town water supply, sewerage, town planning, piers and harbours, sheep-dipping stations, land project schemes, ESB and P&T cables, public lighting, pollution control, maintenance of burial grounds, control of public scavenging, garbage collection and housing loans.

2   The evidence would seem to suggest that many Labour party stalwarts and supporters identified Labour more closely with Fianna Fail than Fine Gael. Certainly, Labour was seen as a threat by Fianna Fail politicians. Trade Union activists from Fianna Fail families, in particular, seemed to gravitate towards Labour. Thus, for example, the two key figures among the militant tugboat shop stewards serving the Gulf Oil tankers came from Fianna Fail backgrounds but saw themselves as Labour men. This was also true of a number of other trade unionists.

3   The traders' attitude is neatly encapsulated in a comment made by a business man from Bantry's neighbouring village, Ballylickey, when organizing his village's festival for the 1977 summer. Half-jokingly he lamented that they could not put ridges across the road, similar to those used by the British Army in Northern Ireland, to slow down the tourist traffic.

4   The organizations which eventually received money were (in addition to the £1000 going to pay for the Fiesta) the Golf Club, the Community Association, the GAA, the Development Association, the Regatta Committee, the Sea Anglers, Comhaltas Ceoltoiri, the West Cork Tourist Association, the Salmon and Trout Anglers Association, the Gurtycloona Theatre and the Town Commissioners.

5   The Submission dealt with a wide range of issues, including the following: Development Planning; an Oil Rig Supply Base; Pier Improvement and Development Preservation of Traditional Fishing Grounds and Amenities; Traffic Control in the Bay; Safety; Environmental Control and Pollution; Complaints, Revenue; Foreshore Ownership; and Land Speculation. The Association wanted the Port Authority to act as a controlling and developing body, arguing that a final decision should be preceded by a conference of all interested parties including Government Departments, along the lines previously proposed by the Bantry Fishermen's and Boat Owners' Association in a letter to the Minister.

6   The positions were rotated as follows:

Executive	President	Vice-President	Secretary
Caretaker Committee	Dentist	Rowa Manager	Draper
First Executive	Rowa Manager	Dentist	Draper
Executive elected at the first AGM	Dentist	Company Secretary	Draper
Executive elected at 1970 AGM	Company Secretary	Dentist	Rowa Manager
Executive elected at adjourned 1971 AGM	Draper	Company Secretary	Dentist (Rowa Manager Asst Secretary)

7   The usual arrangement was that each man took a share of the catch, another share went to the owner of the boat (usually one or more of the crew) and a further share went to the local agent who provided the salt and barrels, arranged the sale of the fish and transport, and who negotiated a price with the buyers. The few businessmen involved in fishing owned larger, half-deck trawlers. They employed a crew and paid them on a share basis. Special provision was made for skippers and for the owners who provided all the gear.

8   At the oral hearing into the refinery proposed for Whiddy Island held in 1973 (see chapter 8, and Eipper, forthcoming), the chief inspector of fisheries for the Cork Board of Conservators estimated that in 1972, 22 000 salmon worth £100 000 were caught in the Bantry district. A local fisherman put the value of the annual scallop catch in the Bay at £20 000, and a part-time fisherman estimated that the herrings caught were worth £100 000 per annum. However, these figures may have been inflated, given the context in which they were produced (*Irish Times*: 7.4.1973).

9   See also *Examiner*: 17.9.1975, 18.9.1975, 25.9.1975, 20.9.1975, 1.10.1975, 8.10.1975, 9.10.1975, 30.10.1975, *Star*: 20.9.1975, 27.9.1975; and the *Irish Times*: 18.11.1975.

10 The first fish of the season were in fact landed by three four-oared yawls at Gerahies. This was regarded by the press as a surprise development since it had previously been understood that not even local men would fish until the dispute was finalized. But the Bantry spokesmen stressed that they had no objection to anyone fishing in an open yawl.

11 The injunction against the outsiders restrained them from attempting to fish over, on or near where the Bantry men were fishing. The local men also claimed that, on the pretext of not seeing any markers, the trawlers drove through their nets, scattering or destroying them. The outsiders got the terms of their injunction against the locals varied when they found the entire fishing area dotted with markers purely for the purpose of excluding them from the fishing grounds.

12 The Bantry 'fishing war' can be compared with a far more dramatic one that climaxed after six years at Fenit in Tralee Bay in November 1975 when 15 boats were burnt and seven set adrift. This incident received national front page press coverage and indicates the intensity of feeling aroused by such disputes. The Fenit oyster beds were the most important in Ireland and reputedly one of the largest and richest in Europe, but the dredging of oysters in the traditional way was now relatively rare. The 'outsiders' were men from fishing villages and towns further around the Kerry coast entering Tralee Bay in half-deck trawlers and smaller open boats. The 1975 season had been the richest in the history of the fishery, with good catches and high prices. Up to 70 boats had been dredging the oyster beds continually, around 50 of these being owned by fishermen from Tralee Bay villages. The six year 'war' had seen continuing outbreaks of trouble, with boats set adrift or damaged and mixtures of sugar and water poured into fuel tanks, but this latest incident was unprecedented for its extent and thoroughness, destroying the bulk of the non-local fishing fleet. The situation at Fenit was extremely complex, but it seems that the major issue of locals versus outsiders was, as in Bantry, complicated by other matters. Apparently many of the outsiders fished from larger, better-equipped boats and this antagonized the local small men who saw themselves being robbed of both oysters and jobs; there were strong feelings that the beds were being threatened by the taking of under-sized oysters, especially by the outsiders; there were also rivalries between the locals themselves related to traditional strife between neighbouring villages. It remains clear, though, that the main thing was resentment at the invasion of large boats owned by outsiders employing outside crews as in Bantry. (The best reports of this incident in the press were by the *Irish Times*: 10.11.1975 and 13.11.1975.)

Notes Chapter 8: Corporate persuasion, state compliance and community impotence

1   Eipper (forthcoming) provides a complete account of Gulf's intervention and supporting evidence for the information upon which this discussion is based can be found there. A condensed version is provided in Eipper (1985). The latter, however, goes further than the book in applying double-bind theory to explicate the precise nature of Gulf's hegemony.

Appendix

Table 1: Population Change 1926–1971 Town and Rural District

	1926	1936	1946	1951	1956	1961	1966	1971
Rural District	11,322	10,335	9,143	8,565	8,061	7,814	7,760	7,918
% Change	−11.08	−8.72	−11.53	−6.32	−5.88	−3.06	−0.69	+2.04
Town	2,685	2,643	2,453	2,319	2,211	2,234	2,341	2,579
% Change	−15.00	−1.56	−7.19	−5.46	−4.66	+1.04	+4.79	+10.17

Source: Census of Ireland

Table 2: Population Change Bantry: Town and Rural District
1961–66, 1966–71

| Area | Population | | | Change | | | | | |
| | 1961 | 1966 | 1971 | 1961–66 | | 1961–71 | | 1966–71 | |
				No.	%	No.	%	No.	%
Rural District	7,814	7,760	7,918	−54	−0.69	+104	+1.33	+158	+2.04
Town	2,234	2,341	2,579	+107	+4.79	+345	+15.44	+238	+10.17

Source: Census of Ireland

Table 3: Population Change — Male and Female Ratios

1961–66, 1966–71 — Town and Rural District

Area		1961	1966	1971	Percentage Change			Females per 1,000 males		
					'61–'66	'61–'71	'66–'71	1961	1966	1971
Rural District	M	4,009	3,915	4,037	−2.39	+0.70	+3.12	949	982	961
	F	3,805	3,845	3,881	+1.10	+2.00	+0.09			
Town	M	1,033	1,033	1,168	0	+13.07	+13.07	1,163	1,266	1,208
	F	1,201	1,308	1,411	+8.91	+17.49	+7.87			

Source: Census of Ireland

Table 4: Workforce Composition 1966 and 1971

(major categories only)

Category	1966	%	1971	%	Change
Males					
Agriculture, Forestry and Fishing	69	11.52	70	10.93	+1
Manufacturing	101	16.86	83	12.97	−18
Building	78	13.02	84	13.13	+6
Commerce, Insurance and Finance	158	26.38	131	20.47	−27
Transport and Communications	51	8.51	100	15.63	+49
Females					
Manufacturing	32	9.55	28	8.38	−4
Commerce, Insurance and Finance	90	26.87	85	25.45	−5
Professional	116	34.63	121	36.23	+5
Other	71	21.19	65	19.46	−6

Source: Census of Ireland

N.B. Gulf's workforce is categorised under 'Transport and Communications', which distorts the so-called Services sector.

Table 5: Town and Rural District — Employment Structure
by Industrial Grouping — 1966 and 1971

Industrial Grouping	Year	Rural District			Town			Remainder		
		M	F	Total	M	F	Total	M	F	Total
Agriculture Forestry and Fishing	1966	1,355	180	1,535	69	6	75	1,286	174	1,460
	1971	1,107	95	1,202	70	2	72	1,037	93	1,130
Mining Quarrying and Turf Production	1966	3	0	3	1	0	1	2	0	2
	1971	2	0	2	0	0	0	2	0	2
Manufacturing	1966	139	50	189	101	32	133	38	18	56
	1971	154	49	203	83	28	111	71	21	92
Building and Construction	1966	226	2	228	78	2	80	148	0	148
	1971	267	1	268	84	0	84	183	1	184
Electricity Gas and Water	1966	20	1	21	9	1	10	11	0	11
	1971	24	1	25	13	1	14	11	0	11
Commerce Insurance and Finance	1966	231	134	365	158	90	248	73	44	117
	1971	240	140	380	131	85	216	109	55	164
Transport and Communication	1966	80	17	97	51	9	60	23	8	37
	1971	187	31	218	100	16	116	87	15	102
Public and Defence Administration	1966	53	9	62	31	6	37	22	3	25
	1971	55	12	67	36	10	46	19	2	21
Professions	1966	93	164	257	48	116	164	45	48	93
	1971	90	177	267	45	121	166	45	56	101
Other	1966	94	215	309	27	71	98	67	144	211
	1971	89	165	254	28	65	93	61	100	161
Total, all Industries	1966	2,294	772	3,066	573	333	906	1,721	439	2,160
	1971	2,215	671	2,886	590	328	918	1,625	343	1,968
'Out of Work'	1966	92	12	104	26	2	28	66	10	76
	1971	118	23	141	50	6	56	68	17	85
Total Labour Force	1966	2,386	784	3,170	599	335	934	1,787	449	2,236
	1971	2,333	694	3,027	640	334	974	1,693	360	2,053

Source: Census of Ireland

Table 6: Rural District, Non-Town and Town Employment Structure by Occupational Grouping, 1971

Occupational Grouping	Rural District			Non-Town			Town		
	M	F	Total	M	F	Total	M	F	Total
Agriculture incl. Forestry & Fishing	1149	95	1244	1067	93	1160	82	2	84
Producers, Makers and Repairers	298	28	326	153	17	170	145	11	156
Labourers and Unskilled Workers	237	0	237	167	0	167	70	0	70
Transport and Communication	189	24	213	89	12	101	100	12	112
Clerical	56	72	128	11	26	37	45	46	91
Commerce, Insurance and Finance	164	126	290	77	59	136	87	67	154
Service, Entertainment and Sport	109	202	311	64	103	167	45	99	144
Professional, Technical & Others	131	147	278	65	50	115	66	97	163
Total Gainfully Occupied	2333	694	3027	1693	360	2053	640	334	974
Total Not Gainfully Occupied*	668	2200	2868	461	1477	1938	207	723	930
Total 14 Years and Over	3001	2894	5895	2154	1837	3991	847	1057	1904
Total Population	4037	3881	7918	2869	2470	5339	1168	1411	1579

* This category includes without breakdown: total at school, or students, total engaged in home duties, the retired, etc.

Source: Census of Ireland

Table 7: Town Employment Listing

Employment Category	M	F	Total
Employers and own Account Workers	133	34	167
Assisting Relatives (i.e. not receiving fixed wage or salary)	12	5	17
Employees	445	289	734
Out of Work	50	6	56
Retired or Not Gainfully Employed	207	723	930
Total	847	1,057	1,904

Source: Census of Ireland

Points to Note

1 The 1966 and 1971 censuses detailed the occupations of those living in the town, but did not take into account those commuting to work from rural areas.

2 The employment of the Rural District was typical for an under-developed area, though Bantry Rural District had a slightly lower proportion of its work force employed in agriculture mainly because of the high service employment and tourist employment in the area (over 41% in the Bantry Rural District). The large number of retail establishments per head of population, though falling, was still high, as was the number employed in commerce in the 1970s (Meehan, 1974: 94, 113).

3 Females comprised 35.87% of the town labour force and 24.73% of the Rural District labour force (which included the town) in 1966, as compared with 34.29% and 22.93% in 1971. The number of women in the work force in the town fell by one between 1966 and 1971, with an additional four of them reporting as out of work. In the same period there appeared an additional 41 males in the work force from the town, with 24 of them reported as 'out of work'. Because of the closure of the Flately and King Shoe plants in 1971 manufacturing figures are lower than those for previous and following years. With the expansion of employment offered by Rowa and the opening of the Chesterton plant the numbers employed in manufacturing would have been closer in 1975 to the 1966 figures.

4 About 40% of the total male labour force was unmarried, and about two-thirds of the working males were under 35. The age composition of the female labour force also shows a predominance in the under 35 year category. Over 80% of the married women employed in the town were shopowners' wives working in the family business. In contrast to the Rural District as a whole, the town had a younger occupational structure (Hourihane, 1971: 167–8).

5 In 1976 there were 287 people listed as unemployed on the social welfare books in Bantry, 220 males and 65 females. Unemployment rates for females on official figures were between one-third and one-half the male figures for Cork County (excluding the city, in 1966). Of course, the official figures always under-estimate the actual amount of unemployment, nor do they give any indication of numbers 'employable' in industry (it goes without saying that this especially applies to women). On official figures, over the 1961–71 period the highest annual rate of unemployment in County Cork as a whole was 3.98% and the lowest was 2.96%. If the city is excluded, the figures for rural County Cork would be nearer those for Kerry, i.e. in the region of 6–10%. In the poorer parts of the county the figure would approach the top end of the scale or exceed it. It would also be subject to large seasonal variations, with a greater incidence recorded among unskilled male workers than among skilled workers (IDA, 1972: 12–13). Due to the availability of seasonal employment in the summer months, unemployment was lower then, reaching its peak in the winter.

Bibliography

Arensberg, C. M. (1937) *The Irish Countryman*. Peter Smith, Mass.

Arensberg, C. M. and Kimball, S. T. (1968) *Family and Community in Ireland*. Harvard University Press, Cambridge, Mass.

Bantry Town Commissioners' Minute Books 1896–1977.

Bax, M. (1970) 'Patronage Irish Style: Irish Politicians as Brokers', *Sociologische Gids*, 17 (3).

Bax, M. (1972) 'Integration, Forms of Communication and Development: Centre – Periphery Relations in Ireland, Past and Present', *Sociologische Gids*, 19.

Bax, M. (1975) 'The Political Machine and its Importance in the Irish Republic', *Political Anthropology*, vol. 1, no. 1.

Bax, M. (1976) *Harpstrings and Confessions: Machine-Style Politics in The Irish Republic*. Van Gorcum, Assen/Amsterdam.

Bax, M. (1982) 'The small community in the Irish political process' in Drudy, P. J. (ed.) *Ireland: Land, Politics and People*, (*Irish Studies 2*). Cambridge University Press, Cambridge. Originally published in 1975 as 'On the small community in the Irish political process' in Boissevain, J. and Friedl, J. (eds) *Beyond the Community: Social process in Europe*. Department of Educational Science of the Netherlands, The Hague.

Bell, C. and Newby, J. (1971) *Community Studies*. Allen and Unwin, London.

Bell, C. and Newby, J. (1978) 'Community, communion and class and community action' in Herbert, D. and Johnson, R. (eds) *Social areas in cities*. Wiley, London.

Bew, P., Gibbon,P. and Patterson, H. (1980) 'Aspects of Nationalism and Socialism in Ireland: 1968–1978' in Morgan, A. and Purdie, B. (eds) *Ireland: Divided Nation Divided Class*. Ink Links, London.

Bew, P. (1982) 'The Land League ideal: achievements and contradictions' in Drudy, P. J. (ed.) *Ireland: Land, Politics and People*, (*Irish Studies 2*). Cambridge University Press, Cambridge.

Binsted, P. B. (1968) (World-wide Co-ordinator – Transportation, Gulf Oil Corp.) 'Mammoth Tankers — The Users' Point of View'. Europoort '68 Congress, Amsterdam, November.

Blackwell, J. and O'Malley, E. (1984) 'The impact of EEC membership on Irish industry' in Drudy, P. J. (ed.) *Ireland and the European Community, (Irish Studies 3)*. Cambridge University Press, Cambridge.

Brody, H. (1974) *Inishkillane: Change and Decline in the West of Ireland*. Penguin, Harmondsworth.

Carty, R. K. (1980a) 'Politicians and Electoral Laws: An Anthropology of Party Competition in Ireland', *Political Studies*, vol. XXVIII, no. 4.

Carty, R. K. (1980b) 'Women in Irish Politics', *Canadian Journal of Irish Studies*, vol. 6, no. 1.

Carty, R. K. (1981) *Party and Parish Pump: Electoral Politics in Ireland*. Wilfred Laurier University Press, Ontario.

Census of Ireland: 1841–1971.

Chubb, B. (1963) ' "Going About Persecuting Civil Servants": The Role of the Irish Parliamentary Representative', *Political Studies*, vol. XI, no. 3.

Chubb, B. (1974) *The Government and Politics of Ireland*. Oxford University Press, Oxford.

Cohan, A. (1972) *The Irish Political Elite*. Gill and MacMillan, Dublin.

Commins, H. and Kelleher, C. (1973) *Farm Inheritance and Succession*. Macre na Feirmè, Dublin.

Commins, P. (1982) 'Land Policies and Agricultural Development' in Drudy, P. J. (ed.) *Ireland: Land, Politics and People, (Irish Studies 2)*. Cambridge University Press, Cambridge.

Connell, R. W. (1977a) *Ruling Class Ruling Culture*. Cambridge University Press, Cambridge.

Connell, R. W. (1977b) 'Logic and Politics in Theories of Class', *Australian and New Zealand Journal of Sociology*, vol. 13, no. 3.

Connell, R. W. and Irving, T. H. (1980) *Class Structure in Australian History*. Longman Cheshire, Melbourne.

Costello, D. (1980) *Report on the Disaster at Whiddy Ireland, Bantry Co. Cork on 8th January, 1979*. Stationary Office, Dublin.

Cox, P. G. and Kearney, B. (1983) 'The Impact of the Common Agricultural Policy' in Coombes, D. (ed.) *Ireland and the European Communities: Ten Years of Membership*. Gill and MacMillan, Dublin.

Crotty, R. (1979) 'Capitalist Colonialism and Peripheralisation: The Irish Case' in Seers, D., Schaffer, B. and Kiljunen, M-L. (eds) *Underdeveloped Europe: Studies in Core – Periphery Relations*. The Harvester Press, Sussex.

Cuddy, M. and Curtin, C. (1983) 'Commercialisation in West of Ireland Agriculture in the 1890s', *Economic and Social Review*, vol. 14, no. 3.

Cullen, L. M. (1972) *An Economic History of Ireland Since 1600*. B. T. Batsford, London.

Drudy, P. J. (1982) 'Land, people and the regional problem in Ireland' in Drudy, P. J. (ed.) *Ireland: Land, Politics and People, (Irish Studies 2)*. Cambridge University Press, Cambridge.

Drudy, P. J. (1984) 'The regional implications of EEC policies in Ireland' in Drudy, P. J. (ed.) *Ireland and the European Community (Irish Studies 3)*. Cambridge University Press, Cambridge.

Eipper, C. (1982) 'Class Processes: Key Issues for Analysis', *Australian and New Zealand Journal of Sociology*, vol. 18, no. 2.

Eipper, C. (1985) 'Double-Binds in the Pursuit of Prosperity: Gulf Oil in Bantry Bay', *Mankind*, vol. 15, no. 3.

Eipper, C. (forthcoming) *Hostage to Fortune — Gulf Oil in Bantry Bay: a case study of the multinational corporation, community change and capitalist development*.

Examiner, The Cork: 1965–80.

Fanning, R. (1978) *The Irish Department of Finance 1922–58*. Institute of Public Administration, Dublin.

Fox, R. (1978) *The Tory Islanders: A People of the Celtic Fringe*. Cambridge University Press, Cambridge.

Gallagher, M. (1976) *Electoral Support for Irish Political Parties 1927–1973*. Sage Publications, London.

Garvin, T. (1974) 'Political Cleavages, Party Politics and Urbanisation in Ireland: The Case of the Periphery-Dominated Centre' in *European Journal of Political Research*, 2 (4).

Garvin, T. (1977) 'Nationalist Elites, Irish Voters and Irish Political Development: A Comparative Perspective', *Economic and Social Review*, vol. 8, no. 3.

Garvin, T. (1978) 'The Destiny of the Soldiers: Tradition and Modernity in the Politics of de Valera's Ireland' in *Political Studies*, 26 (3).

Garvin, T. (1981) *The Evolution of Irish Nationalist Politics*. Holmes and Meier Publishers, Inc., New York.

Garvin, T. (1982) 'Theory, Culture and Fianna Fail: A Review' in Kelly, M. O'Dowd, L. and Wickham, J. (eds) *Power, Conflict & Inequality*, Turoe Press, Dublin.

Gibbon, P. (1973) 'Arensberg and Kimball revisited', *Economy and Society*, vol. 2, no. 4.

Gibbon, P. and Higgins, M. D. (1974) 'Patronage, Tradition and Modernisation: The case of the Irish "Gombeenman"', *Economic and Social Review*, vol. 6, no. 1.

Gibbon, P. and Higgins, M. D. (1977) 'The Irish "Gombeenman": Re-incarnation or Rehabilitation?', *Economic and Social Review*, vol. 8, no. 4.

Gibbon, P. and Curtin, C. (1978) 'The Stem Family in Ireland', *Comparative Studies in Society and History*, vol. 20, no. 3.

Giddens, A. and Parkin, F. (1980) 'Classes, Capitalism and the State' and 'Reply to Giddens', *Theory and Society*, 9.

Gramsci, A. (1975) *Selections from the Prison Notebooks,* Hoare, Q. and Nowell Smith, G. (eds) International Publishers, New York.

Hannan, D. F. (1970) *Rural Exodus: A study of the forces influencing the large-scale migration of Irish rural youth*. Geoffrey Chapman, Dublin.

Hannan, D. F. (1972) 'Kinship, Neighbourhood and Social Change in Irish Rural Communities', *Economic and Social Review*, vol. 3, no. 2.

Hannan, D. F. (1982) 'Peasant models and the understanding of social and cultural change in rural Ireland' in Drudy, P. J. (ed.) *Ireland: Land, Politics and People*, (*Irish Studies 2*). Cambridge University Press, Cambridge.

Hibernia: 1975–77.

Higgins, M. D. (1982) 'The Limits of Clientelism: Towards an assessment of Irish Politics' in Clapham, C. (ed.) *Private Patronage and Public Power*. Frances Pinter, London.

Higgins, M. D. and Gibbons, J. P. (1982) 'Shopkeeper-graziers and land agitation in Ireland, 1895–1900' in Drudy, P. J. (ed.) *Ireland: Land, Politics and People*, (*Irish Studies 2*). Cambridge University Press, Cambridge.

Hourihane, J. K. (1971) Unpublished MA Thesis (Geography). University College, Cork.

Hourihane, J. K. (1977) 'Town Growth in West Cork: Bantry, 1600–1960' *CHASJ*, vol. LXXXII, no. 236.

IDA (1972) 'Regional Industrial Plans: 1973–1977, Parts 1 and 2', Dublin.

IDA (1978) 'Industrial Development in Ireland', Dublin.

Jackson, J. (1967) 'Report on the Skibbereen Social Survey'. Human Sciences Committee, Dublin.

Jackson, J. A. (1968) 'Ireland', in Jackson, J. A. (ed.) *Social Stratification*. Cambridge University Press, Cambridge.

Kane, E. (1968) 'Man and Kin in Donegal: A Study of Kinship Functions in a Rural Irish and an Irish-American Community', *Ethnology,* vol. VII, no. 3.

Kane, E. (1977) *The Last Place God Made: Traditional Economy and New Industry in Rural Ireland.* HRAFlex Books, New Haven.

Kane, E. (1979) 'The Changing Role of the Family in a Rural Irish Community' *Journal of Comparative Family Studies.* Special Issue: Aspects of Family Life in Ireland, vol. X, no. 2, Summer.

Kennedy, L. (1977) 'A Sceptical View on the Reincarnation of the Irish "Gombeen-man" ', *Economic and Social Review,* vol. 8, no. 3.

Kennedy, L. (1978) 'The Roman Catholic Church and Economic Growth in Nineteenth Century Ireland', *Economic and Social Review,* vol. 10, no. 1.

Komito, L. (1984) 'Irish Clientelism: A Reappraisal', *Economic and Social Review,* vol. 15, no. 3.

Larkin, E. (1975) *The Roman Catholic Church and the Creation of the Modern Irish State 1878–1886.* The American Philosophical Society, Philadelphia.

Lee, J. (1973) *The Modernisation of Irish Society.* Gill and MacMillan, Dublin.

Lyons, F. S. L. (1975) *Ireland Since the Famine.* Fontana.

Mair, P. (1979) 'The Autonomy of the Political: The Development of the Irish Party System', *Comparative Politics,* July, 1979.

Manning, M. (1970) *The Blueshirts.* Gill and Macmillan, Dublin.

Manning, M. (1972) *Irish Political Parties: An Introduction.* Gill and MacMillan, Dublin.

Manning, M. (1979) 'Women in Irish National and Local Politics 1927–77' in MacCurtain, M. and O Corrain, D. (eds) *Women in Irish Society: The Historical Dimension.* Greenwood Press, Westport.

Manpower Survey (1976) 'Labour Availability in Bantry: A Report on a Survey Carried out in April 1976'. National Manpower Service, Department of Labour.

Marx, K. (1974) *Capital.* Progress Publishers, Moscow.

Marx, K. (1977) *A Contribution to the Critique of Political Economy.* Progress Publishers, Moscow.

McAleese, D. (1977) 'A Profile of Grant-Aided Industry in Ireland'. IDA Publications Series, Paper 5, Dublin.

McAleese, D. (1982) 'Political independence, economic growth and the role of economic policy' in Drudy, P. J. (ed.) *Ireland: Land, Politics and People, (Irish Studies 2).* Cambridge University Press, Cambridge.

McAleese, D. (1984) 'Ireland and the European Community: the changing pattern of trade' in Drudy, P. J. (ed.) *Ireland and the European Community, (Irish Studies 3).* Cambridge University Press, Cambridge.

Meehan, B. (1974) Unpublished Manuscript (Planning Thesis), Queens University, Belfast.

Meenan, J. (1970) *The Irish Economy Since 1922.* Liverpool University Press, Liverpool.

Messenger, J. C. (1969) *Inis Beag: Isle of Ireland.* Holt, Rinehart and Winston.

Miller, D. W. (1973) *Church, State and Nation in Ireland 1898–1921.* Gill and MacMillan, Dublin.

O'Brien, C. C. (1972) *States of Ireland.* Hutchinson, London.

O'Carroll, J. P. (1973) *Agricultural Records,* vol. 33, Spring.

O'Carroll, J. P. (1976) 'Land Use and Transfer'. Unpublished manuscript.

O'Carroll, J. P., Passchier, N. P. and van der Wusten, H. H. (1978) 'Regional Aspects of the Problem of Restructuring Use and Ownership of Agricultural Land in the Republic of Ireland', *Economic and Social Review,* vol. 9, no. 2.

O'Connell, D. (1982) 'Sociological Theory and Irish Political Research' in Kelly, M., O'Dowd, L. and Wickham, J. (eds) *Power, Conflict & Inequality.* Turoe Press, Dublin.

O'Keefe papers, County Library, Cork.

O'Sullivan, F. (1976) 'The Baron of West Cork', *Hibernia*, 14 June.

O Tuathaigh, M. A. G. (1982) 'The land question, politics and Irish society, 1922–1960' in Drudy, P. J. (ed.) *Ireland: Land, Politics and People, (Irish Studies 2)*. Cambridge University Press, Cambridge.

Oxley, H. (1973) *Mateship in Local Organization*. Queensland University Press, Brisbane.

Parkin, F. (1974) 'Strategies of Social Closure in Class Formation', in Parkin, F. (ed.) *The Social Analysis of Class Structure*. Tavistock, London.

Parkin, F. (1979) *Marxism and Class Theory: A Bourgeois Critique*. Tavistock, London.

Peillon, M. (1982) *Contemporary Irish Society*. Gill and MacMillan, Dublin.

Poulantzas, N. (1973) *Political Power and Social Classes*. NLB, London.

Poulantzas, N. (1975) *Classes in Contemporary Capitalism*. NLB, London.

Pyne, P. (1969–70) 'The Third Sinn Fein Party, 1923–26', *Economic and Social Review*, vol. 1, no. 1 & 2.

Pyne, P. (1974) 'The Bureaucracy in the Irish Republic: Its Political Role and the Factors influencing it', *Political Studies*, vol. XXII, no. 1.

Roche, R. (1982) 'The High Cost of Complaining Irish Style: a Preliminary Examination of the Irish Pattern of Complaint Behaviour and of its Associated Costs', *IBAR — Journal of Irish Business and Administrative Research*, vol. 4, no. 2.

Rowse, T. (1978) 'Connell on the Ruling Class', *Intervention*, 10/11, August.

Ruane, J. (1979) 'The Analysis of Dependency in rural Ireland: a critique of current approaches' in Spencer, A. (ed.) *Dependency: Social, Political, Cultural. The Proceedings of the Fifth Annual Conference of the Sociological Association of Ireland*. Belfast: Queen's University, Department of Social Studies.

Rumpf, E. and Hepburn, A. C. (1977) *Nationalism and Socialism in 20th Century Ireland*. Barnes and Noble Books, New York.

Sacks, P. M. (1970) 'Bailwicks, Locality and Religion: Three Elements in an Irish Dail Constituency Election', *Economic and Social Review*, vol. 1, no. 4.

Sacks, P. M. (1976) *The Donegal Mafia: An Irish Political Machine*. Yale University Press, New Haven and London.

Schaffer, B. (1979) 'Regional Development and Institutions of Favour: Aspects of the Irish Case' in Seers, D., Schaffer, B. and Kiljunen, M-L. (eds) *Underdeveloped Europe: Studies in Core – Periphery Relations*. The Harvester Press, Sussex.

Scheper-Hughes, N. (1979a) 'Inheritance of the Meek: Land, Labour and Love in Western Ireland', *Marxist Perspectives*, vol. 2, no. 1, Spring.

Scheper-Hughes, N. (1979b) 'Breeding Breaks Out in the Eye of the Cat: Sex Roles, Birth Order and the Irish Double-Bind', *Journal of Comparative Family Studies*. Special Issue: Aspects of Family Life in Ireland, vol. X, no 2, Summer.

Scheper-Hughes, N. (1979c) *Saints, Scholars and Schizophrenics: Mental Illness in Rural Ireland*. University of California Press, Berkeley and Los Angeles.

Sheehy, S. J. (1984) 'The Common Agricultural Policy and Ireland' in Drudy, P. J. (ed.) *Ireland and the European Community, (Irish Studies 3)*. Cambridge University Press, Cambridge.

Stanton, R. (1979) 'Foreign Investment and Host Country Politics: The Irish Case' in Seers, D., Schaffer, B. and Kiljunen, M-L. (eds) *Underdeveloped Europe: Studies in Core – Periphery Relations*. The Harvester Press, Sussex.

Star, The Southern: 1965–80.

Symes, D. G. (1972) 'Farm Household and Farm Performance: A Study of Twentieth Century Changes in Ballyferriter, Southwest Ireland', *Ethnology*, vol. XI, no. 1.

Therborn, G. (1978) *What Does the Ruling Class do When it Rules?* NLB, London.

Thompson, E. P. (1968) *The Making of the English Working Class*. Penguin, Harmondsworth.

Thompson, E. P. (1978a) 'Eighteenth-century English Society: class struggle without class?' *Social History*, vol. 3, no. 2.

Thompson, E. P. (1978b) *The Poverty of Theory*. Merlin Press, London.

Tovey, H. (1982) 'Milking the Farmer? Modernisation and Marginalisation in Irish Dairy Farming' in Kelly, M., O'Dowd, L. and Wickham, J. (eds) *Power, Conflict & Inequality*. Turoe Press, Dublin.

Weber, M. (1968) *Economy and Society*. Roth, G. and Wittich, C. (eds), Bedminster Press, New York.

West Cork Resource Survey (1963) An Foras Taluntais (The Agricultural Institute), Dublin.

White, J. (1975) *Minority Report: The Protestant Community in the Irish Republic*. Gill and MacMillan.

Whyte, J. H. (1971) *Church and State in Modern Ireland 1923 – 1970*. Gill and MacMillan, Dublin.

Whyte, J. H. (1974) 'Ireland: Politics without Social Bases' in Rose, R. (ed.) *Electoral Behaviour: A Comparative Handbook*. Collier-MacMillan, New York.

Wickham, J. (1980) 'The Politics of Dependent Capitalism: International Capital and the Nation State' in Morgan, A. and Purdie, B. (eds) *Ireland: Divided Nation Divided Class*. Ink Links, London.

Wild, R. A. (1974) *Bradstow: A Study of Status, Class and Power in a Small Australian Town*. Angus and Robertson, Sydney.

Wild, R. A. (1981) *Australian Community Studies and Beyond*. Allen and Unwin, Sydney.

Williams, R. (1976) *Keywords*. Fontana.

Williams, R. (1977) *Marxism and Literature*. Oxford University Press, Oxford.

Wright, E. O. (1978) *Class, Crisis and the State*. NLB, London.